By JEAN MANDRELL BENSON

Farm Journal, Inc.
Philadelphia, Pennsylvania

Distributed to the trade by
Doubleday & Company, Inc.
Garden City, New York

OTHER FARM JOURNAL CRAFT BOOKS

Patterns for Appliqué and Pieced Work

Knit Sweaters the Easy Way

Scrap Saver's Stitchery Book

More Scrap Saver's Stitchery

Let's Make a Patchwork Quilt

Farm Journal's Homespun Christmas

Farm Journal's Design-and-Sew Children's Clothes

Easy Sewing with Knits

Modern Patchwork

Book Design: Michael P. Durning
Photography: Fred Carbone Studio, Inc.

Library of Congress Cataloging in Publication Data

Benson, Jean Mandrell.
Soft toys to stitch and stuff.

Includes index.
1. Soft toy making. I. Title.
TT174.3.B46 1983 745.592'4 82-45099
ISBN 0-385-18136-1

Printed in the United States of America

Contents

Introduction *v*

I. HELPFUL GUIDES FOR MAKING SOFT TOYS

Choosing Fabrics 1
Tracing Patterns 2
Enlarging Patterns 2
Cutting Fabric 2
Stitching Seams 3
Making Fur "Spots" 3
Stuffing 4
Wire Supports 4
Final Hand Stitching 5
Facial Features 5
Basic Supplies 6

II. CRITTERS TO STITCH

Country Critters 7
Rooster 7
Mice 10
Pig 15
Black Sheep 21
Squirrel 26
Worm & Apple Pillow 29
Simple Circle Critters 30
Rabbit 35
Leopard 35
Kitten 36
Puppy 37
Robin 37
Bluebird 37
Chick 37
Duck 38

Pond Dwellers 42
Fish & Fish Pole 42
Ducks & Goose 44
Snake 50

Dolls 52
Baby 52
Girl 53
Boy 55
Mom & Grandma 56
Dad & Grandpa 57

Hand Puppets 71
Frog 71
Fox 75
Parrot 78

Hen Pajama Bag & Slippers 82

Pets 88
Shag Dog 88
Siamese Cat 91
Monkey 96

Lovey Bear 100

Pony & Friends 109
Pony 109
Burro 111
Unicorn 111
Stick Pony 112

Large Animals 120
TV Horse 120
Ape 130

III. A TOY BOX TO BUILD

Barn & Fence 135

Index 138

Introduction

Making soft toys is rewarding for all ages. Stuffed animals—I call mine critters—are fun to stitch for special gifts, and they're popular items at craft shows and bazaars. Whether you sew by hand or machine, and whether you want to make something simple or challenging, there is a critter pattern here for you.

You'll find that every critter you stitch will become a unique character. Even when I use the same pattern several times, I find that each new toy is a bit different from the last. Much of my enjoyment is in watching a new personality emerge from a piece of fabric. The materials, facial features, clothes or other accessories you choose will make every critter individually yours.

My own interest in soft toys began about ten years ago, when I visited a friend at her newly opened toy shop. The toys were all handmade and child-safe, but none of the stuffed animals were the furry kind—my favorite type. Ideas began forming in my mind. I stopped in another store to buy some patterns and materials and went home to sew.

In a few days I returned with my sample toys. "Mother Hen," as my friend called herself, was enthusiastic. She took what I had and asked for more. Her customers also responded favorably, and soon I was busy filling orders. That was the beginning of my Critter Crafts business venture.

As I worked, I began to modify existing patterns, eliminating unnecessary pieces and changing shapes and features to suit myself. I also began to take special orders. One of the first was for a black cat made to resemble the favorite pet of a hospitalized teenager.

Then a man who raises show horses asked me to make a large Appaloosa pony for his granddaughter. He suggested that the horse should be on the ground with its legs bent, and it should be wearing a saddle and bridle. That was the first of my TV Horses.

Later, the same man ordered a one-color thoroughbred model of the Horse, and since then I have turned out several color variations. A few years ago, each of my eight grandchildren received a TV Horse as a birthday present. (One vivacious little girl insisted on dragging her Horse up to the top bunk every night to sleep with her. The Horse was large, but she was determined.)

After designing the TV Horse, I began to eliminate commercial patterns and build an inventory of my own creations. Since I grew up on a farm and have lived much of my married life in the country, I've had the opportunity to observe many different animals. These have been the inspiration for most of the toys in this book.

Along with these local look-alikes, I've included a few special-request critters that are more at home in other parts of the world. For instance, there's a Parrot and an Ape. You'll also find a set of soft dolls.

Seeing the loving response of children to my efforts gives me great pleasure. An unexpected surprise has been the enthusiastic reaction of adults, especially men. They seem pleased to find unique gifts, and often order custom-made mascots for their vans.

I most enjoy working with fake furs, but many of these patterns can be adapted to knits and woven fabrics, in either solid colors or prints.

I hope you will experience as much pleasure in using these patterns as I have had in creating them.

—Jean Mandrell Benson

Helpful guides for making soft toys

CHOOSING FABRICS

Fake furs are my favorite fabrics for making toy animals, and I use them for all my critters. (Even my dolls have fur fabric hair.) Fur fabrics give the toys a more realistic look, and I think it's especially important to use them for large animals, such as the TV Horse.

For me, fake fur is easier to use than flat woven fabrics. The knitted back on fur pile has "give," so matching and pinning seams goes quickly. After stitching, the fur pile covers the seams—*and* any little mistakes. You can't see puckering or rippling that would be conspicuous on a flat fabric.

You may want to try other fabrics for some of the small animal patterns, however, and you'll find finished samples of the Mouse done in both fake fur and a cotton print. Just remember that any pattern made in a flat fabric will look smaller than the same design made in fake fur—the fur pile adds to the apparent size. To keep the smooth-fabric Unicorn from looking too skinny, you'll find I added ¼" to the basic pattern.

Felt is used for small trims, such as a bird's beak and a dog's tongue. I buy a washable felt, but any type you can find will do.

FUR FABRICS

Fake fur comes in a variety of pile lengths, and I use them all.

Long pile, often sold as Fantasy Fur or Shag, has fibers about 2½" long. I used this for the Monkey, page 96, and for the mane and tail on the TV Horse, page 120. In my part of the country, this long-pile fabric is sold in pre-cut pieces in craft shops and by the yard in some fabric shops.

Medium-length pile has fibers about 1" to 1½" long, and it's used for the Rooster, page 7.

Short pile, with fibers running ½" to ¾" long, works well for the body of the TV Horse, page 120.

Plush, a short velvety pile about ¼" long, is a good choice for the Frog, page 71.

Fake lamb's wool has a close, curly texture, and it's perfect for the Black Sheep on page 21.

All these fur fabrics are relatively inexpensive, as compared to those that look like mink or fox. Even less expensive, however, are fabrics printed with tiger stripes, zebra stripes or leopard spots. These have a pile but are more like flannel than a plush fabric, and you'll find several Fish made in tiger stripes on page 12.

For most critters shown in this book, the colors and types of fur fabric are listed. However, you can substitute another color or type of pile, depending on your preference and what you can find locally.

Always consider the size of the toy when selecting fabric, and remember that a lightweight short pile is easier to use for critters with very small parts (those little ears and legs must be stitched and turned). If you find your fabric choice is too thick for some areas, you often can trim the pile in those areas before stitching.

Trimming the pile can be used to advantage at times—to create hoofs or to define a mouth. I often trim the pile on a small face before embroidering a nose or mouth.

TRACING PATTERNS

Most of the patterns in this book are actual size, ready for tracing. Lay a sheet of paper over the book page and copy the pattern outline and all details, such as slash lines, arrows for fur direction and points for matching pieces. Then cut out the traced pattern. Any paper you can see through will work, including typing paper and tracing paper.

Sometimes only half a pattern is given. For this, use a sheet of paper large enough for a full pattern and fold the paper in half. Open the paper and place the fold over the broken pattern line in book (it's labeled "fold line for paper pattern"). Trace the half pattern. Refold your paper and cut out a full pattern piece.

In some cases patterns are divided into sections and printed on several different pages. To trace these, use a sheet of paper large enough for the complete pattern. (Tape together smaller sheets, if necessary.) Trace the various sections, joining them on the broken lines.

ENLARGING PATTERNS

A few pattern pieces are too large to be given actual size, and they will have to be enlarged. These pieces are drawn on grids.

To enlarge a pattern, take a sheet of paper large enough for the whole piece. You can use any paper available, even brown wrapping paper. For my large patterns, I use roll ends of paper I get from a newspaper printer. The 5′-wide rolls still have a lot of paper left on them, and the price is unbelievably small. (Besides being marvelous for patterns, this roll paper is great for art projects, shelf paper and wrapping paper. At today's prices, it's a bargain.)

On the paper, draw horizontal and vertical lines to form a grid the size needed (use 1½″ or 2″ squares as indicated on the pattern grid). Then copy the pattern, line by line, square by square, as in Fig. 1.

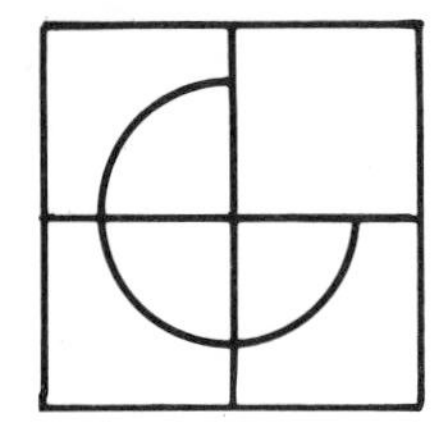

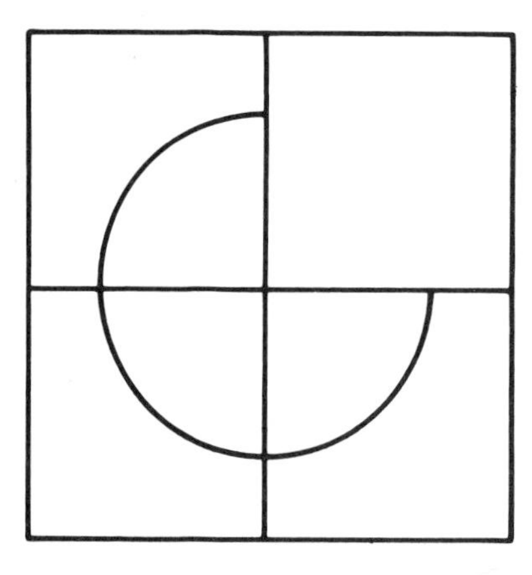

Fig. 1 *Enlarging pattern*

The main problem I run into when enlarging patterns is keeping track of which square I am copying. By numbering the squares horizontally and vertically, both in the book and on your enlarged grid, you will have a frame of reference at a glance (Fig. 2).

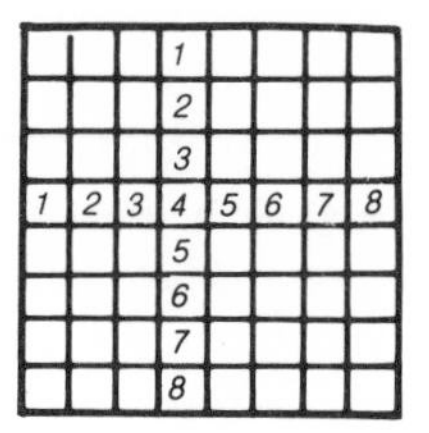

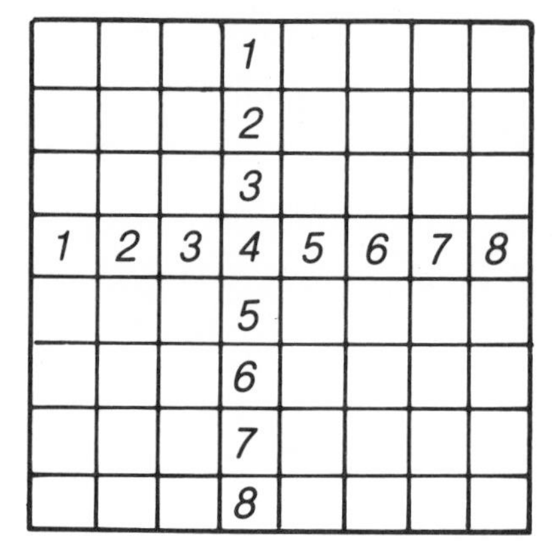

Fig. 2 *Numbering grid squares*

CUTTING FABRIC

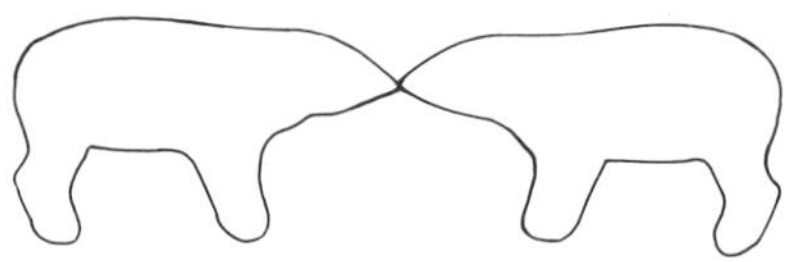

Fig. 3 *Reversing one pattern piece*

Duplicate parts of a pattern must be laid out with one piece reversed, as in Fig. 3, to give you a right and left side. (Fabric is not always wide enough to lay matching pieces across the width as shown, but they can be stacked or arranged another way.)

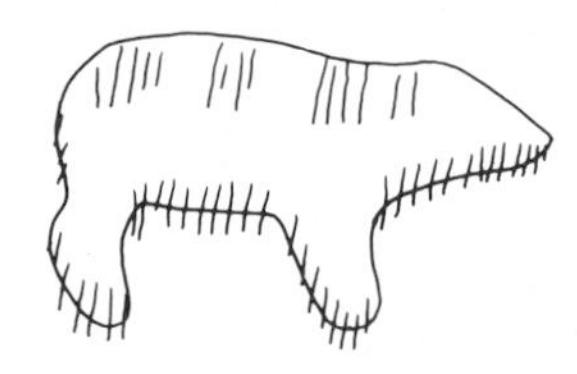

Fig. 4 *Direction of fur pile*

Fibers on fake fur and other pile fabrics will tend to run in one direction. Determine the direction, and lay out pattern pieces according to arrows on each piece. If in doubt, lay pattern pieces so the fur pile runs from top (or back) of the animal downward, as in Fig. 4.

Since lamb's wool fabric has no definite pile direction, you can use the knitted backing as a guide. Place pattern pieces so all arrows run in one direction, following the lines of the knit.

Trace pattern pieces on the back (wrong side) of the fabric. Use a lead pencil to mark light colors, and white chalk or white dressmaker's pencil to mark dark colors. Transfer all markings you will need for construction.

To cut fur fabric, use shears that have a sharp point on the lower blade. Run the blade in close to the backing (Fig. 5), and cut only the knitted backing. Part, never cut, the fur fibers.

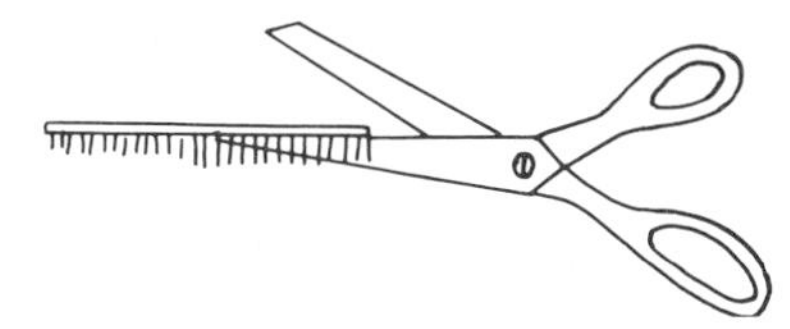

Fig. 5 *Cutting fur fabric*

Brush fur fibers away from cut edges. This prepares fabric for stitching and removes loose hairs that could get caught in the seams. Later, while pinning and stitching, continually work fur away from the seams.

STITCHING SEAMS

On fur fabrics, I use a transparent thread for machine stitching. It's strong and blends with any color fur. I set the machine for a zigzag stitch (Fig. 6) so that seams will have more "give" than if made with a straight stitch.

Fig. 6 *Zigzag machine stitch*

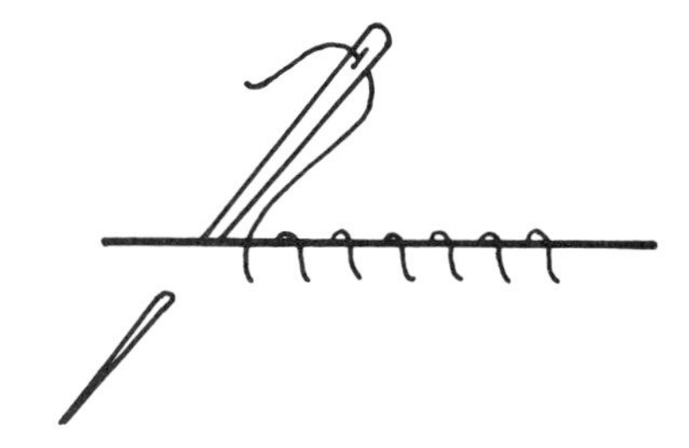

Fig. 7 *Overcast stitch*

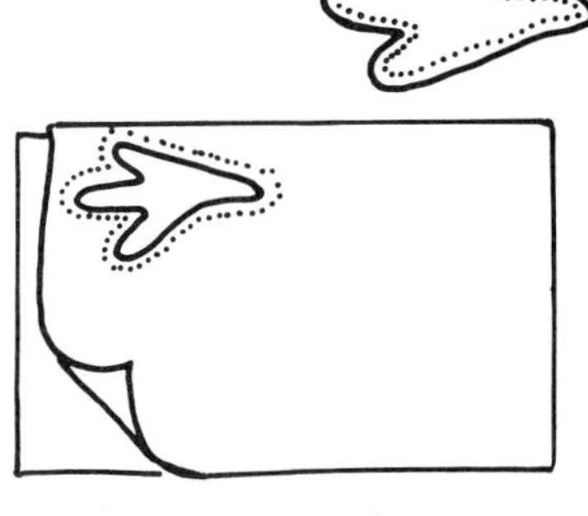

Fig. 8 *Stitching small shapes of felt before cutting*

For hand-stitching fur fabrics together on the wrong side, I like heavy button-and-carpet thread. The colors are limited, but your stitches are hidden by the pile. Just choose the closest color or shade and use an overcast (or whipping) stitch shown in Fig. 7. (To hand-stitch seams together from the right side, I make an invisible stitch discussed on page 5.)

A combination of machine and hand stitching is needed for some seams. Pile fabrics are thick, and if several seams end at one point, you may not be able to machine-stitch each seam all the way to the point. Zigzag as far as you can by machine, then finish by hand with overcast stitches.

After stitching fur fabric, brush seams briskly with a stiff brush to loosen trapped fur.

On flat fabrics, I often use transparent thread for both machine and hand stitching, but you may want to use matching thread. With some knitted fabrics, I set the machine for a zigzag stitch. With other knits (my polyester dolls, for instance), and with felt and woven fabrics, I use a straight machine stitch, then slash into any V areas and inside curves so seams will be smooth when turned.

For small parts made of felt, such as feet and ears, you can take a double thickness of felt and lay the pattern on top. Trace it first or simply straight-stitch around it, letting one side of the presser foot ride on the pattern. Then cut out the shape, leaving a narrow seam, about 1/8" wide (Fig. 8). This is much easier and more accurate than trying to sew around a small cut-out shape.

I like to let the seams show on some of these small pieces, so I don't turn the fabric. If the felt is to be turned, be sure to leave an opening for turning.

The doubleknit dolls also should be stitched together before cutting. Shaping the small areas is easily done in this manner. You can trace the pattern onto the knit fabric, or you can pin the pattern in place and stitch close to it, as with felt.

MAKING FUR "SPOTS"

Occasionally I luck into a piece of spotted fur like the one used for the Leopard Appaloosa Horse page 104. However, you can have fun custom-making spots. Here's how to make a "star" mark, similar to the one on the face of the black TV

Horse shown on page 105.

Take the fabric piece on which you wish to add a spot (such as the face for the TV Horse). On the back (wrong side) of the fabric, mark and cut out the size and shape spot you want. Make a pattern by laying the fabric spot on paper, pile side up, and tracing around it. Cut out the paper pattern, turn it face down on the back (wrong side) of the contrasting fur fabric, and trace around it. Cut out the shape with no seam allowance.

Position the contrasting spot in the matching "hole." Hand-stitch the edges together with overcast stitches (Fig. 9), us-

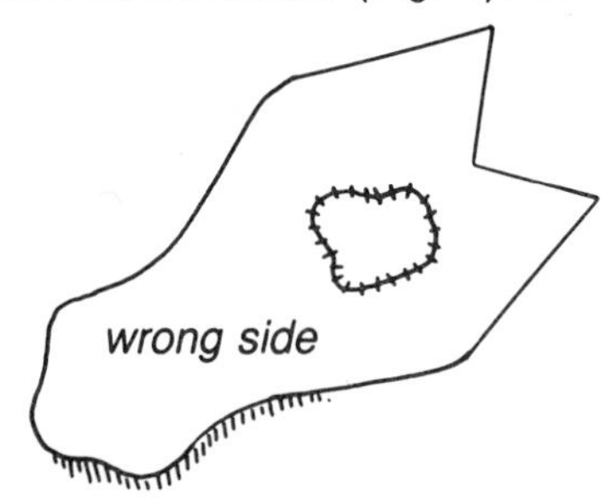

Fig. 9 *Adding a contrasting spot to fur fabric*

ing heavy button-and-carpet thread. With sturdy pile material, there is no need to overlap edges. Just pull them firmly together with stitches. If you cut your fabric carefully without destroying the fur pile, you will have a beautiful, natural-looking spot that will be as durable as the rest of the fabric.

STUFFING

Careful attention to turning and stuffing is important to a good-looking finished project. When turning a stitched piece right side out, use a wooden spoon handle to turn the narrow parts and to push out corners and remote areas.

Stuff heads, necks and legs of animals firmly and evenly where support is needed. Do this by pressing small wads of stuffing in place, using the wooden spoon handle. For a standing animal, be sure stuffing is packed tightly where legs join body. Shape each part as you stuff, trying to give the animal a pleasing, realistic look. Toys that do not stand can be stuffed more loosely to make a cuddly toy.

For stuffing, select a material that is resilient and that doesn't matt or lump. I list polyester fiberfill as the stuffing in my instructions because it is the one I use most and it's easy to find. Most critters in the book take less than one bag (12 oz.). If a project requires more, the approximate amount is given.

WIRE SUPPORTS

Most toys in this book can be made without reinforcement. However, a few long-legged animals, such as the Pony, page 109, tend to slide down on their haunches, even when they are made of fake fur and are firmly stuffed. Adding an inner support of wire will help them stand on all four legs.

I use inner supports mostly with fur fabrics. When I make animals of soft flat fabrics, I usually keep them soft and don't worry if they won't stand up. I just let them flop if they want to—like the Unicorn on page 111.

Adding an inner support does involve an additional construction step, and you may want to wait until you've stitched and stuffed one or two critters before you try it.

For wire, I often use 16-gauge copper wire, cut in single lengths. This is something we have on the farm, and it's flexible. The finished support can be bent for inserting, and then reshaped to fit the critter.

You can use any similar-size wire, or even lightweight coat hangers. If a wire seems too light and flexible, try using it double.

When you do plan to make a wire support, first assemble the critter and turn it to the right side. (Leave the opening large enough to insert the support.) Lay the stitched fabric on the table and measure the length of wire needed. Allow space beyond the wire for stuffing—so the animal will be rounded and the wire concealed.

Cut a length of wire for the body (or for the body and the neck curve). Bend a loop in each end so there will be no sharp points (Fig. 10). Cut a length of wire for the front legs and another length for the hind legs; add the end loops. Then bend leg wires in half and tape them to the body wire (use cloth, plastic or duct tape).

Fig. 10 *Making loop in end of wire*

With coat hangers, let the wire length determine how you shape the support. For instance, one hanger might form a hind leg, the body and a front leg. Use two such shapes, and tape them together along the body length. You can improvise to get the shape you want.

Wrap the finished wire shape with old nylons or strips of knit fabric to pad it (Fig. 11); tape to hold in place. Then add a layer of fiberfill, keeping the shape rounded and even.

Insert the wire frame in the fabric. As you stuff the animal, work the fiberfill into place evenly so that all sides of the wire are well padded.

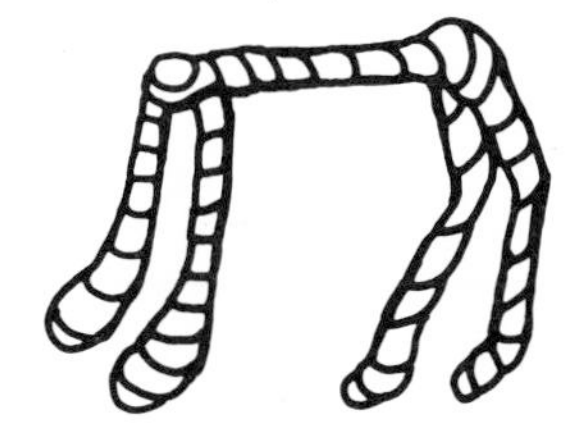

Fig. 11 *Wrapping wire support*

FINAL HAND STITCHING

Close seam openings from the right side by hand. Use heavy button-and-carpet thread for sewing fur fabrics, and transparent or matching thread for flat fabrics. Make a parallel stitch that I call an invisible stitch (Fig. 12).

Fig. 12 *Joining edges with invisible (parallel) stitches*

Align the seam edges and take a stitch on one side of the seam, parallel to the cut edge. Cross over and take a stitch on the other side, also parallel to the cut edge. Continue crossing over from one side to the other, taking one parallel stitch on each side as you go. As stitches are pulled together, the raw edges will automatically roll inward, producing an invisible seam.

On fur, keep brushing pile away from the stitching line on both parts as you sew.

Use this same invisible stitch when attaching parts (Fig. 13). If you want to keep the part (such as a head or arm) from moving, sew in a circular line around the part (Fig. 14) to give a broad base and prevent the part from flopping.

If you want a part to move (for example, the Frog's front legs, page 71), keep edges of the part together when sewing.

Another way to attach small parts (sometimes an ear) is with an overcast stitch, handling both edges as one. The cut edges are not turned under, but the fur pile will hide both the edges and the stitches.

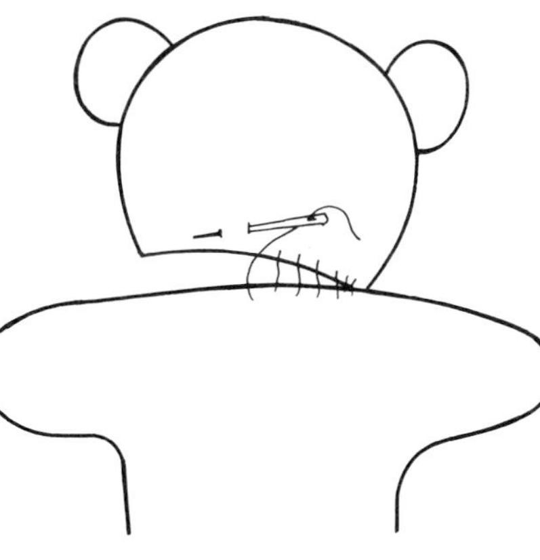

Fig. 13 *Joining stuffed parts with invisible (parallel) stitches*

Fig. 14 *Parts joined with circular seams*

FACIAL FEATURES

You can make eyes of felt, and embroider noses, and I do this for most of my critters. Other choices for these features may be buttons, or purchased animal eyes and noses available at craft shops.

Keep in mind the age of the person who will receive the toy. I prefer the safety of felt or embroidered features if the child is small.

A plastic animal eye or nose with a post on the back must be installed before a critter is stuffed. First, make a small hole in the fabric. Then insert the post, and anchor it on the back with a metal disc (supplied with the part).

If a plastic eye is made to be stitched or glued on, add the part after the critter is stuffed.

To make a felt eye, trace eye pattern. From a plastic lid (such as a coffee can lid), cut the full eye shape (Fig. 15-a). Cover the plastic with felt cut ¼" larger all around it (Fig. 15-b). Sew the edge of the felt with a running stitch, draw the thread tightly to pull felt over the plastic (Fig. 15-c) and secure thread on the back.

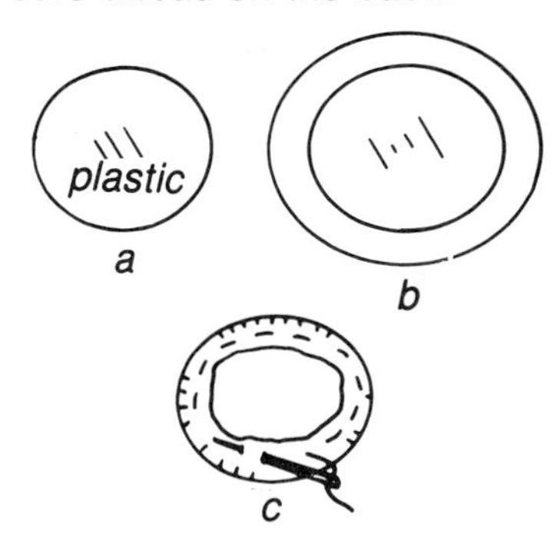

Fig. 15 *Making felt eyes*

Cut out any smaller eye pieces (number of layers will vary, depending on the particular pattern), and glue them to

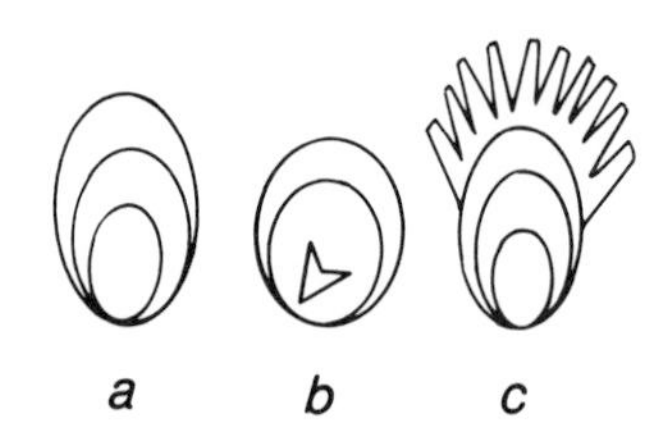

Fig. 16 *Gluing on layers of felt, adding eyelash*

the felt base (Fig. 16-a). Use white or craft glue for this and let it dry completely. To add a highlight, glue on a small white felt V or triangle (Fig. 16-b).

Eyelashes can be cut from felt or you can buy plastic ones. These are glued to the back of the finished felt eye (Fig. 16-c).

Attach completed felt eye to face using button-and-carpet thread on fur fabrics, and transparent or matching thread on flat fabrics.

Other small felt features, such as a tongue or nostrils, can be attached with thread or with glue.

To embroider features, use yarn or several strands of embroidery thread. For eyes and noses, work a satin stitch (Fig. 17). To embroider straight lines, as for a mouth or eyelashes, use a stem stitch (Fig. 18) or a chain stitch (Fig. 19).

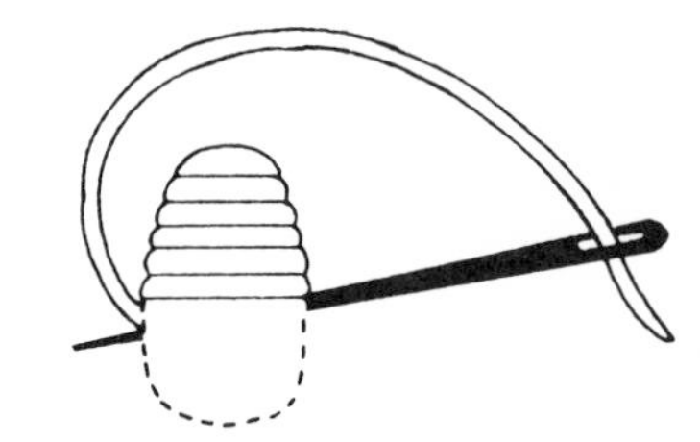

Fig. 17 *Satin stitch*

Fig. 18 *Stem stitch*

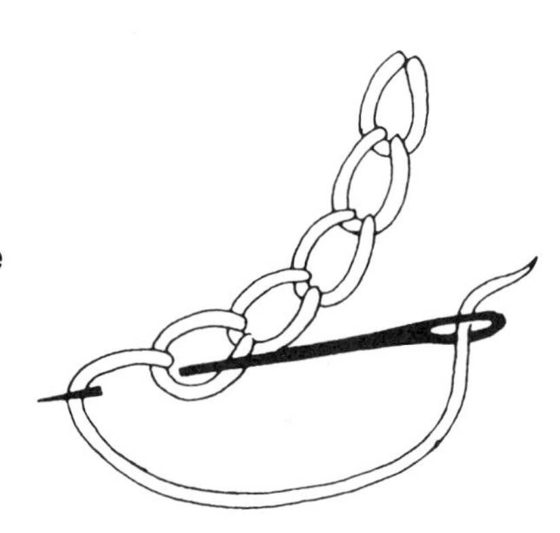

Fig. 19 *Chain stitch*

BASIC SUPPLIES

Below is a summary of items you'll need for making soft-toy critters:

- **Paper** for tracing and enlarging patterns
- **Sewing machine** with a zigzag stitch
- **Needles** for hand stitching, some large enough to handle heavy button-and-carpet thread
- **Straight pins,** 1¾″ long
- **Sharp-pointed shears**
- **Thread for fur-fabric** critters: transparent for machine stitching; button-and-carpet thread for handwork
- **Thread for flat-fabric** critters: transparent or matching color for all sewing
- **Soft lead pencil** for marking light color fabrics
- **White chalk** or white dressmaker's pencil for marking dark color fabrics
- **Stiff brush** for brushing fur fibers away from seams
- **Wooden spoon,** with handle ¼″ wide and 12″ long, for turning and stuffing critters
- **Plastic lids** (from coffee cans, margarine containers, etc.) for reinforcing felt eyes
- **White or craft glue** for making felt eyes and attaching small features

Country critters

ROOSTER

(color photo, page 105)

Let's begin our tour of Country Critters by meeting the fellow who heralds the dawning of each new day. Who else but Mr. Rooster?

He's a rusty brown color, cut from fake fur with a medium-length pile. All the trims, including the big yellow feet, are made of felt. This cuddly Rooster is about 8x10".

MATERIALS

brown medium-length pile fur fabric, 14½x14½"
yellow felt, 8½x10", for trim
red felt, 9x12", for trim
blue and black felt scraps, for eyes
transparent thread, for machine stitching
button-and-carpet thread, for handwork
polyester fiberfill, for stuffing
plastic lid, for eyes
glue

DIRECTIONS

For tips on tracing patterns and working with fur fabric, see *Helpful Guides,* page 1.

Make pattern pieces

1. Trace patterns for body, foot and feathers, page 9. Trace beak, comb, wattle and under gusset, page 8; join under gusset sections on broken lines.
2. Cut out pattern pieces.

Cut fabric

1. Lay pattern pieces on back of fur fabric, making sure fur is running in correct direction. Trace 2 body pieces (1 reversed) and 1 under gusset.
2. Cut out fabric on traced lines; ¼" seam allowances are included.

Assemble

Use ¼" seams and a zigzag machine stitch.

1. Pin under gusset to one body piece, right sides together, matching points A and B. Stitch between points.

Pin and stitch under gusset to other body piece.

2. Pin and stitch body pieces together along neck, head, back and tail; leave a small opening on back for turning. Turn to right side.

Stuff and finish

1. Stuff head firmly. Stuff neck and body more loosely so toy is cuddly. Close opening with invisible stitches.
2. To make felt trims, work with double layers of felt. Place each pattern piece on the felt and straight-stitch around it. Then cut out the shape ⅛" from the stitching line.

On yellow, stitch 1 beak and 2 feet. On red, stitch 1 center tail feather, 2 side tail feathers and 2 wattles.

For the comb, use red felt and stitch along the scallops only; leave bottom curve open.

3. Sew tip of each tail feather to body; place center feather at top of seam and a side feather at each side.
4. On each wattle, gather the top (straight edge) slightly and attach to body.
5. For comb, stuff a little fiberfill between the layers, close opening, and stitch comb to top of head.
6. Fold beak across center and attach to body just above wattles. Sew along fold, catching inner layer of felt.

7. Attach feet to bottom of under gusset by sewing across center of foot, catching inner layer of felt.

8. Make and attach eyes; see *To make a felt eye,* page 5. Cut the large circle from the plastic lid and cover it with blue felt. Glue on a small black felt circle.

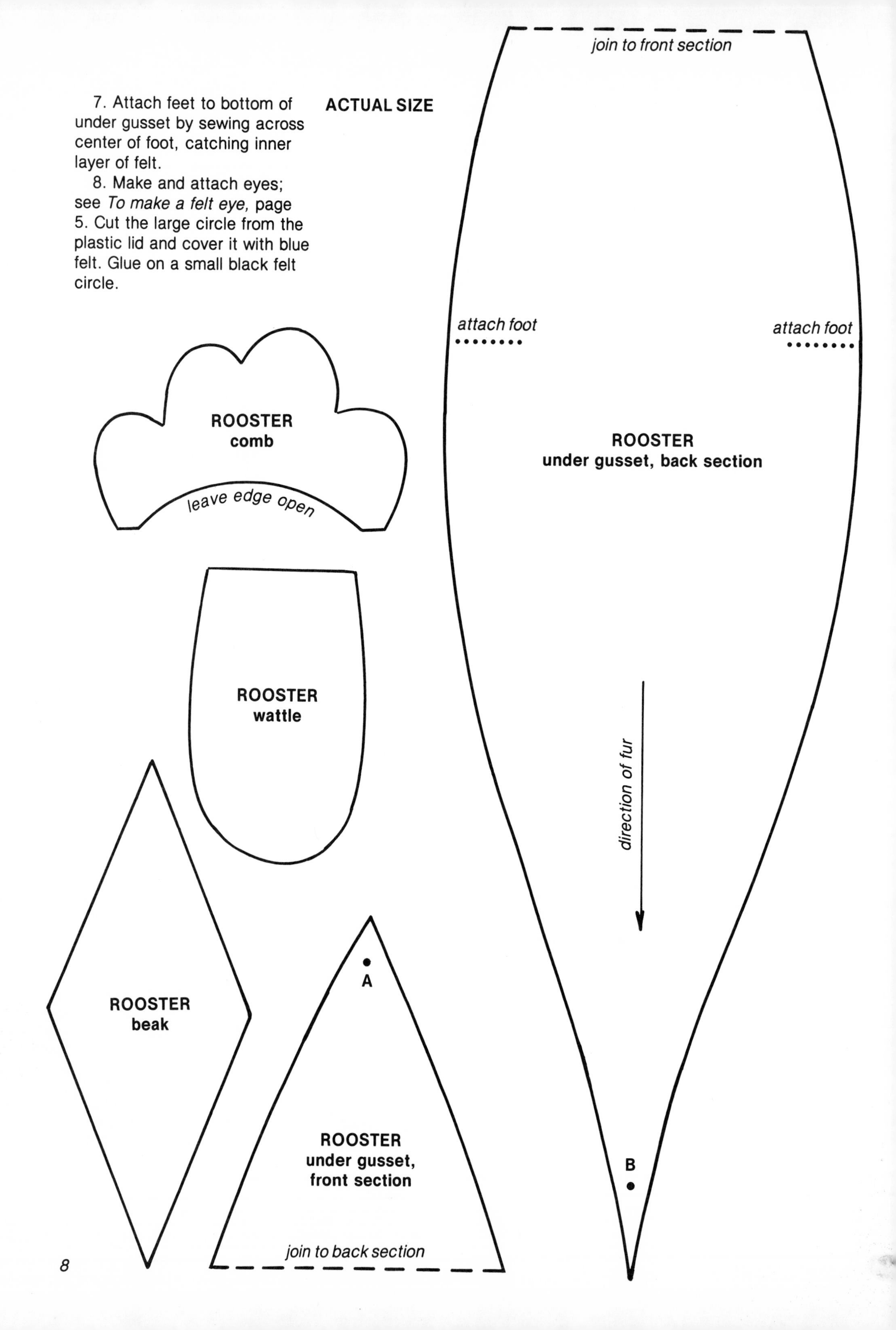

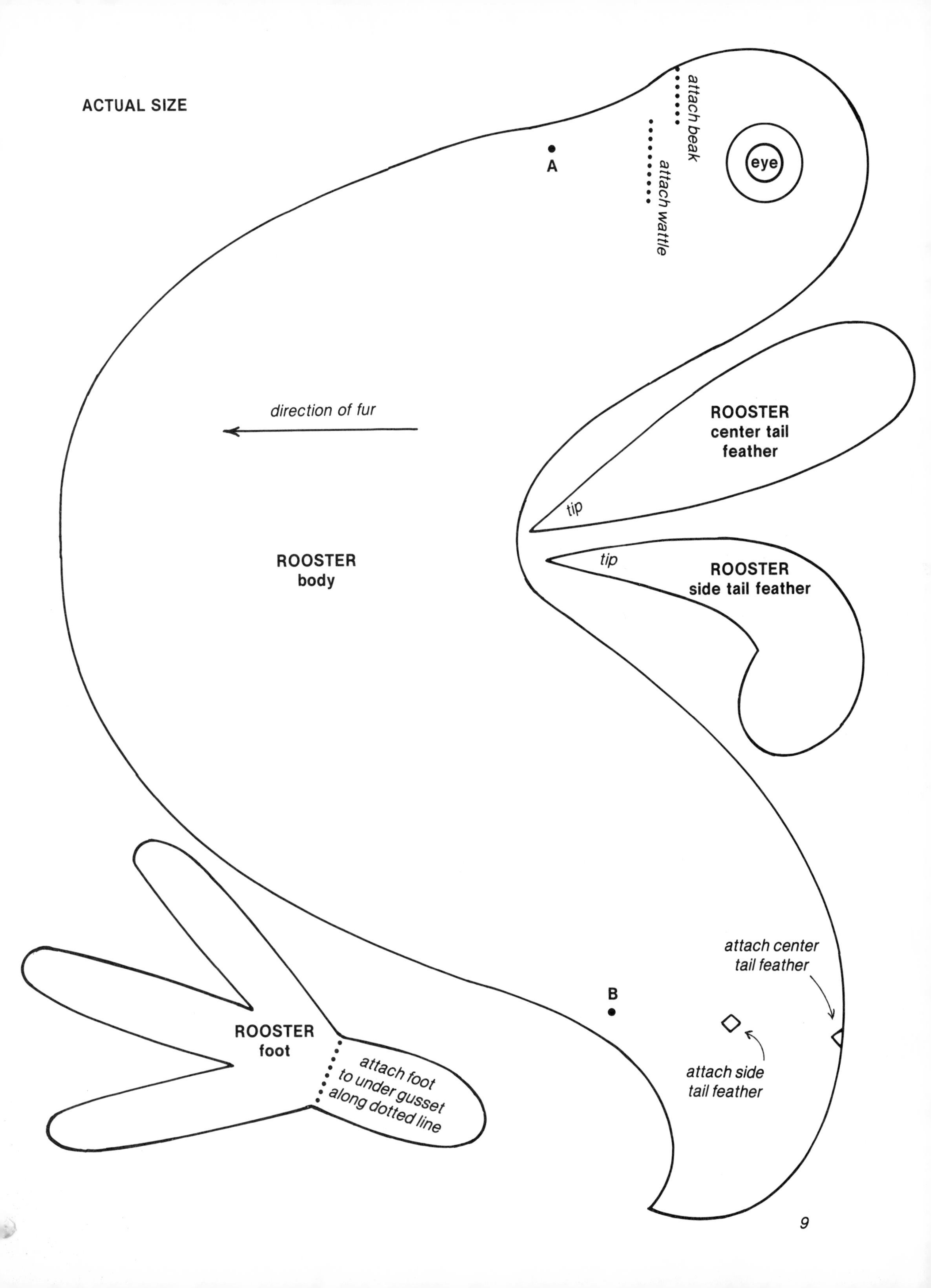
ACTUAL SIZE
attach beak
attach wattle
A
eye
direction of fur
ROOSTER
center tail
feather
tip
tip
ROOSTER
side tail feather
ROOSTER
body
attach center
tail feather
B
attach side
tail feather
ROOSTER
foot
attach foot
to under gusset
along dotted line

MICE

In the country, there are always mice for cats to chase. These whimsical fellows with floppy ears are somewhat larger than their real-life counterparts, and they're much nicer to have around.

Make a fur fabric Mouse with contrasting tail and ear linings, or cut all pattern pieces from one cotton print.

You have a choice of two ear sizes—medium or large—as well as the option of adding four big feet. You also can choose from three types of eyes: large felt eyes, like the ones shown on the Gray Fur Mouse; buttons, used on the Peach Fur Mouse; or plastic animal eyes, purchased for the Cotton Print Mouse.

Gray Fur Mouse

(color photo, page 14)

This timid fellow has medium-size ears, four big feet and eyes made of felt.

MATERIALS

gray short-pile fur fabric, 9x16", for body and medium-size ears (pile should run along the 9" length)
pink fabric, 9x21", for inner ears, tail and feet
black, white and pink felt scraps, for eyes
black felt scrap, for nose
yellow felt scrap, for teeth
transparent thread, for machine stitching
button-and-carpet thread, for handwork
black button-and-carpet thread, for whiskers
polyester fiberfill, for stuffing
plastic lid, for eyes
glue

DIRECTIONS

For tips on tracing patterns and working with fur fabric, see *Helpful Guides,* page 1.

Make pattern pieces

1. Trace patterns for body, hind foot, medium-size ear, nose, teeth and eye, page 17. Trace tail and front foot, page 18.
2. Cut out full pattern pieces.

Cut fabric

1. Lay pattern pieces on back of fur fabric, making sure fur is running in correct direction. Trace 2 body pieces (1 reversed) and 2 ears.
2. On wrong side of contrasting fabric, trace 2 ears, 1 tail, 4 front feet and 4 hind feet.
3. Cut out fabric on traced lines; ¼" seam allowances are included.

Assemble

Use ¼" seams and a zigzag machine stitch.

1. Pin body pieces right sides together. Stitch, leaving a small opening for turning. Turn to right side.
2. For each ear, pin a fur piece to a contrasting lining piece, right sides together. Stitch, leaving the straight edge open for turning. Turn to right side.

Stuff and finish

1. Stuff body and close opening with invisible stitches.
2. For each ear, tuck raw edges to inside and close opening by hand, gathering edge tightly. Stitch ear to body along gathered edge.
3. Make and attach eyes; see *To make a felt eye,* page 5. Cut the large eye oval from the plastic lid and cover it with pink felt. Glue on a small black oval and add a tiny white felt triangle as a highlight.
4. Cut teeth from yellow felt and stitch to body.
5. Cut a nose from black felt. By hand, sew a running stitch around the edge and gather tightly. Stitch nose to body so that it covers top edge of teeth.
6. For whiskers, use black button-and-carpet thread. With doubled thread in needle, take a small stitch at each side of

(continued on page 15)

Brown lamb's wool fabric and black felt combine to make this Black Sheep (page 21).

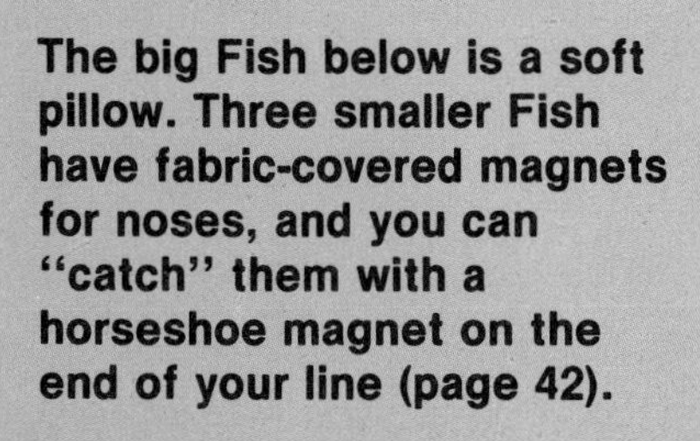
The big Fish below is a soft pillow. Three smaller Fish have fabric-covered magnets for noses, and you can "catch" them with a horseshoe magnet on the end of your line (page 42).

Four Ducks and a Goose, opposite page, are made from one basic pattern. At top is a Wild Duck (page 44) with a white neck ring. The three Cotton Print Ducks (page 45) are made from coordinated fabrics. At right is a plush Goose with its own golden egg (page 46).

Here are three ways to stitch one mouse pattern (beginning on page 10). For the Cotton Print Mouse at center, all pattern pieces are cut from one fabric, and purchased eyes are used. The Gray Fur Mouse at left shows off big felt eyes and big pink feet. The Peach Fur Mouse at right has a contrasting print for inner ears and tail, and brown buttons for eyes.

(continued from page 10)

nose. Tie thread in a knot close to fabric and cut off, leaving 1″ lengths.

7. To make tail, fold fabric in half lengthwise, right side inside. Stitch across narrow end and along length. Turn to right side and stuff.

Turn raw edge of tail to inside and stitch tail to body.

8. To make each foot, join two matching pieces, right sides together; leave the short straight edge open for turning. Slash seam allowance to stitching in V areas at toes.

Turn foot to right side and stuff lightly. Turn raw edges to inside and close opening with invisible stitches.

Stitch feet to body, positioning them at a forward angle.

Peach Fur Mouse

(color photo, opposite page)

The large ears are lined with a print fabric that matches the tail. Brown buttons are used for eyes, and the feet are omitted.

MATERIALS

peach lamb's wool or short-pile fur fabric, 9x20½″, for body and large ears (pile should run along the 9″ length)
coordinated print fabric, 9x10½″, for inner ears and tail
white felt scrap, for teeth
brown felt scrap, for nose
transparent thread, for machine stitching
button-and-carpet thread, for handwork
black button-and-carpet thread, for whiskers
polyester fiberfill, for stuffing
2 brown shank buttons, ¾″ diameter, for eyes

DIRECTIONS

Follow directions for Gray Fur Mouse, page 10, substituting materials above.

Trace pattern for the large ear, and omit the feet. Sew on brown buttons for eyes.

Cotton Print Mouse

(color photo, opposite page)

A single fabric is used for the body, ears and tail, and the plastic eyes are purchased. Feet, nose, teeth and whiskers are omitted in the sample, but you could add any of these features (along with felt eyes) if you wish.

MATERIALS

print fabric, 9x30″, for body, tail and large ears
transparent or matching thread, for all stitching
polyester fiberfill, for stuffing
plastic animal eyes with posts, ½″ diameter (available at craft shops)

DIRECTIONS

Follow directions for Gray Fur Mouse, page 10, substituting print fabric for all body, tail and ear pieces.

Trace pattern for large ear; omit patterns for eye, teeth, nose and feet.

Install plastic eyes before stuffing Mouse.

PIG

(color photo, page 69)

Pigs have personalities all their own, and when they get excited, they can be unruly.

A pig we called Grunts would get upset whenever we had to load him on the truck at Fair time. To calm him, my daughter would use the end of a stick to scratch his side. With that, he'd forget all fear and frustration and lie down to be scratched, while the rest of us reinforced the loading chute and patched the fence he'd torn down. Finally, Grunts would get up and slowly walk onto the truck.

My fake fur Pig is a copy of Grunts, a black and white Hampshire. If you would rather have a one-color Pig (maybe pink), overlap the three body pieces to eliminate seam allowances and make one pattern piece.

MATERIALS

black short-pile or plush fur fabric, 12x48″, for body and ears (pile should run along the 12″ length)
white short-pile or plush fabric, 8x11½″, for body (pile should run along the 8″ length)
black felt, 7½x7½″, for tail, snout, inner ears and eyes
blue and white felt scraps, for eyes
red felt scrap, for nostrils
transparent thread, for machine stitching

button-and-carpet thread, for handwork
polyester fiberfill, for stuffing
plastic lid, for eyes
glue
pipe cleaner, for tail
½ yd. narrow ribbon, for trimming tail (optional)

DIRECTIONS

For tips on tracing patterns and working with fur fabric, see *Helpful Guides,* page 1.

Make pattern pieces

1. Trace separate patterns for body front and inner front leg, page 19, joining sections on broken lines. Trace patterns for eye and snout, page 19; for body center, page 18; and for body back, inner hind leg, tail and ear, page 20.

2. Cut out pattern pieces. On body front and body back pieces, slash along lines at legs as indicated on pattern.

Cut fabric

1. Lay pattern pieces on back of fur fabric, making sure fur is running in correct direction. On black, trace 2 body front pieces (1 reversed), 2 body back pieces (1 reversed), 2 inner front legs (1 reversed), 2 inner hind legs (1 reversed) and 2 ears (1 reversed). On white, trace 2 body center pieces (1 reversed).

2. On black felt, trace 2 ear pieces (1 reversed), 1 snout and 1 tail.

3. Cut out fabric on traced lines; ¼" seam allowances are included. Slash front and back body pieces at legs.

Assemble

Use ¼" seams and a zigzag machine stitch.

1. Pin each body center piece to the matching front and back pieces, right sides together. Machine-stitch the seams.

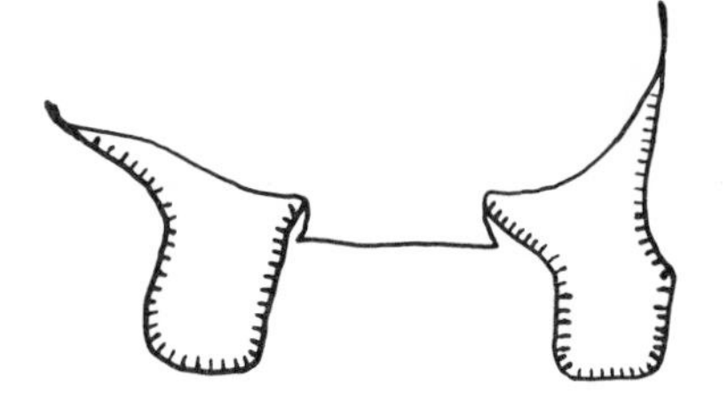

Fig. 1 *Stitching inner legs to body*

2. Pin each inner leg to matching body piece, right sides together. Stitch around leg, tapering seam at top edges; leave top curve of inner leg open (Fig. 1).

3. On each body piece, lift the belly flap between legs. Pin front cut edge to top curve of inner front leg, right sides together (Fig. 2, a). Stitch, tapering seam at each end.

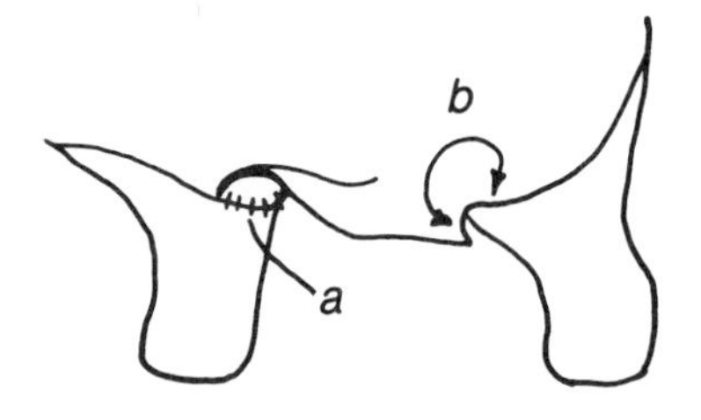

Fig. 2 *Stitching belly flap to inner legs*

Pin back cut edge of belly flap to top curve of inner hind leg, right sides together (Fig. 2, b). Stitch in same manner.

4. To join body pieces, match body seams, right sides together. Pin along head, back, inner legs and underside. Begin at snout and stitch around pig; leave opening on underside between legs for turning, and leave snout open. Turn to right side.

Stuff and finish

1. Stuff legs firmly, making sure fiberfill is packed tightly where legs join body. Stuff rest of body, and close opening with invisible stitches.

2. Turn raw edges at snout opening to center. Pin felt snout in place and hand-stitch to body with overcast stitches.

3. Cut 2 oval nostrils from red felt (see pattern on page 19 for size). Glue or stitch to snout.

4. To make each ear, pin one felt piece to a plush piece, right sides together. Stitch, leaving an opening for turning. Turn to right side. Stitch ears to head so they point toward snout.

5. Make and attach eyes; see *To make a felt eye,* page 5. Cut the large eye shape from the plastic lid and cover it with blue felt. Glue on the middle shape of white felt and the small shape of black felt.

6. To make tail, fold felt piece in half lengthwise, and straight-stitch a lengthwise seam, starting at the tip. Turn to right side.

Cut pipe cleaner the same length as the tail. Fold wire over at each end to make it rounded, and wrap entire length with a little fiberfill. Insert pipe cleaner in tail, stitch tail to body and twist it to make a curl. Add ribbon bow for trim if you wish.

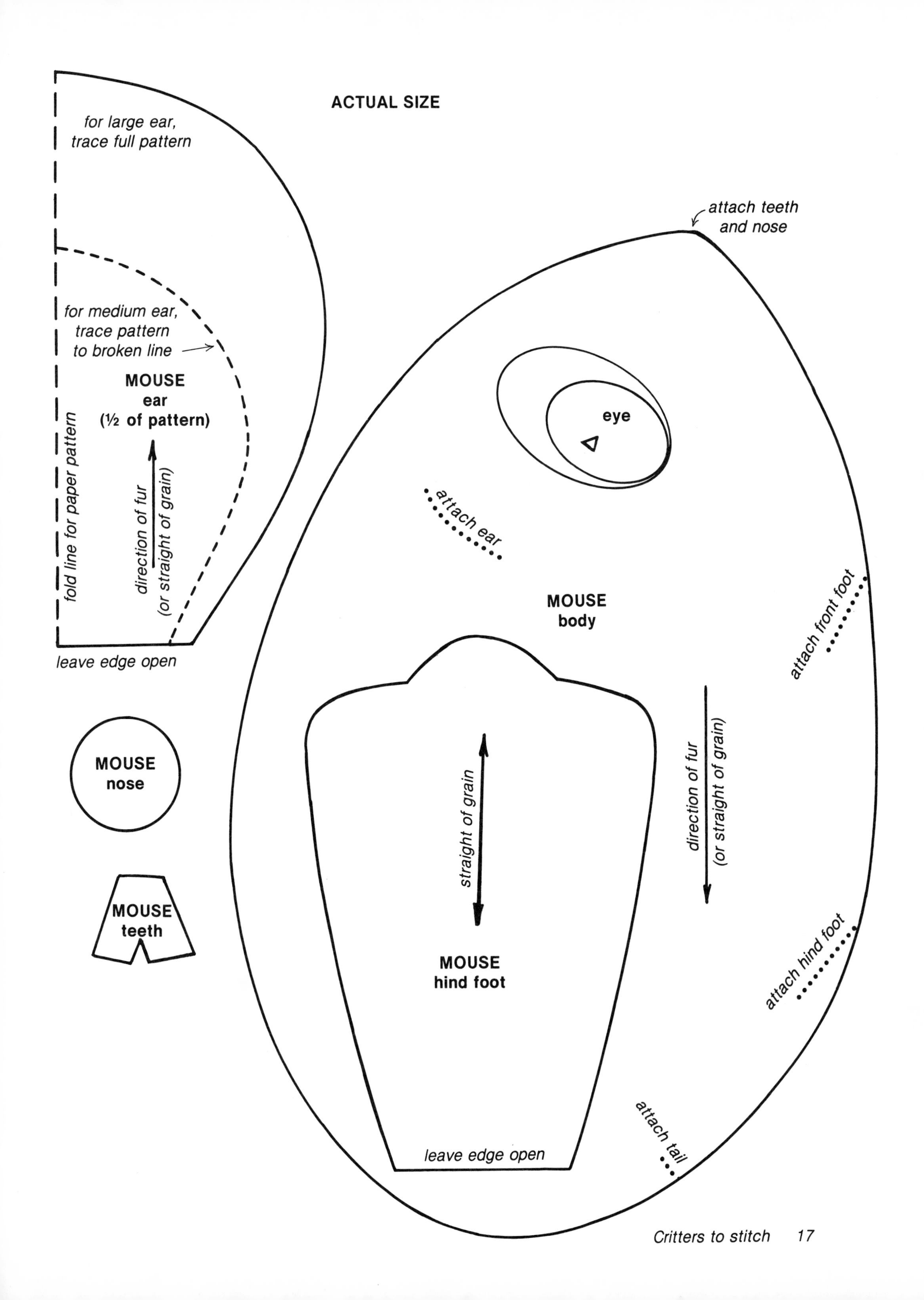
ACTUAL SIZE
for large ear, trace full pattern
for medium ear, trace pattern to broken line
MOUSE ear (½ of pattern)
direction of fur (or straight of grain)
fold line for paper pattern
leave edge open
MOUSE nose
MOUSE teeth
attach teeth and nose
eye
attach ear
MOUSE body
attach front foot
direction of fur (or straight of grain)
straight of grain
MOUSE hind foot
attach hind foot
attach tail
leave edge open

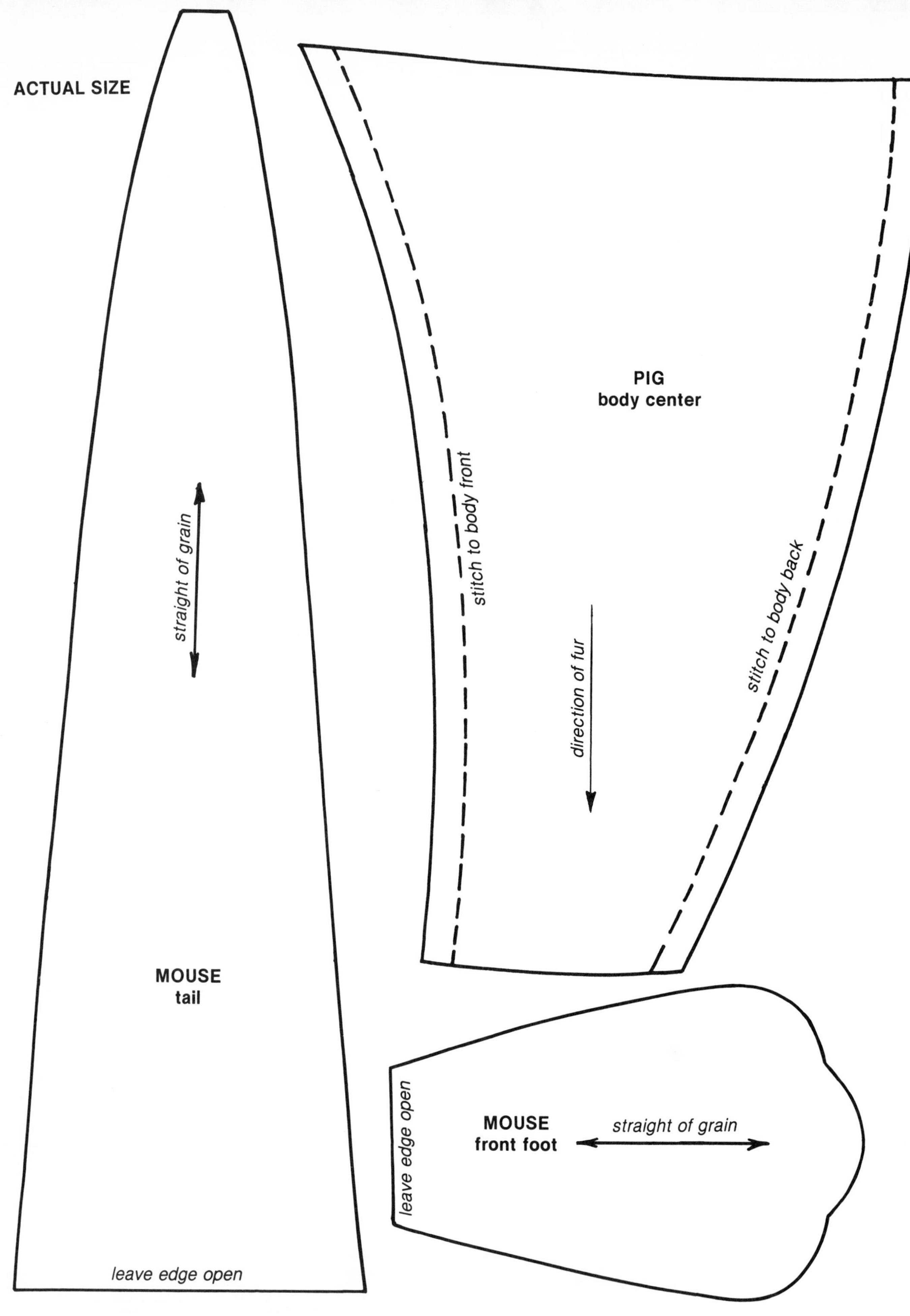
ACTUAL SIZE
straight of grain
MOUSE
tail
leave edge open
stitch to body front
PIG
body center
direction of fur
stitch to body back
leave edge open
MOUSE
front foot
straight of grain

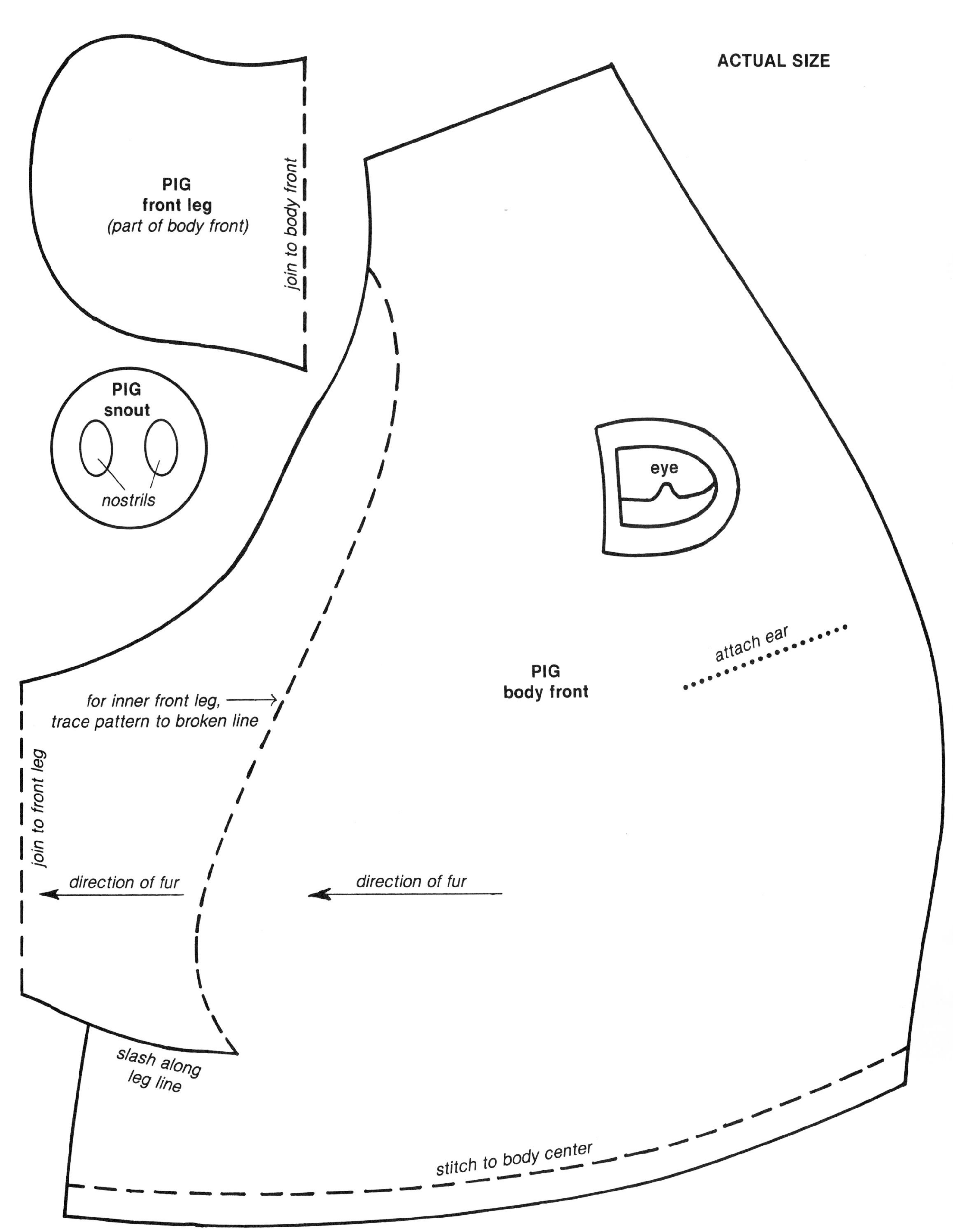
ACTUAL SIZE
PIG
front leg
(part of body front)
join to body front
PIG
snout
nostrils
eye
attach ear
PIG
body front
for inner front leg,
trace pattern to broken line
join to front leg
direction of fur
direction of fur
slash along
leg line
stitch to body center

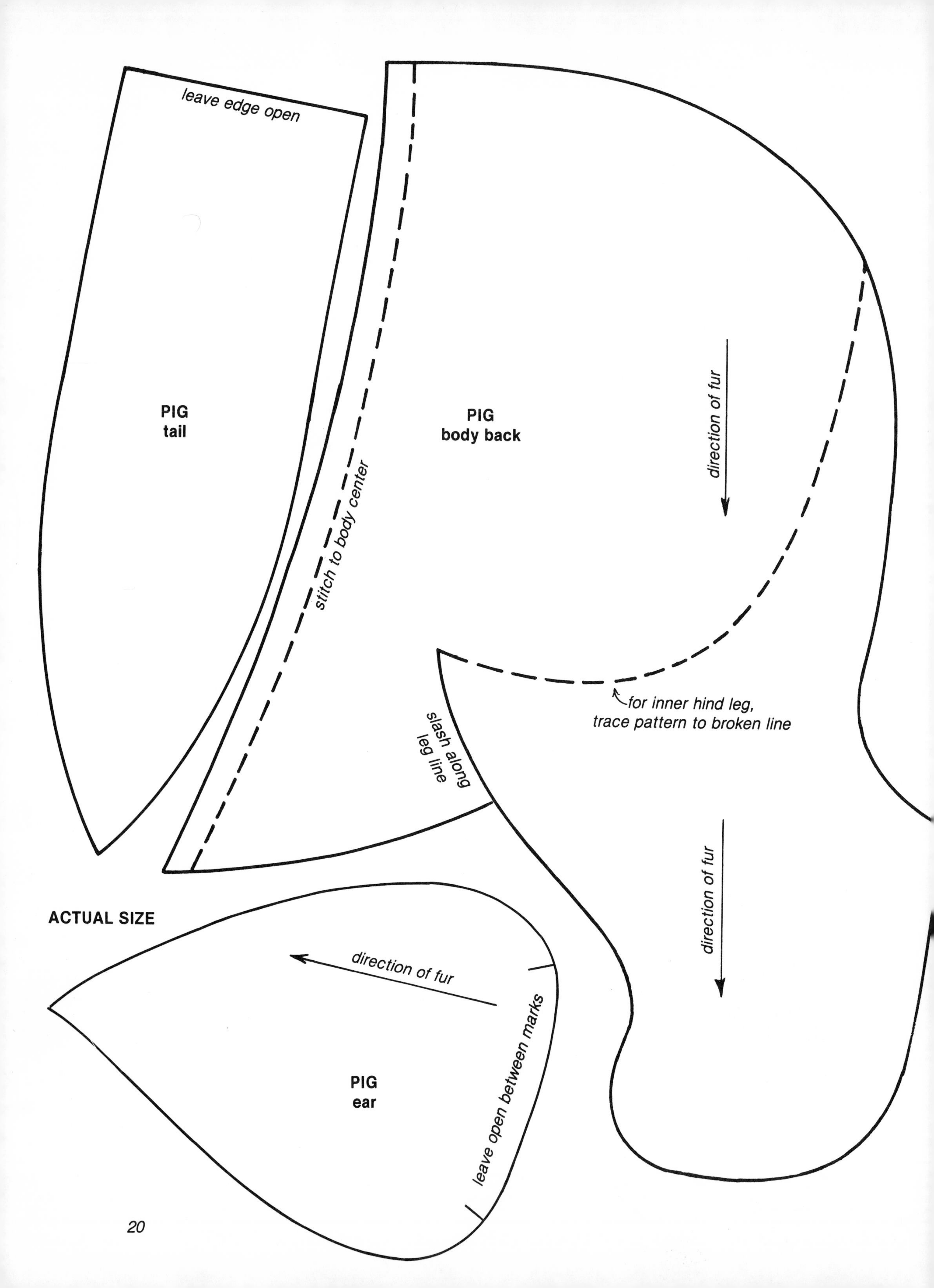
leave edge open
PIG
tail
stitch to body center
PIG
body back
direction of fur
for inner hind leg,
trace pattern to broken line
slash along
leg line
direction of fur
ACTUAL SIZE
direction of fur
PIG
ear
leave open between marks

BLACK SHEEP

(color photo, page 11)

Beside the farm pond, there's a green pasture where sheep like to graze. Most of the flock are white, but occasionally you'll see a black sheep—and that's the one I copied.

This Black Sheep (it's really a brown color) is made of lamb's wool fabric, with head and legs of black felt. To keep it standing on those slim legs, add an inner support of wire.

MATERIALS

brown lamb's wool fur fabric, 18x20", for body (if pile has a direction, it should run along the 18" length)
black felt, 9x36" (or three 9x12" pieces), for face, legs, inner ears and eyes
brown felt scraps, for eyes and nostrils
transparent thread, for machine stitching
button-and-carpet thread, for handwork
polyester fiberfill, for stuffing
plastic lid, for eyes
glue
for inner support: wire; tape; old nylons or strips of knit fabric

DIRECTIONS

For tips on tracing patterns, working with fur fabric and making an inner support of wire, see *Helpful Guides*, page 1.

Make pattern pieces

1. Trace patterns for body, pages 24-25, and for under gusset, page 23; join sections on broken lines.

Trace patterns for tail, and for inner and outer hind leg, page 22; for inner and outer front leg, page 23; and for face and ear, page 25.

2. Cut out pattern pieces. On body piece, slash along lines at legs as indicated on pattern.

Cut fabric

1. Lay pattern pieces on back of fur fabric, making sure fur is running in correct direction. (If fur has no definite direction, have all pattern arrows running in the same direction along the knit lines on the back.) Trace 2 body pieces (1 reversed), 1 under gusset, 1 tail and 2 ears.

2. On felt, trace 2 face pieces (1 reversed), 2 outer front legs (1 reversed), 2 inner front legs (1 reversed), 2 outer hind legs (1 reversed), 2 inner hind legs (1 reversed) and 2 ears.

3. Cut out fabric on traced lines; ¼" seam allowances are included. Slash body pieces at legs.

Assemble

Use ¼" seams and a zigzag machine stitch.

1. Pin each outer leg piece to matching body piece, right sides together, lining up one edge of leg with slash line. Stitch across top of leg (Fig. 1); begin stitching at slash end of seam, and taper seam to make it narrower at opposite end.

2. Pin each inner leg to matching outer leg, right sides together, letting inner leg extend along body to end of slash. Stitch around leg, tapering seam at each end; leave

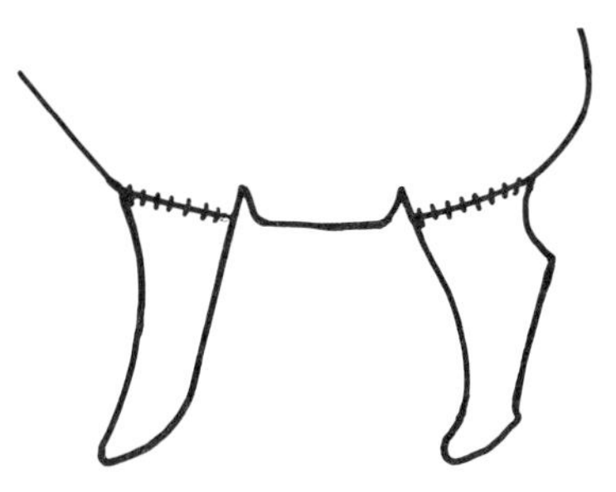

Fig. 1 *Stitching outer legs to body*

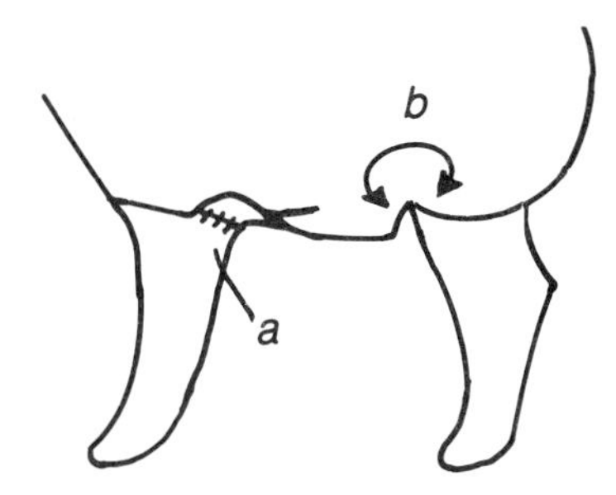

Fig. 2 *Stitching belly flap to inner legs*

top curve of inner leg open.

3. On each body piece, lift belly flap between legs. Pin front cut edge to top curve of inner front leg, right sides together (Fig. 2, a). Stitch, tapering seam at each end.

Pin back cut edge of belly flap to top curve of inner hind leg, right sides together (Fig. 2, b). Stitch in same manner.

4. Pin each face piece to a body piece, right sides together, matching points A and B. Stitch the seam.

5. Pin under gusset to one body unit, right sides together. Match points C (on body) and D (on inner hind leg), pinning along top curves of inner legs. Stitch, tapering seam at D.

Pin under gusset to other body piece and stitch, leaving about 6" open between legs for turning.

6. Pin body units together. Stitch from C, around head and body to D. Turn to right side.

Stuff and finish

1. Stuff head and neck firmly. Stuff each leg for about 1".

2. Prepare inner wire support, referring to page 4. Cut a 9″ length of wire for body and a 17″ length for each pair of legs. Make a small loop in each wire end, and tape wires together to hold in place. Wrap with nylon or knit fabric, then wrap with fiberfill. Keep wrappings smooth and slim to avoid bulges.

Position support in Sheep, adding fiberfill on all sides to keep support centered. Finish stuffing toy firmly, and close opening with invisible stitches.

3. To make tail, fold fabric in half, with fur inside. Stitch, leaving opening at rounded end for turning. Turn to right side, stuff lightly, and stitch to body.

4. To make each ear, pin a felt piece to a fur piece, with fur inside. Stitch around curves, leaving bottom edge open. Turn to right side.

Fold each ear in half, felt inside. Stitch to head so ear slants downward.

5. Make and attach eyes; see *To make a felt eye,* page 5. Cut the large oval from the plastic lid and cover it with brown felt. Glue on a black felt center.

6. For nostrils, cut two strips of brown felt, each 1/8x½″. See pattern for position and glue or stitch to face.

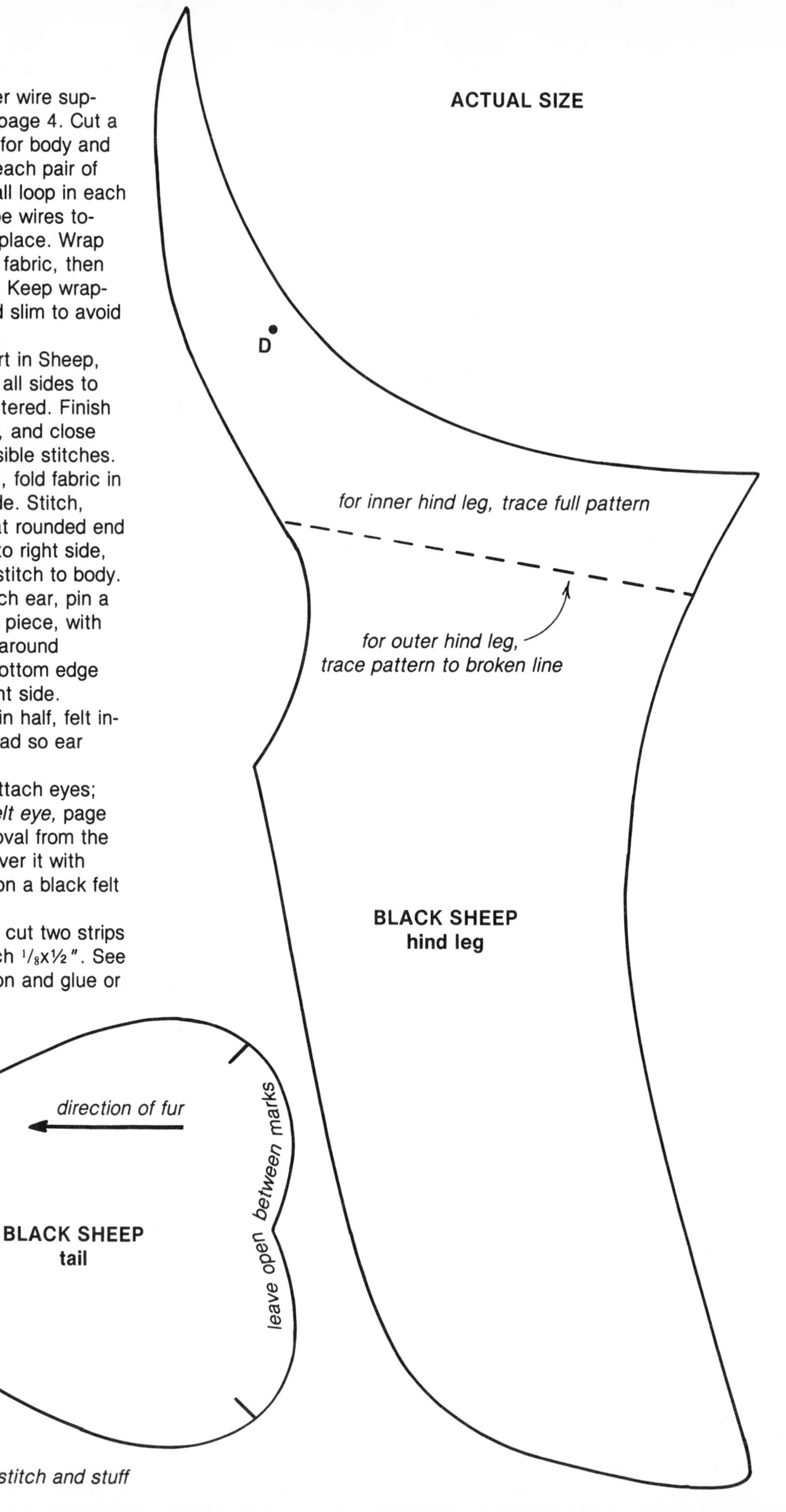

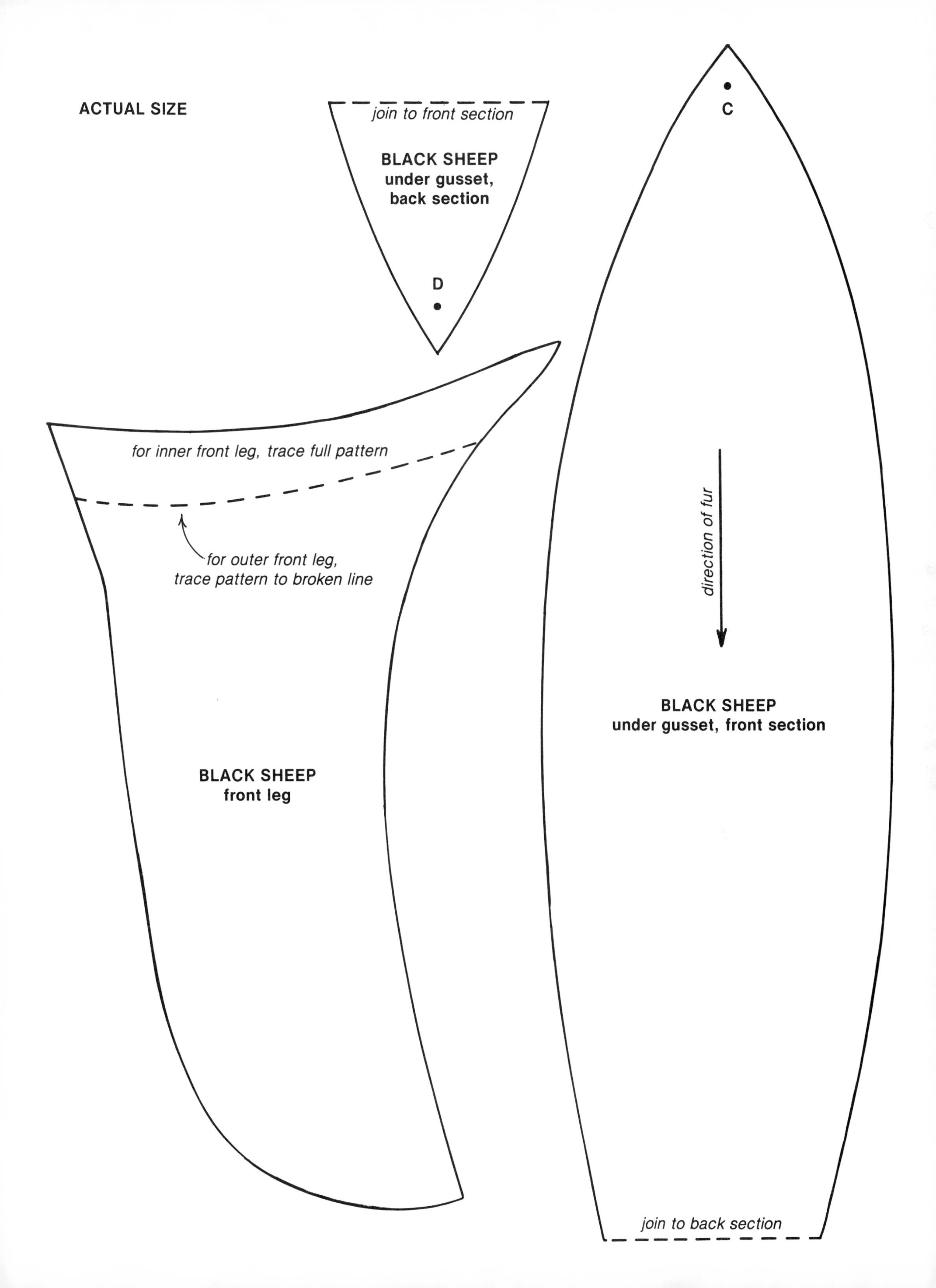
ACTUAL SIZE
join to front section
BLACK SHEEP
under gusset,
back section
D
C
for inner front leg, trace full pattern
for outer front leg,
trace pattern to broken line
BLACK SHEEP
front leg
direction of fur
BLACK SHEEP
under gusset, front section
join to back section

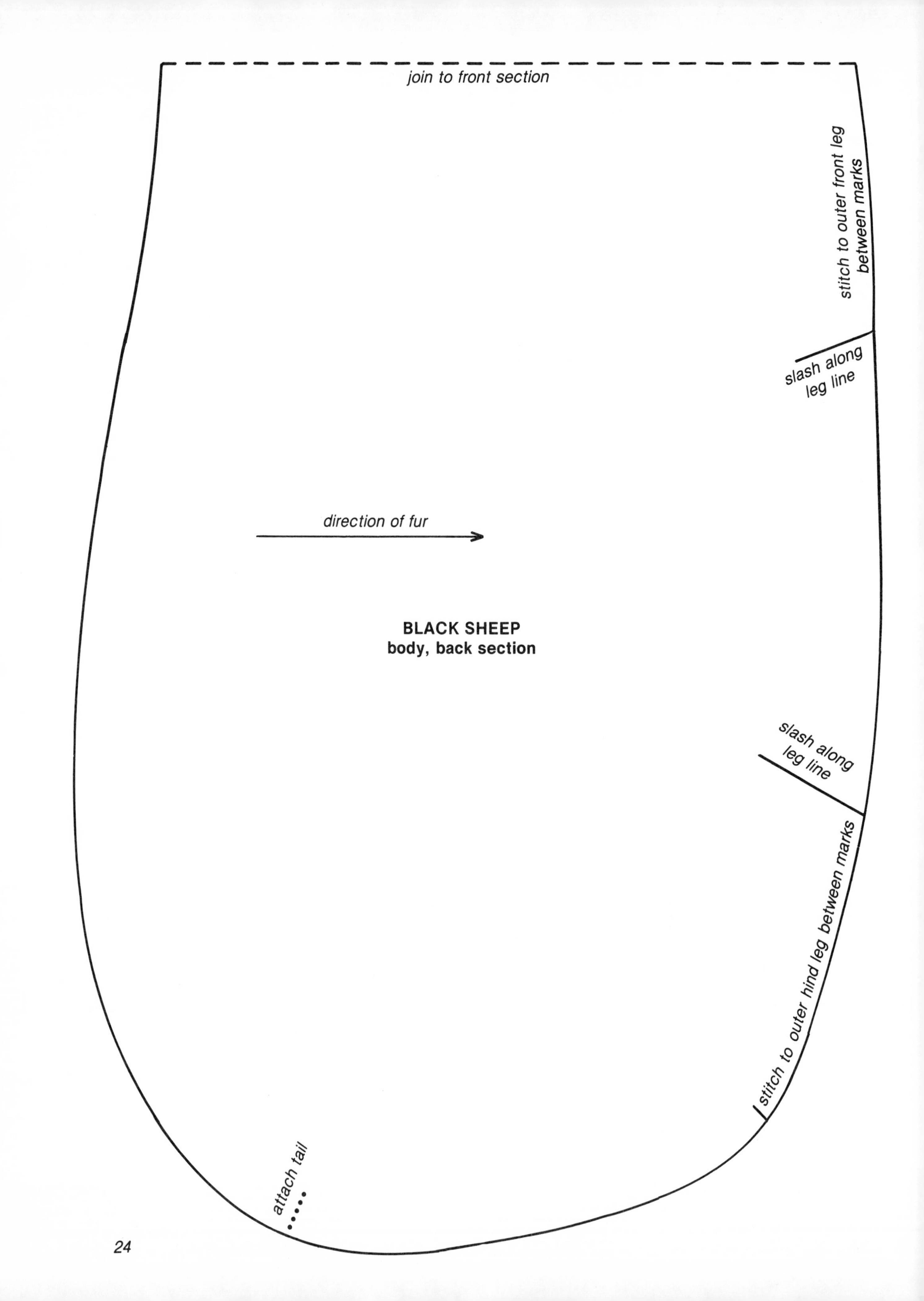
join to front section
stitch to outer front leg between marks
slash along leg line
direction of fur
BLACK SHEEP
body, back section
slash along leg line
stitch to outer hind leg between marks
attach tail

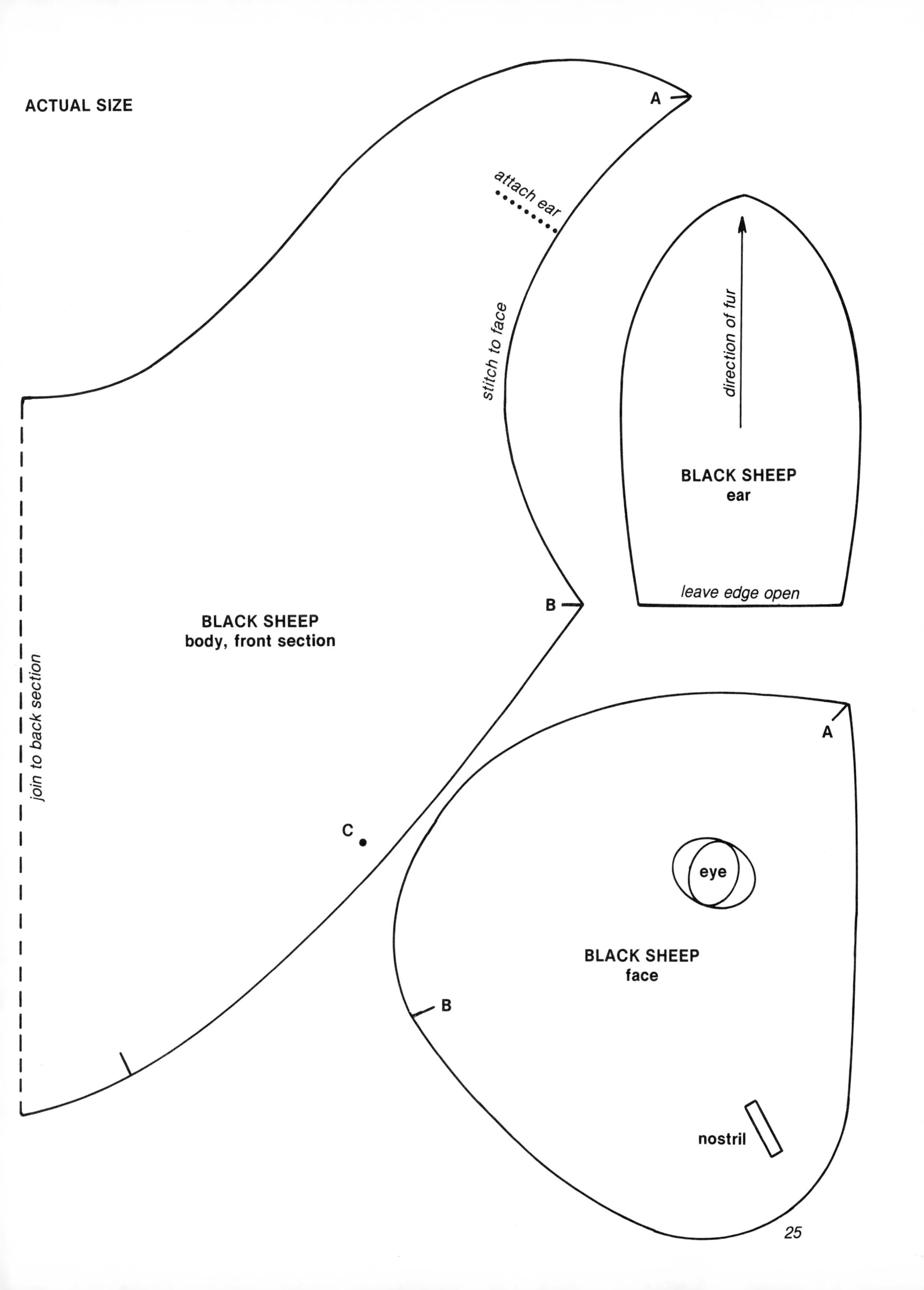
ACTUAL SIZE
A
attach ear
stitch to face
B
BLACK SHEEP
body, front section
join to back section
C
direction of fur
BLACK SHEEP
ear
leave edge open
A
eye
BLACK SHEEP
face
B
nostril

SQUIRREL

(color photo, page 105)

One spring day when I was a child, my brother and I found an injured squirrel under a tree. We warmed him, loved him and fed him drops of milk from the end of a straw.

Scuffy grew up, lived in the attic, and became a member of our household. He packed away incredible numbers of nuts and pine cones in places where our mother didn't want them, but Mom overlooked a lot because Scuffy meant so much to us kids.

You can use any fur fabric for this toy Squirrel, but one with a medium or long pile makes a nice, bushy tail. (I was lucky to find some fake fox fur for mine.) Since the animal is small, you'll have to clip these longer piles on the legs, under gusset, face and ears. Do this before assembling to help shape the body and to make stitching and turning easier. If necessary, you can do some final trimming, after the critter is finished.

The inner ears are felt and the plastic eyes are purchased. If you want to make felt eyes, see *To make a felt eye,* page 5.

MATERIALS

tan fur fabric, 14x28" (pile should run along the 14" length)
brown felt scrap, for inner ears
transparent thread, for machine stitching
button-and-carpet thread, for handwork
plastic animal eyes with posts, 3/8" diameter (available at craft shops)
polyester fiberfill, for stuffing

DIRECTIONS

For tips on tracing patterns and working with fur fabric, see *Helpful Guides,* page 1.

Make pattern pieces

1. Trace pattern for body, page 27. Trace separate patterns for inner front leg, inner hind leg, ear and under gusset, page 27. Also trace the two tail patterns, page 28; join sections for tail top pattern on broken lines.

2. Cut out full pattern pieces. On body piece, slash along lines at legs, as indicated on pattern.

Cut fabric

1. Lay pattern pieces on back of fur fabric, making sure fur is running in correct direction. Trace 2 body pieces (1 reversed), 2 inner front legs (1 reversed), 2 inner hind legs (1 reversed), 1 under gusset, 2 ears, 2 under tail pieces (1 reversed) and 1 tail top.

2. On felt, trace 2 ears.

3. Cut out fabric on traced lines; seam allowances are included. Slash body pieces at legs.

Assemble

Use ¼" (or narrower) seams, with a zigzag machine stitch or an overcast hand stitch.

1. Pin each inner leg to matching body piece, right sides together. Machine-stitch around leg, tapering seam at top edges; leave top curve of inner leg open.

2. On each body piece, lift belly flap between legs. Pin front cut edge to top curve of inner front leg, right sides together (see Fig. 2, a for Pig, page 16). Hand-stitch the short seam.

Pin cut edge of belly flap to top curve of inner hind leg, right sides together (see Fig. 2, b for Pig, page 16). Hand-stitch in same manner.

3. Pin under gusset to one body piece, right sides together; match points A and B, and pin along curves on inner legs. Hand-stitch between points.

Pin under gusset to other body piece. Stitch seam, leaving an opening in the middle for turning.

4. Pin body pieces together along head and back, and machine-stitch. Turn to right side.

5. To make tail, pin the top piece to each under tail piece; match points C and D and stitch.

Pin the two under tail pieces together along the center seam. Begin at C and stitch the seam, leaving 4" open above D for turning. Turn to right side.

Stuff and finish

1. Install plastic eyes.

2. Stuff legs firmly, making sure stuffing is packed tightly where legs join body. Stuff rest of body, and close opening with invisible stitches.

3. Stuff tail lightly to hold shape, and close end of center seam with invisible stitches.

4. Pin tail to body. Align base of tail with inner hind leg seams on body, and let tail run up the body. Stitch tail to body for about 2". (Tail should allow Squirrel to stand on all four legs and to sit up.)

5. To make each ear, pin a felt piece to a fur piece, right sides together. Stitch a narrow seam, leaving bottom edge open. Turn to right side. Gather bottom edge of ear and stitch to head.

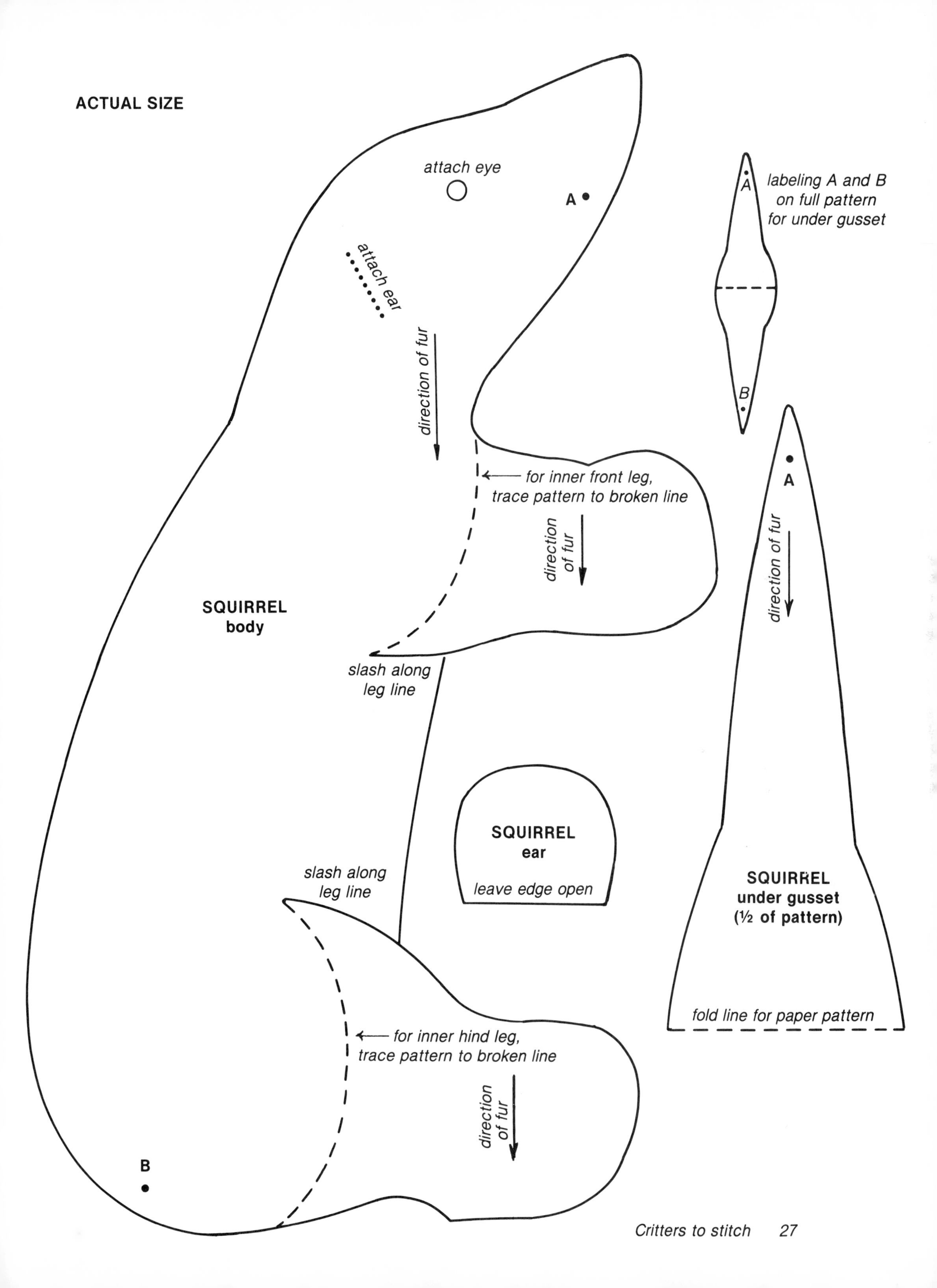
ACTUAL SIZE
attach eye
A
attach ear
direction of fur
for inner front leg,
trace pattern to broken line
direction of fur
SQUIRREL
body
slash along
leg line
slash along
leg line
for inner hind leg,
trace pattern to broken line
direction of fur
B
SQUIRREL
ear
leave edge open
A
labeling A and B
on full pattern
for under gusset
B
A
direction of fur
SQUIRREL
under gusset
(½ of pattern)
fold line for paper pattern

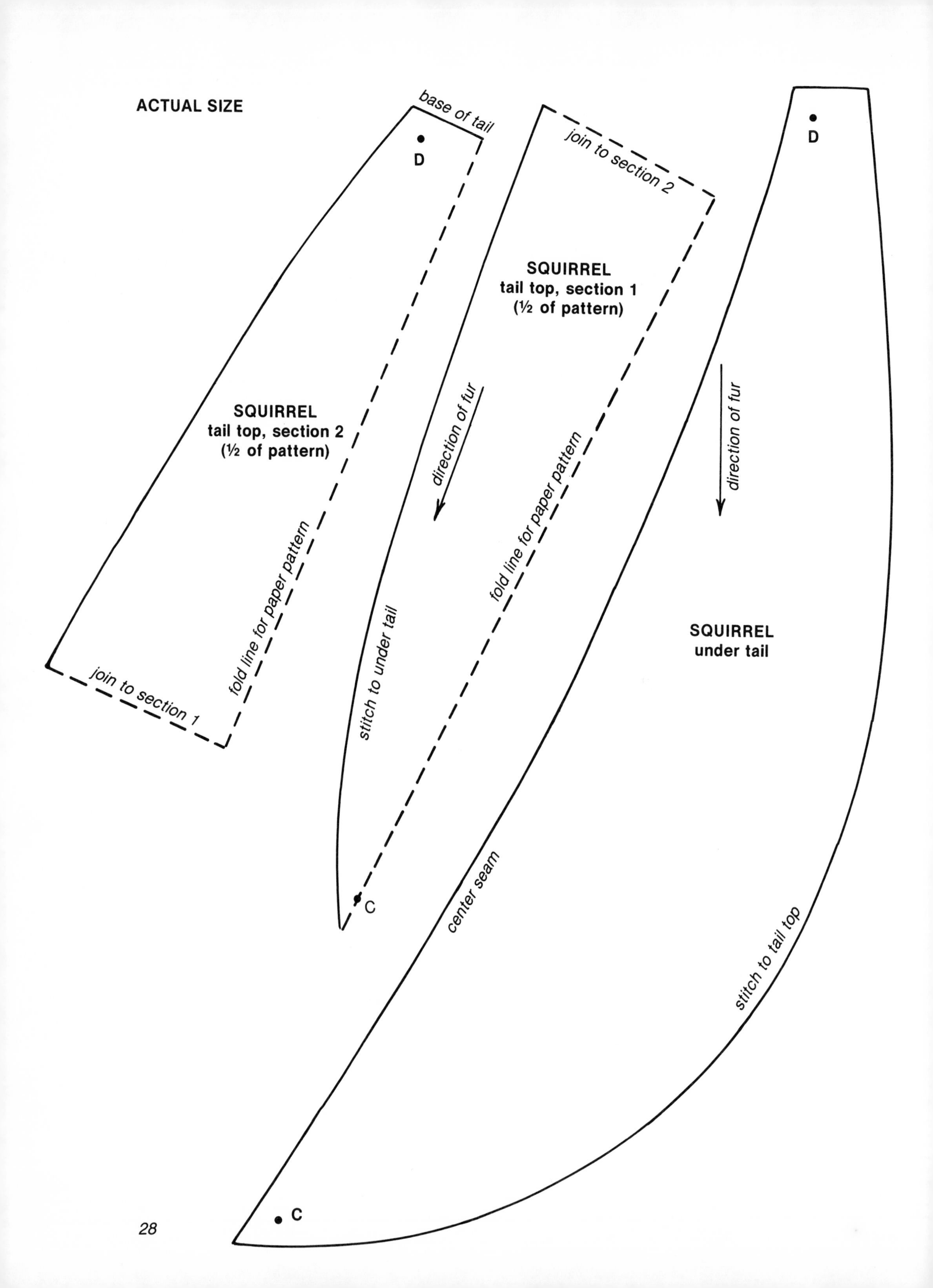
ACTUAL SIZE
base of tail
D
SQUIRREL
tail top, section 2
(½ of pattern)
fold line for paper pattern
join to section 1
join to section 2
SQUIRREL
tail top, section 1
(½ of pattern)
direction of fur
fold line for paper pattern
stitch to under tail
C
D
direction of fur
SQUIRREL
under tail
center seam
stitch to tail top
C

WORM & APPLE PILLOW

(color photo, page 31)

(The Apple also may be made into a pajama bag.)

What a thrill when a child finds his first real furry caterpillar or wiggly worm! Even though the sight of such a "treasure" in a chubby fist may startle some grandmas, I've tried never to discourage these exciting encounters.

I must admit, however, that I'm more comfortable with my own creation. Squirmy is cute and cuddly, complete with its own Apple Pillow (or pajama bag) to delight a little person.

To make an Apple Pillow, you can use a plush pile fabric or a lively cotton print. For a pajama bag, however, you should choose the plush.

MATERIALS

red or yellow plush fabric, 18x40", for Apple (pile should run along the 18" length)
green plush fabric, 11x21", for leaves (pile should run along the 11" length)
brown plush fabric, 6½x6½", for stem
transparent thread, for machine stitching
button-and-carpet thread, for handwork
polyester fiberfill, for stuffing
green or brown plush fabric, 9x22", for Worm (pile can run along either length)
white, black and brown (or green) felt scraps, for eyes
pink felt scrap, for tongue (optional)
plastic lid, for eyes
glue
2 lengths yellow bump chenille, each 4" long, for antennae
self-gripping fastener, ½x1", for attaching Worm to Apple
9" zipper to match Apple fabric (for pajama bag only)

DIRECTIONS

For tips on tracing and enlarging patterns, and working with fur fabric, see *Helpful Guides,* page 1.

Make pattern pieces

1. Use a 22x24" sheet of paper (marked in 2" squares) to enlarge pattern for Apple, page 39.
2. Trace patterns for leaf, stem, Worm eye and critter circle, page 40.
3. Cut out full pattern pieces.

Cut fabric

1. Lay pattern pieces on back (wrong side) of fabric, making sure fur is running in correct direction. On red or yellow, trace 2 Apple pieces. On green, trace 4 leaves (2 reversed). On brown, trace 2 stems (1 reversed).
2. For Worm, place critter circle pattern on back of plush fabric and trace 10 times.
3. Cut out fabric on traced lines; ¼" seam allowances are included.

Assemble Apple

Use ¼" seams and a zigzag machine stitch on fur fabric.

1. *For pillow,* pin Apple pieces right sides together. Stitch, leaving an opening for turning. Turn to right side.

For pajama bag, first make a 9" slash down the center of one Apple piece (the back) and insert matching zipper, as in Fig. 1. (Do not turn fur fabric under; stitch raw edge to zipper tape.) Open zipper and stitch Apple front to back, right sides together. Turn to right side through zipper opening.

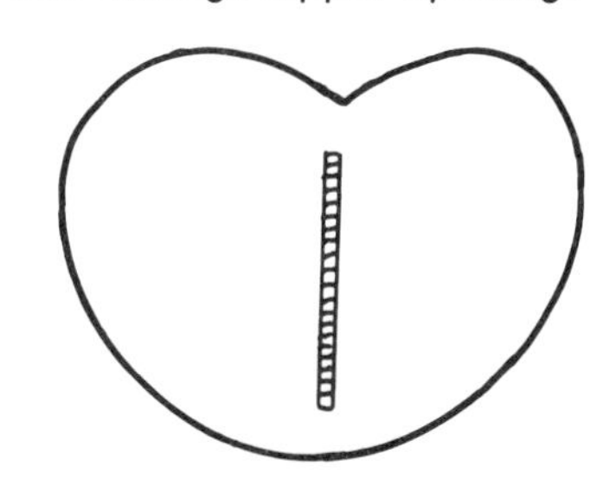

Fig. 1 *Inserting zipper for pajama bag*

2. To make each leaf, pin two matching leaf pieces right sides together. Stitch, leaving an opening for turning. Turn to right side.
3. To make stem, follow directions under Step 2 for leaf.

Stuff and finish Apple

1. *For pillow,* stuff to medium fullness, and close opening with invisible stitches. *(Skip this step for pajama bag.)*
2. Stuff leaves and stem loosely, and close openings with invisible stitches.
3. Stitch stem and leaves to top of Apple.

Assemble Worm

Use ¼" seams and a zigzag machine stitch.

1. Pin circles together in pairs, with fur inside. Machine-stitch, leaving a 2½" opening at the bottom.
2. Turn to right side. This gives you five circle units.

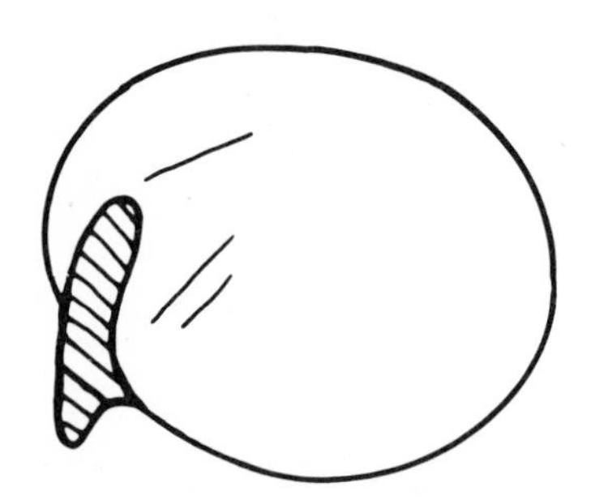

Fig. 2 *Folding raw edges of opening crosswise to circle seam*

Stuff and finish Worm

1. Take four circle units and stuff the top half of each one to make it medium-firm. Fold opening crosswise to the circle seam (Fig. 2). Stitch edges together by hand. If fabric backing is soft enough to roll under, use invisible stitches. Otherwise, sew cut edges together with an overcast stitch.

2. Arrange stuffed units in a line, with legs down (Fig. 3); circle seams run down the center, from front to back. Sew together with a few hand stitches.

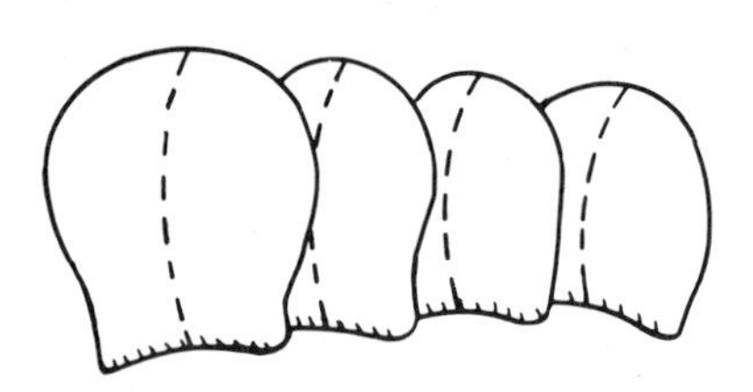

Fig. 3 *Lining up units to form Worm body, with circle seams at center*

3. For head, stuff last unit. Turn raw edges in and close opening along the circle seam with invisible stitches.

4. Stitch head to body, with circle seam at center front (see Fig. 4).

Fig. 4 *Adding trims to Worm*

5. Make and attach eyes; see *To make a felt eye*, page 5. Cut the large oval from the plastic lid and cover it with white felt. Glue on a middle-size brown (or green) felt oval and a small black felt oval.

6. Sew on two lengths of bump chenille to form the antennae.

7. If you wish to make a tongue, cut a strip of pink felt ¼x1¾" and stitch to front seam on head.

8. Add self-gripping fastener. Sew one section of fastener to bottom of Worm body (second circle unit), and sew matching section to center of Apple.

SIMPLE CIRCLE CRITTERS

After completing the Worm, I was intrigued with the possibilities of the circle pattern. So I made a few other characters with the same pattern.

Here are a little Rabbit, Leopard, Kitten, Puppy, Robin, Chick and Duck. Once you make a Circle Critter, you'll probably go on to create your own menagerie.

This is a good way to use up fur scraps, combining whatever colors you have on hand. My standard critter circle is 4" in diameter. You might try using 2" or 3" circles to make baby animals for the 4" Moms and Dads.

BASIC MATERIALS

transparent thread, for machine stitching
button-and-carpet thread, for handwork
polyester fiberfill, for stuffing
plastic lid, for eyes
glue
fur fabric, felt and trims (see Additional Materials for individual critters)

GENERAL DIRECTIONS

For tips on tracing patterns and working with fur fabric, see *Helpful Guides,* page 1.

1. For both head and body units, work with pairs of circles. Pin two circles right sides together. Machine-stitch with a ¼" zigzag seam, leaving 2½" open at bottom. Turn to right side and stuff to make it medium-firm.

2. *To make a round unit* for head or body, close opening along the circle seam. Use an

(continued on page 35)

This Siamese Cat (page 91) combines tan and black fur fabrics, but you could use the same pattern for a one-color cat. Each Worm is made of ten circles—and each one has its own Apple Pillow (page 29).

Dolls are easy to stitch with polyester doubleknit fabrics, and here are three generations, from Grandpa to Baby (page 52). Tuck Baby dolls into buntings, and give the other dolls hair cut from long-pile fur fabrics.

Only two major pattern pieces are needed to whip up this 11"-high Shag Dog (page 88). The Simple Circle Critters, left to right, are a Puppy, Rabbit, Leopard and Kitten (beginning on page 30), all cut from the same circle pattern.

(continued from page 30)

invisible stitch, turning raw edges to the inside.

3. *To make a unit with two peaks* (for legs or ears), fold opening crosswise to the circle seam (see Fig. 2, page 30). Stitch edges together by hand. If fabric backing is soft enough to roll under, use an invisible stitch. Otherwise, sew cut edges together with an overcast stitch.

Rabbit

(color photo, page 34)

Combine white and pink fur fabric to make this wide-eyed critter. You can make the tail or use a pink pompon.

ADDITIONAL MATERIALS

(Check Basic Materials, page 30)
white long-pile fur fabric, 9x15" (pile can run along either length)
pink long-pile fur fabric, 4½x8½", for ears and tail (or 4½x5" for ears only); pile should run along the 4½" length
blue and black felt scraps, for eyes
pink yarn, for nose and mouth
pink pompon, 2½" diameter, for tail (optional)

ADDITIONAL DIRECTIONS

Make pattern pieces

1. Trace pattern for critter circle, page 40. Trace patterns for Rabbit ear, tail and eye, page 41.
2. Cut out pattern pieces.

Cut fabric

1. Lay pattern pieces on back of fur fabric, making sure fur is running in correct direction. On white, trace 6 critter circles and 2 ears. On pink, trace 2 ears and 1 tail.
2. Cut out fabric on traced lines; seam allowances are included.

Assemble, stuff and finish

1. Stitch fur circles together to make three units (see *General directions,* Step 1).
2. Complete one unit for a round head (see *General directions,* Step 2). Complete two units with peaks (legs) for the body (see *General directions,* Step 3).
3. Join two units with peaks (legs) down for body, circle seams touching. Add round unit for head, with circle seam at center front.
4. To make each ear, pin a white fur piece to a pink piece, right sides together. Stitch a narrow seam, leaving bottom edge open for turning. Turn to right side.

Fold each ear down center, bringing curved edges forward, and stitch to head.

5. To make tail, hand-stitch a gathering thread around edge of tail circle. Stuff a little fiberfill in center of circle, then pull thread tightly to make a ball. Stitch to body.

(If you prefer, use pompon for tail and stitch to body.)

6. Make and attach eyes; see *To make a felt eye*, page 5. Cut the large oval from the plastic lid and cover it with blue felt. Glue on a smaller black felt circle.
7. Add nose and mouth lines. With pink yarn, make two 5/8"-long straight stitches along the circle seam. At each end of these stitches, take two 3/8"-long diagonal stitches.

Leopard

(color photo, page 34)

Spotted fabric makes this critter a Leopard. Substitute black and yellow (or black and white) striped fabric, and you turn him into a tiger.

ADDITIONAL MATERIALS

(Check Basic Materials, page 30)
spotted fur fabric with flat nap, 9x16½" (pile should run along the 9" length)
green and black felt scraps, for eyes
pink yarn, for nose and mouth

ADDITIONAL DIRECTIONS

Make pattern pieces

1. Trace pattern for critter circle, page 40. Trace patterns for Leopard ear, tail and eye, page 38.
2. Cut out pattern pieces.

Cut fabric

1. Lay pattern pieces on back of fur fabric, making sure fur is running in correct direction. Trace 6 critter circles, 4 ears and 1 tail.
2. Cut out fabric on traced lines; seam allowances are included.

Assemble, stuff and finish

1. Stitch fur circles together to make three units (see *General directions,* Step 1).
2. Complete one unit to make a round head (see *General directions,* Step 2). Complete two units to make peaks (legs) for body (see *General directions,* Step 3).
3. Join body units with peaks (legs) down, circle seams touching. Add head circle, with seam at center front.
4. To make each ear, pin two ear pieces right sides together. Stitch a narrow seam, leaving straight edge open for turning. Turn to right side.

   Fold each ear down center, bringing curved edges forward, and stitch to head.
5. To make tail, fold fabric in half lengthwise, right side out. Turn raw edges to the inside and close lengthwise seam and one end with invisible stitches. Stitch to body, letting tail curve over the back.
6. Make and attach eyes; see *To make a felt eye*, page 5. Cut circle from the plastic lid and cover it with green felt. Glue on a black felt center piece.
7. Add nose and mouth. With pink yarn, make two 5/8"-long straight stitches along the circle seam. Across the top, take four satin stitches for the nose. At the bottom, take two 3/8"-long diagonal stitches for the mouth.

Kitten

(color photo, page 34)

The sample is made of beige long-pile fur fabric, but you could use any color and fur type you choose.

ADDITIONAL MATERIALS

(Check Basic Materials, page 30)

beige long-pile or other fur fabric, 9x17" (pile should run along the 9" length)

turquoise and black felt scraps, for eyes

black yarn, for mouth, nose and whiskers

ADDITIONAL DIRECTIONS

Make pattern pieces

1. Trace pattern for critter circle, page 40. Trace patterns for Kitten tail and eye, page 41.
2. Cut out pattern pieces.

Cut fabric

1. Lay pattern pieces on back of fur fabric, making sure fur is running in correct direction. Trace 6 critter circles and 2 tails (1 reversed).
2. Cut out fabric on traced lines; seam allowances are included.

Assemble, stuff and finish

1. Stitch fur circles together to make three units (see *General directions,* Step 1).
2. Complete all three units with peaks (see *General directions,* Step 3).
3. Join two units with peaks (legs) down for body, circle seams touching. Add third unit with peaks (ears) up for head.
4. Pin tail pieces right sides together. Stitch a narrow seam, leaving straight edge open for turning. Turn to right side and stitch to body.
5. Make and attach eyes; see *To make a felt eye*, page 5. Cut the circle from the plastic lid and cover it with turquoise felt. Glue on a black felt center piece.
6. Add nose and mouth. (You may want to clip pile in face area first.) With black yarn, make two 5/8"-long straight stitches along the circle seam. Across the top, make four satin stitches for the nose. At the bottom, take two 3/8"-long diagonal stitches for the mouth.

   For whiskers, take a small stitch on each side of the face. Tie yarn in knot and cut off, leaving ½" lengths.

Puppy

(*color photo, page 34*)

The sample is made of long-pile fur fabric in shades of gray. Follow directions for Kitten, substituting patterns for Puppy tail and eye.

Attach tail (Step 4) so it curves over back of Puppy. For eye (Step 5), cover the plastic circle with black felt. For rest of face (Step 6), add only a nose, using black yarn and a few satin stitches.

Robin

(*color photo, page 68*)

The arrival of this brown bird with a red breast announces spring in many parts of the country.

ADDITIONAL MATERIALS

(Check Basic Materials, page 30)

brown plush fabric, 4½x14" (pile can run along either length)

red plush fabric, 4½x4½", for breast

yellow felt, 8x9", for eyes, beak and feet

black felt scrap, for eyes

ADDITIONAL DIRECTIONS

Make pattern pieces

1. Trace pattern for critter circle, page 40. Trace patterns for bird tail, beak, eye and foot, page 41.
2. Cut out pattern pieces.

Cut fabric

1. Lay pattern pieces on back of brown plush, making sure fur is running in correct direction. Trace 3 critter circles and 2 tail pieces. On back of red plush, trace 1 critter circle.
2. Cut out fabric on traced lines; seam allowances are included.

Assemble, stuff and finish

1. Stitch fur circles together to make two units (see *General directions,* Step 1).
2. Complete both units to make them round (see *General directions,* Step 2).
3. Join head to body; have red breast (body) and circle head seam at front.
4. Pin tail pieces right sides together. Stitch a narrow seam, leaving straight edge open for turning. Turn to right side and stitch tail to body about ¾" from seam.
5. Make and attach felt eyes; see *To make a felt eye,* page 5. Cut large circle from the plastic lid and cover it with yellow felt. Glue on a smaller black felt circle.
6. To make beak and each foot, place each pattern piece on double layer of yellow felt and straight-stitch around it. Cut out felt 1/8" from stitching.
7. Fold beak in half and sew to head, catching back layer of felt.
8. Attach feet, sewing center of each foot to circle seam.

Bluebird

(*color photo, pages 104, 105*)

Follow directions for Robin, using blue plush for body and tail, orange plush for breast, and orange felt for the large eye circle, beak and feet.

Chick

(*color photo, page 68*)

Cut circles of yellow plush to make this baby chicken.

ADDITIONAL MATERIALS
(Check Basic Materials, page 30)
yellow plush fabric, 9x9"
yellow felt, 8x9", for beak and feet
green and black felt scraps, for eyes

ADDITIONAL DIRECTIONS

Make pattern pieces

1. Trace pattern for critter circle, page 40. Trace patterns for Chick beak, foot and eye, page 41.
2. Cut out pattern pieces.

Cut fabric

1. Lay pattern pieces on back of yellow plush, making sure fur is running in correct direction. Trace 4 critter circles.
2. Cut out fabric on traced lines; seam allowances are included.

Assemble, stuff and finish

1. Pin and stitch fur circles together to make two units (see *General directions*, Step 1).
2. Complete one unit for a round head (see *General directions*, Step 2). Complete second unit with peaks (legs) for body (see *General directions*, Step 3).
3. Join head to body, with both circle seams at center front.
4. Make and attach felt eyes; see *To make a felt eye*, page 5. Cut the large circle from the plastic lid and cover it with blue felt. Glue on a black felt circle.
5. To make beak and each foot, place each pattern piece on double layer of yellow felt and straight-stitch around it. Cut out felt 1/8" from stitching.
6. Fold beak in half and sew to head, catching back layer of felt.
7. Attach feet, sewing each foot under a leg.

Duck

(color photo, page 68)

Follow directions for Chick, at left, substituting pattern pieces for Duck bill and foot, below. Use orange felt for bill and feet, and blue felt for the large eye circle.

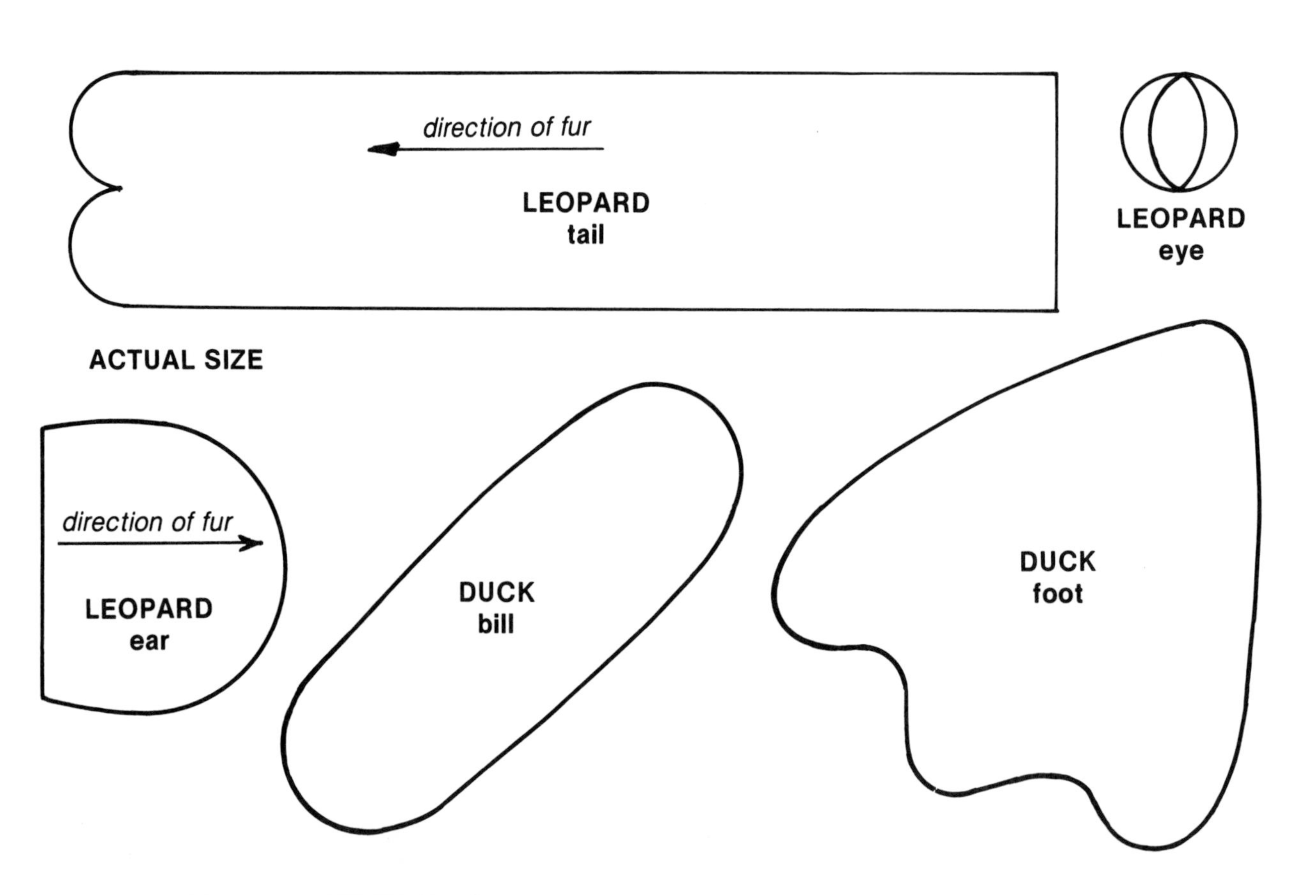

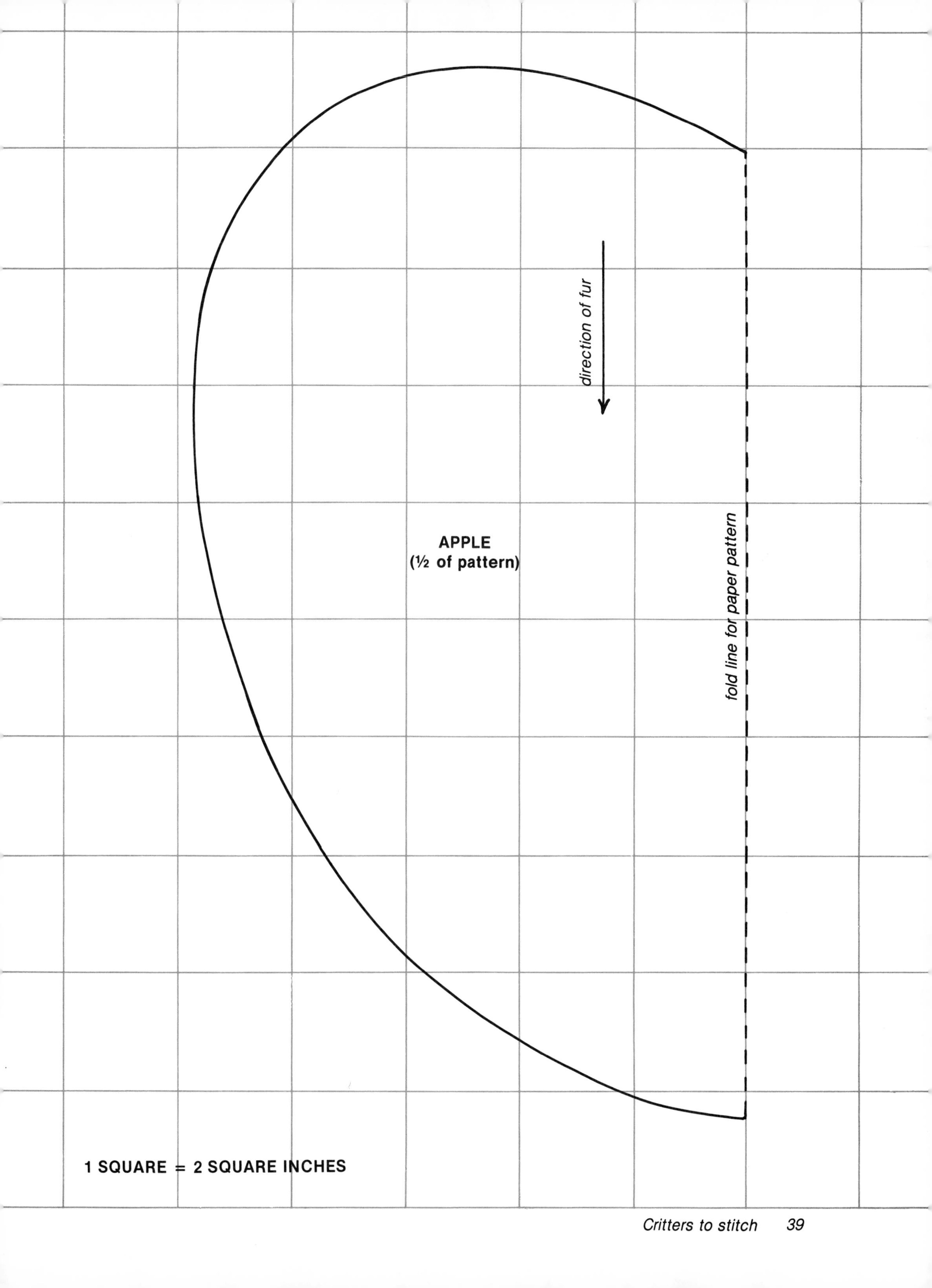
direction of fur
APPLE
(½ of pattern)
fold line for paper pattern
1 SQUARE = 2 SQUARE INCHES

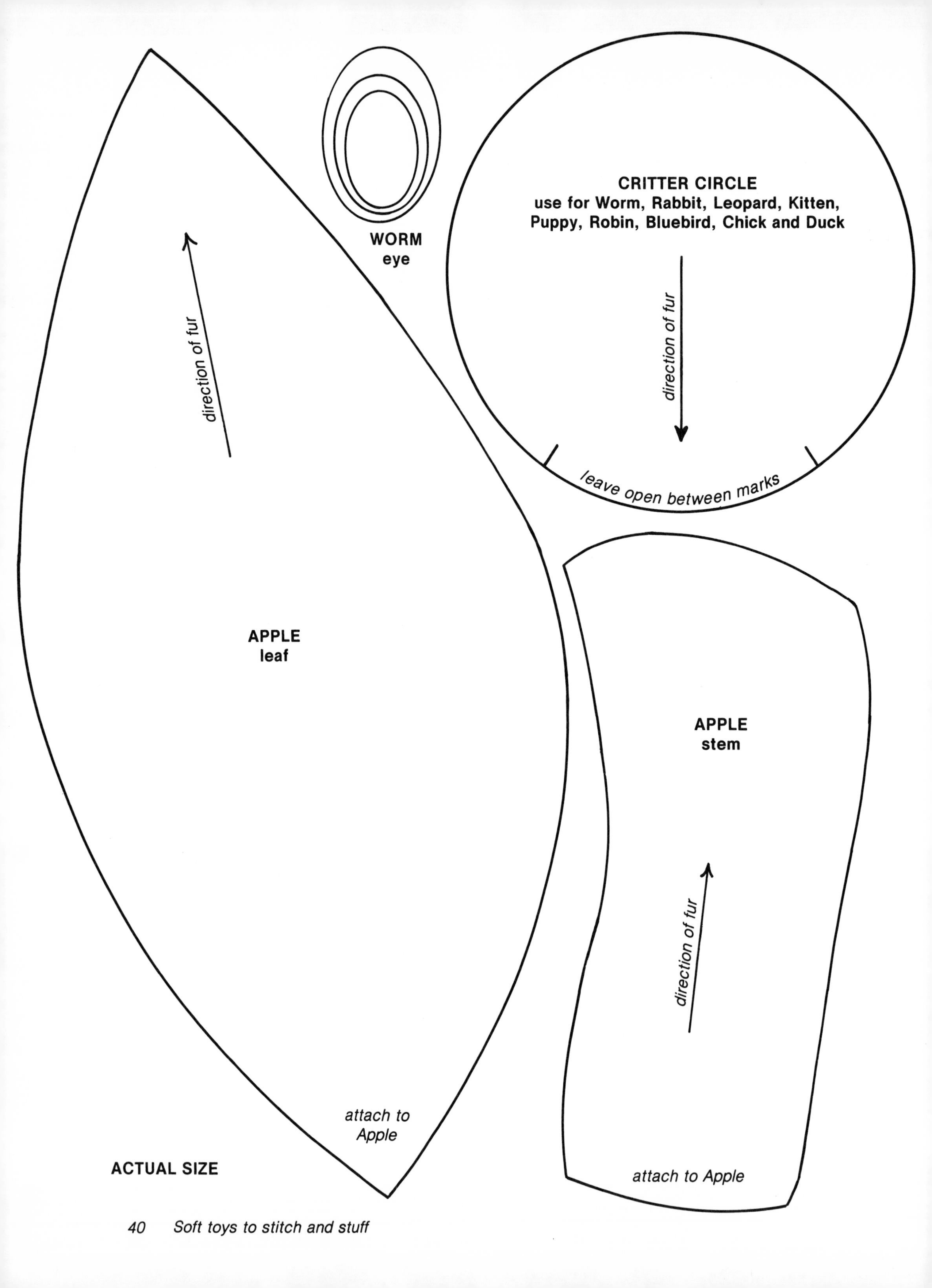
WORM
eye
CRITTER CIRCLE
use for Worm, Rabbit, Leopard, Kitten, Puppy, Robin, Bluebird, Chick and Duck
direction of fur
leave open between marks
direction of fur
APPLE
leaf
attach to Apple
ACTUAL SIZE
APPLE
stem
direction of fur
attach to Apple

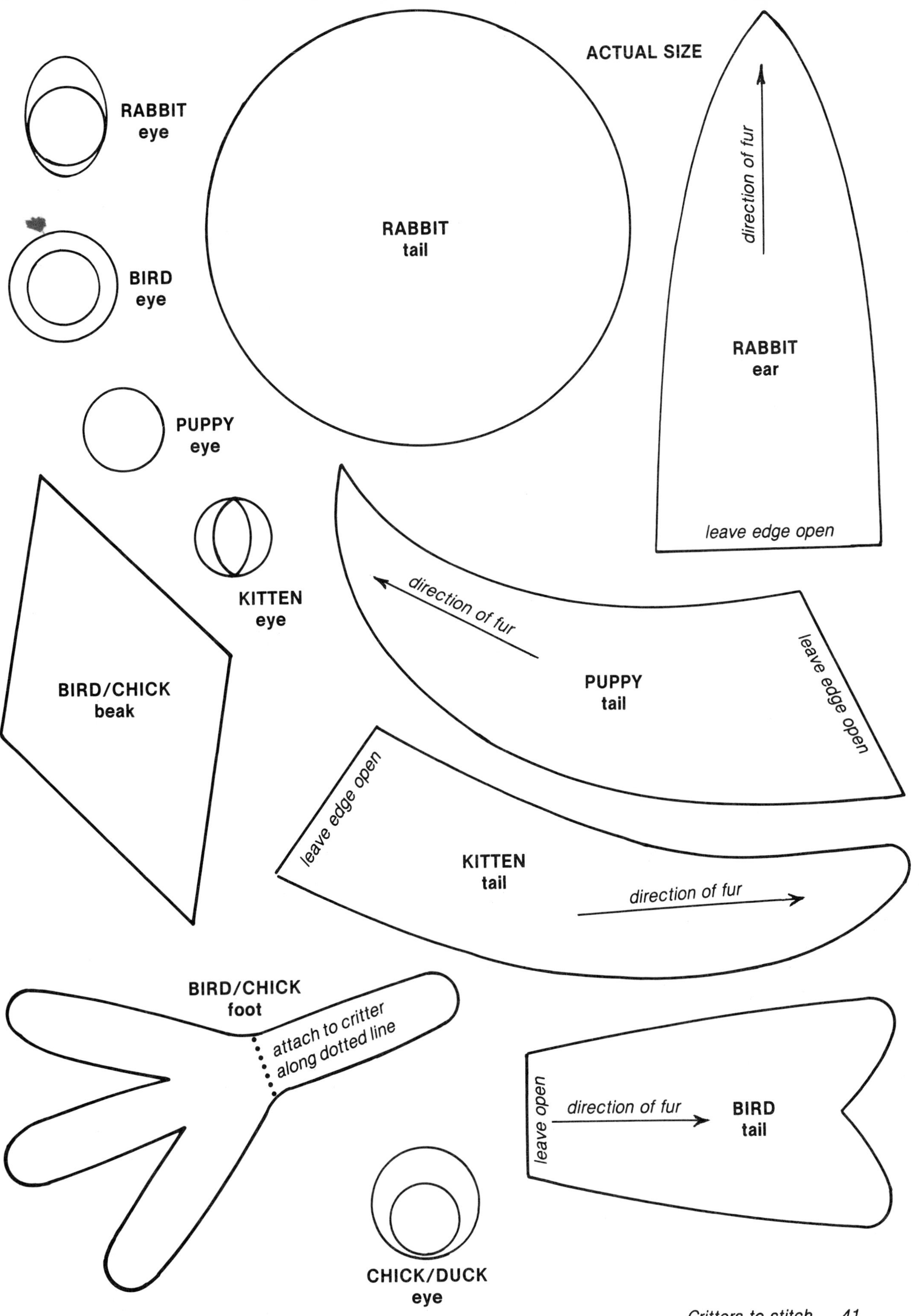
ACTUAL SIZE
RABBIT
eye
RABBIT
tail
direction of fur
RABBIT
ear
leave edge open
BIRD
eye
PUPPY
eye
KITTEN
eye
direction of fur
PUPPY
tail
leave edge open
BIRD/CHICK
beak
leave edge open
KITTEN
tail
direction of fur
BIRD/CHICK
foot
attach to critter
along dotted line
leave open
direction of fur
BIRD
tail
CHICK/DUCK
eye

Pond dwellers

FISH & FISH POLE

(color photo, page 12)

(The Fish may be made into a small stuffed toy or a large pillow.)

On our farm, we use irrigation for the crops, so a pond with real fish is a part of our environment. We can go fishing without leaving home.

Here's a toy Fish that youngsters can "catch" in the house—no water needed. The 9½" toy has a fabric-covered magnet on its nose, and you go fishing with a horseshoe magnet tied to your line. Stitch up three furry Fish in assorted colors and add a plush-covered pole to complete the set.

By enlarging the basic pattern, you also can make an attractive pillow about 29" long. Choose fur fabric in a solid color or tiger stripes, or use a decorator print. It's an inexpensive way to add color and a new look to a room.

MATERIALS

fabric in tiger stripes or solid-color plush, 9x24", for each toy Fish (pile should run along the 9" length)
¾ yd. fabric in tiger stripes or solid-color plush, 60" wide, for pillow
beige plush fabric, 3½x26", to cover fish pole (pile can run along either length)
black felt scraps, plus gold (or white or orange) felt scraps, for eyes
fabric scraps to match Fish body or eyes, for covering magnet
transparent thread, for machine stitching
button-and-carpet thread, for handwork
polyester fiberfill, for stuffing
1 yd. narrow ribbon, for fish line
plastic lid, for eyes
glue
24" wooden dowel or P.V.C. (plastic) pipe, ¾" outside diameter, for fish pole
3 round magnets, ¾" diameter (one for each toy Fish)
horseshoe magnet, 1¼" wide, for fish pole

DIRECTIONS

For tips on tracing and enlarging patterns, and working with fur fabric, see *Helpful Guides*, page 1.

Make pattern pieces

1. *For toy Fish*, trace patterns for body, top fin and bottom gusset on opposite page.

For pillow, use a 24x34" sheet of paper (marked in 1½" squares) to enlarge the patterns. Use another sheet of paper to trace the enlarged top fin (this gives you a separate top fin pattern).

2. Cut out pattern pieces.

Cut fabric

1. Lay pattern pieces on back of fur fabric, making sure fur is running in correct direction. For each Fish, trace 2

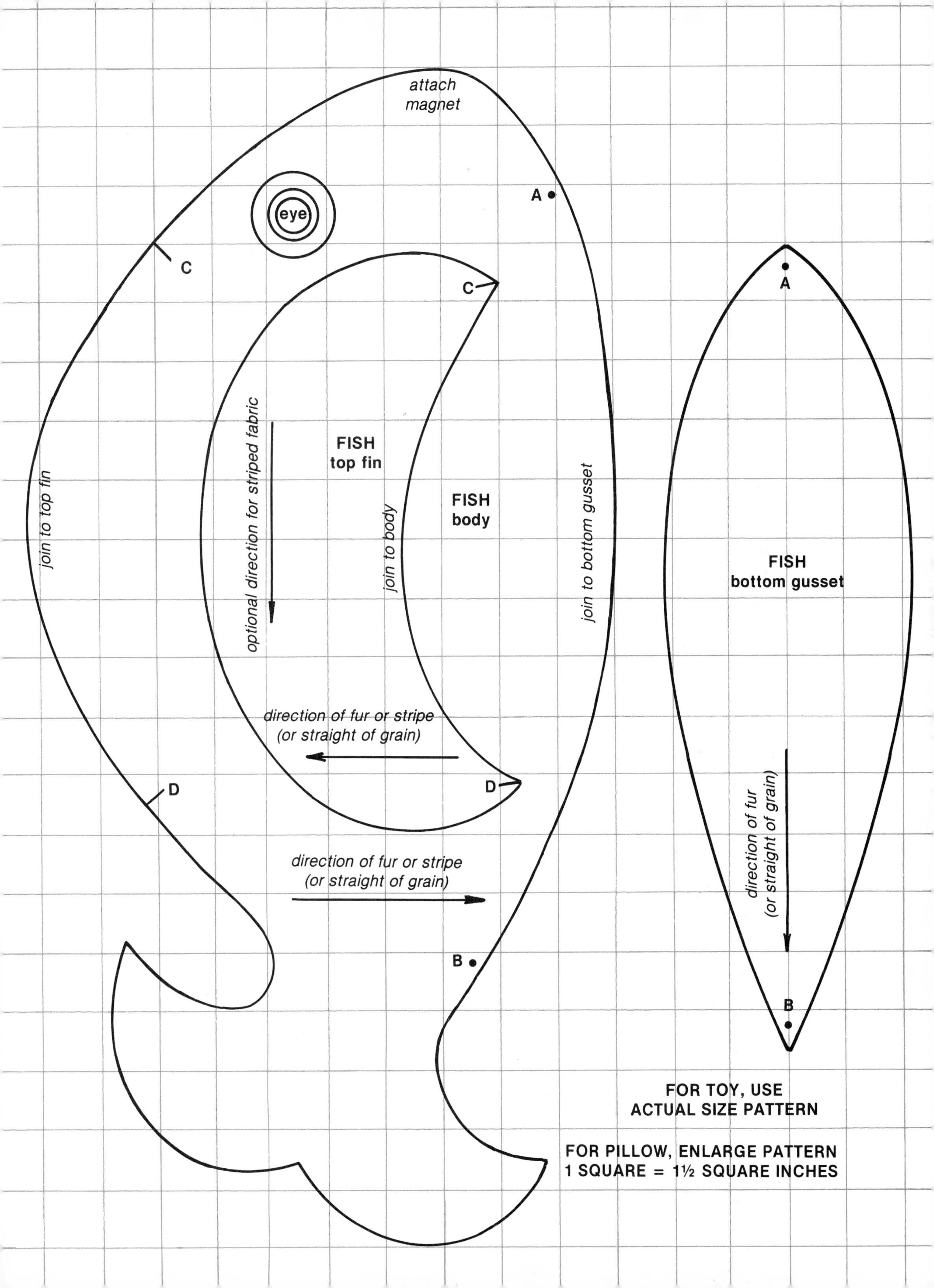

attach magnet
A
eye
C
FISH top fin
optional direction for striped fabric
join to top fin
join to body
FISH body
join to bottom gusset
direction of fur or stripe (or straight of grain)
D
direction of fur or stripe (or straight of grain)
B
FISH bottom gusset
direction of fur (or straight of grain)
FOR TOY, USE ACTUAL SIZE PATTERN
FOR PILLOW, ENLARGE PATTERN 1 SQUARE = 1½ SQUARE INCHES

body pieces (1 reversed), 2 top fins (1 reversed) and 1 bottom gusset. (On striped fabric, fin pattern can be placed so stripes run either up and down or across; see examples on page 12.)

2. Cut out fabric on traced lines; ¼" seam allowances are included.

Assemble each Fish

Use ¼" seams and a zigzag machine stitch.

1. Pin bottom gusset to one body piece, right sides together; match points A and B. Stitch between points.

Pin gusset to other body piece and stitch.

2. Pin fin pieces, right sides together, and stitch around outside curve. Turn to right side and stuff lightly. Pin raw edges together.

3. Pin fin to right side of one body piece; match points C and D and have raw edges even. Join by hand with overcast stitches.

4. Pin body pieces right sides together. Machine-stitch, leaving fin area open. Turn to right side.

Stuff and finish

1. Stuff with fiberfill. Close opening with invisible stitches, turning raw edge on body to inside.

2. To cover round magnet for nose on toy Fish, use fabric to match body or eyes. Cut a 2" circle and sew a running stitch around the edge by hand. Place magnet on wrong side, pull thread to gather fabric tightly around magnet and secure thread.

Position magnet at nose of Fish and sew in place around back edge of magnet.

3. Make and attach eyes; see *To make a felt eye*, page 5. Cut the large eye circle from the plastic lid.

For gold-striped Fish, cover plastic with black felt, then glue on a middle-size gold felt circle and a small black felt circle.

For white-striped Fish, cover plastic with orange felt, then glue on a black middle-size felt circle.

For blue Fish, cover plastic with white felt, then glue on a black middle-size felt circle.

Assemble fish pole

1. Fold the 3½x26" plush fabric in half lengthwise, with fur inside. Stitch across one end and along the length. Turn to right side.

2. Slip fur fabric over dowel or pipe, and close open end by hand.

3. Sew one end of ribbon around horseshoe magnet. Stitch other end of ribbon to pole.

DUCKS & GOOSE

From the edge of a rippling pond, you can often see ducks and geese paddling across the surface. My fabric creations include a furry Wild Duck with a white neck ring, three Cotton Print Ducks in fall colors, and a long-neck gray Goose with a golden egg.

Wild Duck

(color photo, page 13)

Three different colors of plush fabric distinguish this handsome bird. A bright blue head tops a dark blue body, and a patch of brown runs along the back. The white neck ring is a separate strip, added after the bird is finished.

MATERIALS

dark blue plush fabric, 19x21", for body (pile should run along the 21" length)
bright blue plush fabric, 5½x11", for head (pile should run along the 5½" length)
dark brown plush fabric, 4x11", for back (pile should run along the 11" length)
7" strip of white plush fabric or velvet ribbon, ½" wide, for neck ring
yellow felt, 4x6", for beak
white and blue felt scraps, for eyes
transparent thread, for machine stitching
button-and-carpet thread, for handwork
polyester fiberfill, for stuffing
plastic lid, for eyes
glue

DIRECTIONS

For tips on tracing patterns and working with fur fabric, see *Helpful Guides*, page 1.

Make pattern pieces

1. Trace separate patterns for head, page 48, and body, pages 48-49; join body sections on broken lines. Add ¼" to each pattern piece at neck line for seam allowance.

Trace separate patterns for face and front gusset, page 47; join three gusset sections on broken lines. Add ¼" to each pattern piece at neck line for seam allowance.

Also trace patterns for back and small eye, page 47, and for Duck beak, page 49.

2. Cut out full pattern pieces.

Cut fabric

1. Lay pattern pieces on back of plush fabric, making sure fur is running in correct direction. On bright blue, trace 1 face and 2 head pieces (1 reversed). On dark blue, trace two body pieces (1 reversed) and 1 front gusset. On brown plush, trace 1 back.

2. On yellow felt, trace 2 beak pieces.

3. Cut out fabric on traced lines; ¼" seam allowances are included.

Assemble

Use ¼" seams and a zigzag machine stitch.

1. Pin face piece to front gusset at neck, right sides together, and stitch.

2. Pin each head piece to a matching body piece, right sides together, and stitch.

3. Pin front gusset (with face) to one body piece (with head), right sides together, matching points A and B. Stitch between points.

Pin and stitch front gusset to other body piece, leaving opening for turning.

4. Pin back to one body piece, right sides together; match points B and C, easing in fullness on body piece. Stitch between points.

Pin back to other body piece and stitch.

5. Pin body pieces together from A (top of head) down neck to C, and stitch. Turn to right side.

Stuff and finish

1. Press balls of fiberfill into head; use a wooden spoon handle to make head firm. Stuff neck evenly, then stuff body to make it medium-firm. Close opening with invisible stitches.

2. Make and attach eyes; see *To make a felt eye*, page 5. Cut the large circle from the plastic lid, and cover it with white felt. Glue on a blue felt circle.

3. To make beak, pin the two felt pieces together. Join with a straight machine stitch, leaving a small opening for turning. Turn to right side. Stuff lightly with fiberfill if you wish, and close opening by hand.

4. Fold beak in half and stitch to face along the fold. Bend free ends into desired position.

5. To finish Wild Duck, wrap strip of white plush or velvet ribbon around neck to cover seam, and stitch ends together.

Cotton Print Ducks

(color photo, page 13)

Three prints in brown and gold are used for each Duck, but they're combined in different ways. Make one Duck, or use three together as a fall decoration for your mantel.

MATERIALS
(for one Duck)

first cotton print, 12x30", for body
second cotton print, 4x25", for front gusset
third cotton print, 4x11", for back
orange felt, 4x6", for beak
white and brown felt scraps, for eyes
transparent or matching thread, for all stitching
polyester fiberfill, for stuffing
plastic lid, for eye
glue

Note: For three Ducks, use three different prints, 15x30" each, and arrange them differently for each Duck.

DIRECTIONS
(for one Duck)

For tips on tracing patterns and working with fabric, see *Helpful Guides*, page 1.

Make pattern pieces

1. Trace pattern for body, pages 48-49, joining front and back sections on broken lines. Trace patterns for back and front gusset, page 47; join gusset sections on broken lines. Trace patterns for large eye, page 48, and for Duck beak, page 49.

2. Cut out full pattern pieces.

Cut fabric

1. Place pattern pieces on wrong side of fabric. On first print, trace 2 body pieces (1 reversed). On second print, trace 1 front gusset, and on third print, trace 1 back.

2. On orange felt, trace 2 beak pieces.

3. Cut out fabric on traced lines; ¼" seam allowances are included.

Assemble, stuff and finish
Use ¼" seams and a straight machine stitch.

Follow directions for the Wild Duck, beginning with *Assemble*, Step 3, page 45.

After stitching all seams (Step 5), clip seam allowances to stitching along inside curves on neck and back. Press seams open, and turn to right side.

For eyes (Step 2 under *Stuff and finish*), cover the plastic shape with white felt, then glue on a brown felt oval.

Goose with Egg

(color photo, page 13)

The Goose is shaped like the Ducks, but its neck is 3" longer and it has a different beak.

MATERIALS

gray plush fabric, 19x30" (pile should run along the 30" length)
yellow fur fabric, 7x14", for egg (pile can run along either length)
orange felt, 6x6½", for beak
light blue and black felt scraps, for eyes
transparent thread, for machine stitching
button-and-carpet thread, for handwork
polyester fiberfill, for stuffing
plastic lid, for eye
glue

DIRECTIONS

For tips on tracing patterns and working with fur fabric, see *Helpful Guides*, page 1.

Make pattern pieces

1. Trace pattern for body, pages 48-49, joining front and back sections on broken lines; add 3" to elongate neck at neck line. Trace front gusset, page 47, joining sections on broken lines; add 3" to elongate neck at neck line.

Also trace patterns for back and small eye, page 47; the Goose egg, page 48; and the three beak pieces (top beak, bottom beak and Goose inner beak), page 49.

2. Cut out full pattern pieces.

Cut fabric

1. Lay pattern pieces on back of gray plush, making sure fur is running in correct direction. Trace 2 body pieces (1 reversed), 1 front gusset and 1 back. On yellow fur fabric, trace 4 egg pieces.

2. On orange felt, trace 1 top beak, 1 bottom beak and 1 inner beak.

3. Cut out fabric on traced lines; ¼" seam allowances are included.

Assemble

Follow directions for Wild Duck, beginning with *Assemble*, Step 3, page 45.

Stuff and finish

1. Press balls of fiberfill into head; use a wooden spoon handle to make head firm. Stuff neck evenly, then stuff body to make it medium-firm. Close opening with invisible stitches.

2. Make and attach eyes; see *To make a felt eye*, page 5. Cut the large circle from the plastic lid, and cover it with blue felt. Glue on a smaller black felt circle.

3. To make beak, pin one end of inner beak to bottom beak, matching arrows. Straight-stitch around curve by machine.

Pin free end of inner beak to top beak, right sides together, matching arrows. Stitch from one arrow, around curve, to other arrow. Turn to right side and stuff lightly.

4. Pin beak to face. By hand, stitch free edge of bottom beak to body (this seam will be hidden). Then stitch around curve of top beak, turning under seam allowance. Tuck a little fiberfill into top area of beak as you work.

Bend free ends into desired position.

5. To make egg, pin two pieces, right sides together. Stitch. Pin a third piece to the egg, and stitch. Then add the last piece, leaving a small opening for turning. Turn to right side, stuff and close opening with invisible stitches.

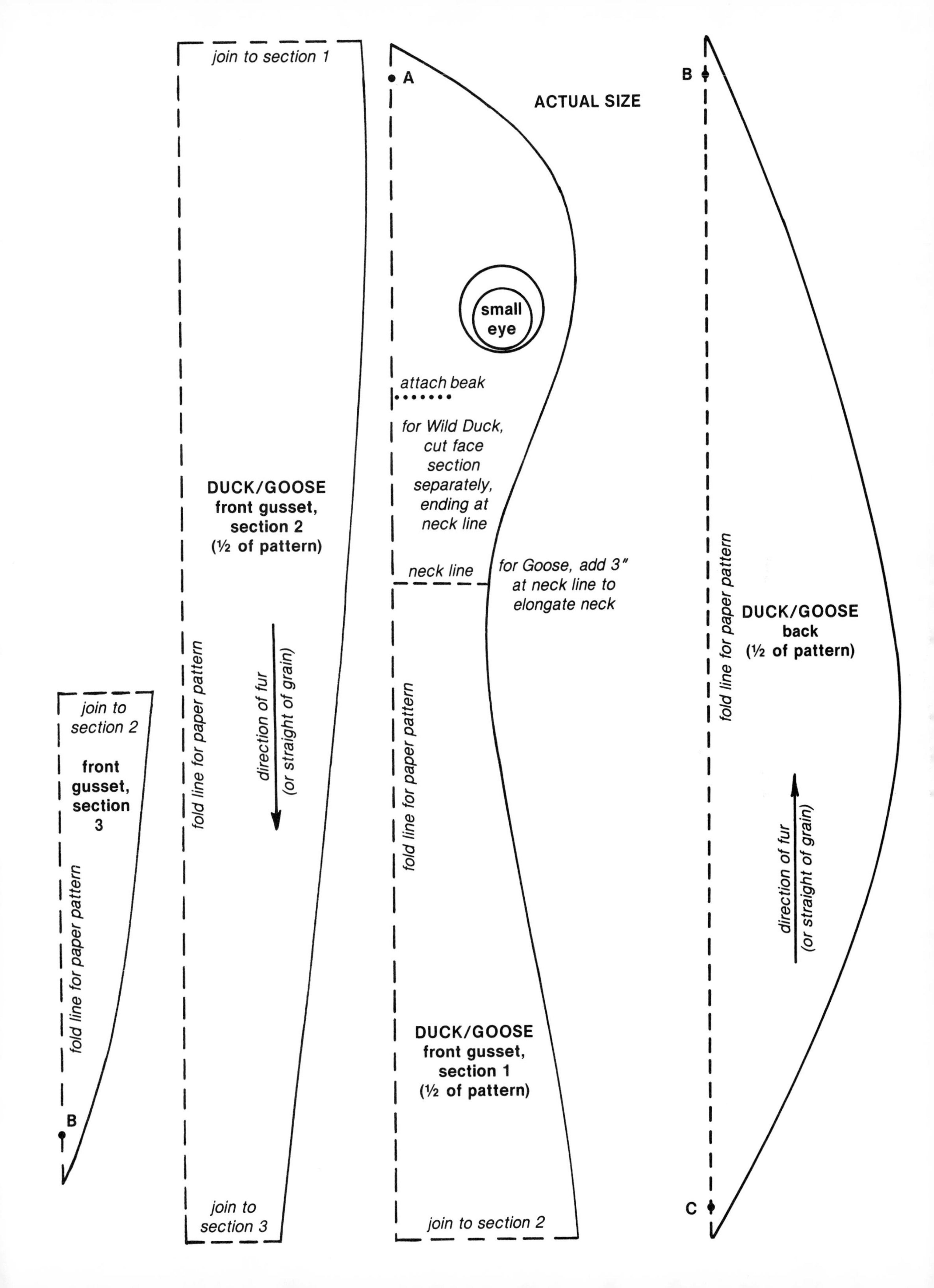

ACTUAL SIZE
join to section 1
DUCK/GOOSE
front gusset,
section 2
(½ of pattern)
fold line for paper pattern
direction of fur
(or straight of grain)
join to section 3
join to
section 2
front
gusset,
section
3
fold line for paper pattern
B
A
small
eye
attach beak
for Wild Duck,
cut face
section
separately,
ending at
neck line
neck line
for Goose, add 3″
at neck line to
elongate neck
fold line for paper pattern
DUCK/GOOSE
front gusset,
section 1
(½ of pattern)
join to section 2
B
C
fold line for paper pattern
DUCK/GOOSE
back
(½ of pattern)
direction of fur
(or straight of grain)

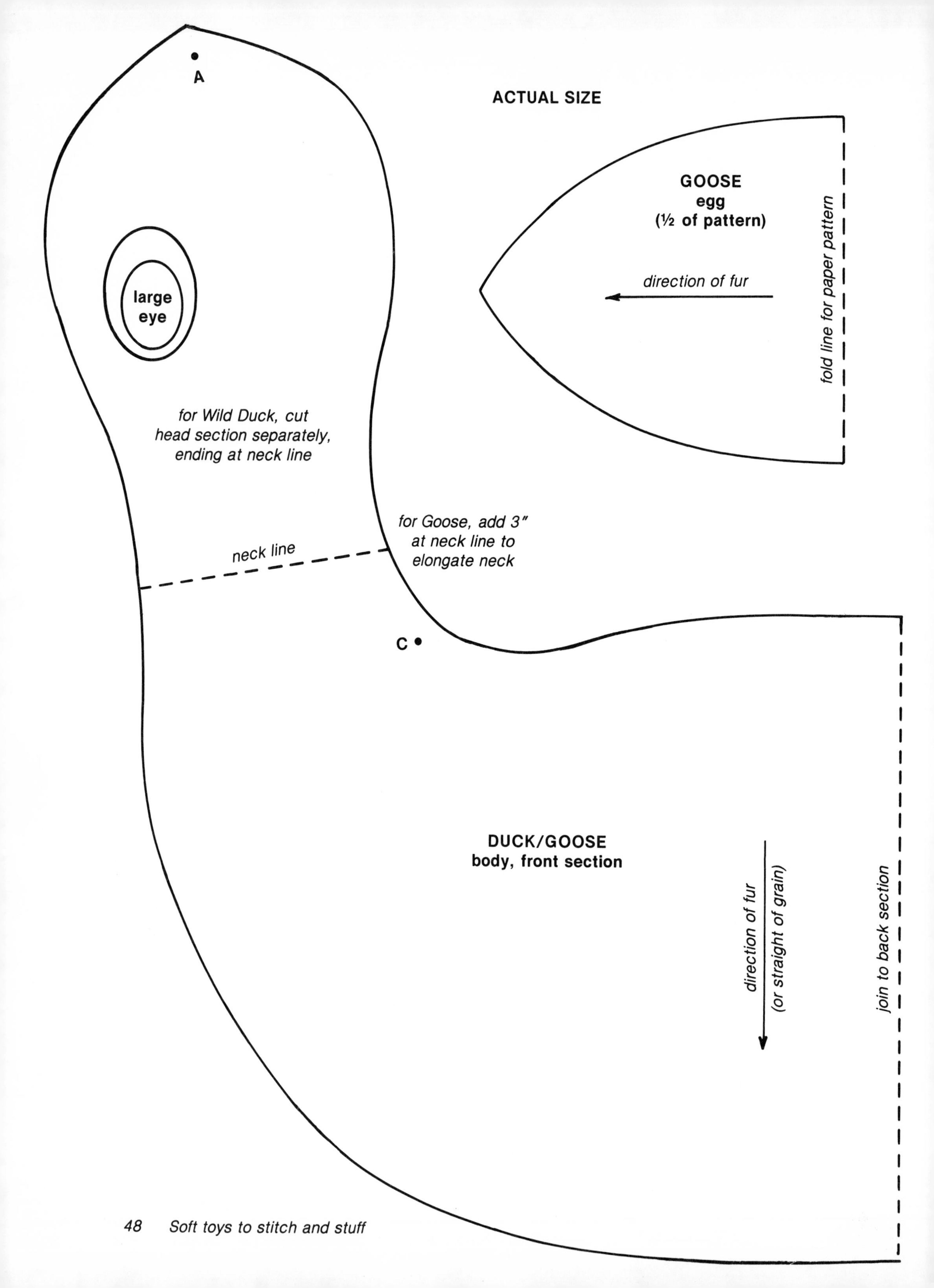
A
ACTUAL SIZE
GOOSE
egg
(½ of pattern)
direction of fur
fold line for paper pattern
large
eye
for Wild Duck, cut
head section separately,
ending at neck line
for Goose, add 3″
at neck line to
elongate neck
neck line
C
DUCK/GOOSE
body, front section
direction of fur
(or straight of grain)
join to back section

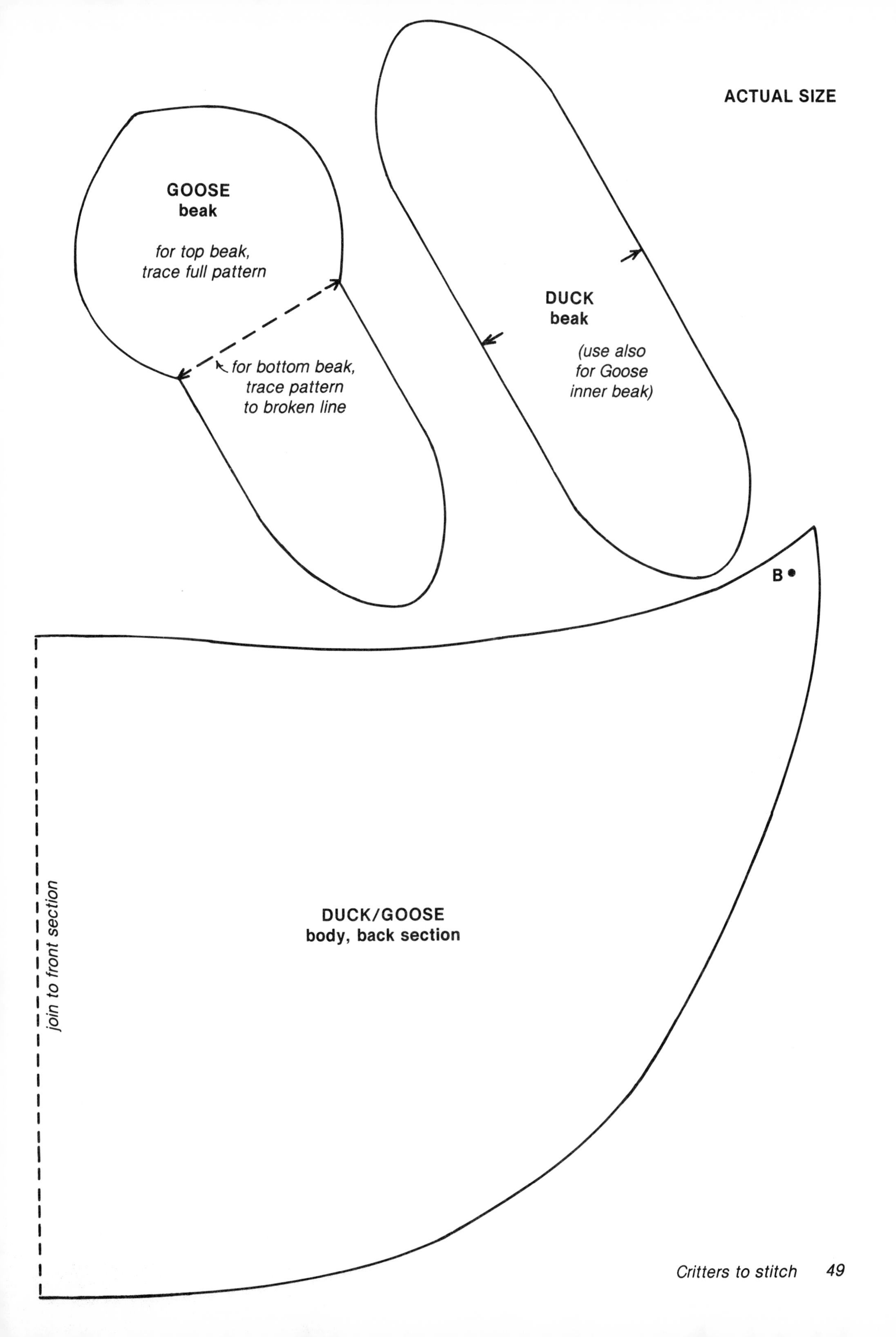
ACTUAL SIZE
GOOSE
beak
for top beak,
trace full pattern
for bottom beak,
trace pattern
to broken line
DUCK
beak
(use also
for Goose
inner beak)
B
DUCK/GOOSE
body, back section
join to front section

SNAKE

(color photo, page 69)

When you walk through grass around a farm pond, don't be surprised to find a snake. Most are harmless to people, and luckily, I've never seen a poisonous one on our place.

Snakes are sometimes considered outcasts, but often they are the good guys, eating mice and insects that destroy the crops. So, here is my tribute to the snake—unlike any snake I've ever seen. I think you'll find the sleepy-looking fellow fun to make and have around.

MATERIALS

rust plush fabric, 7x14", for head (pile can run along either length)
print plush fabric, 4½x35", for body (pile running along the 35" length is preferable, but not necessary)
red plush fabric or felt scrap, for inner mouth
green, rust and black felt scraps, for eyes
red felt scrap, for tongue
transparent thread, for machine stitching
button-and-carpet thread, for handwork
polyester fiberfill, for stuffing
plastic lid, for eyes
glue

DIRECTIONS

For tips on tracing patterns and working with fur fabric, see *Helpful Guides*, page 1.

Make pattern pieces

1. Trace patterns for head, eye, eyelid, inner mouth and tongue on opposite page.
2. Cut out pattern pieces.

Cut fabric

1. Lay head pattern on back of rust fur fabric, making sure fur is running in correct direction. Trace 2 heads (1 reversed, to correctly position the points A and C).

On red plush or felt, trace 1 inner mouth.

2. Cut out fabric on traced lines; ¼" seam allowances are included.

Assemble

Use ¼" seams and a zigzag machine stitch.

1. To make body, fold the strip of print fur fabric in half lengthwise, with fur inside, and pin. Stitch along the length; about 8" from the end, begin tapering toward the fold to form tip of tail. Turn to right side.

2. To make head, pin inner mouth to one head circle, right sides together; match points C and B. By hand, sew a narrow seam between points with overcast stitches. Then pin points A together and continue seam from B to A.

Pin and stitch free edge of inner mouth to other head circle in some manner. Finish mouth by sewing head pieces together at each corner of mouth (points A and C); stitch along head pieces about ¼".

3. Pin head circles right sides together, and machine-stitch; leave about 3" open for turning. Turn to right side.

Stuff and finish

1. Stuff head lightly and close opening with invisible stitches.

2. To make tongue, place pattern on double layer of red felt and straight-stitch around pattern. Cut out tongue ⅛" from stitching.

Sew tongue to center of inner mouth.

3. Make and attach eyes; see *To make a felt eye*, page 5. Cut the oval from the plastic lid and cover it with green felt. Glue on a strip of black felt. Then glue on a rust felt eyelid, letting eyelid extend beyond eye on each side.

4. Stuff body lightly with fiberfill. Pin to head, positioning body about 1½" from seam at back of head. Sew together in a circular seam, using invisible stitches.

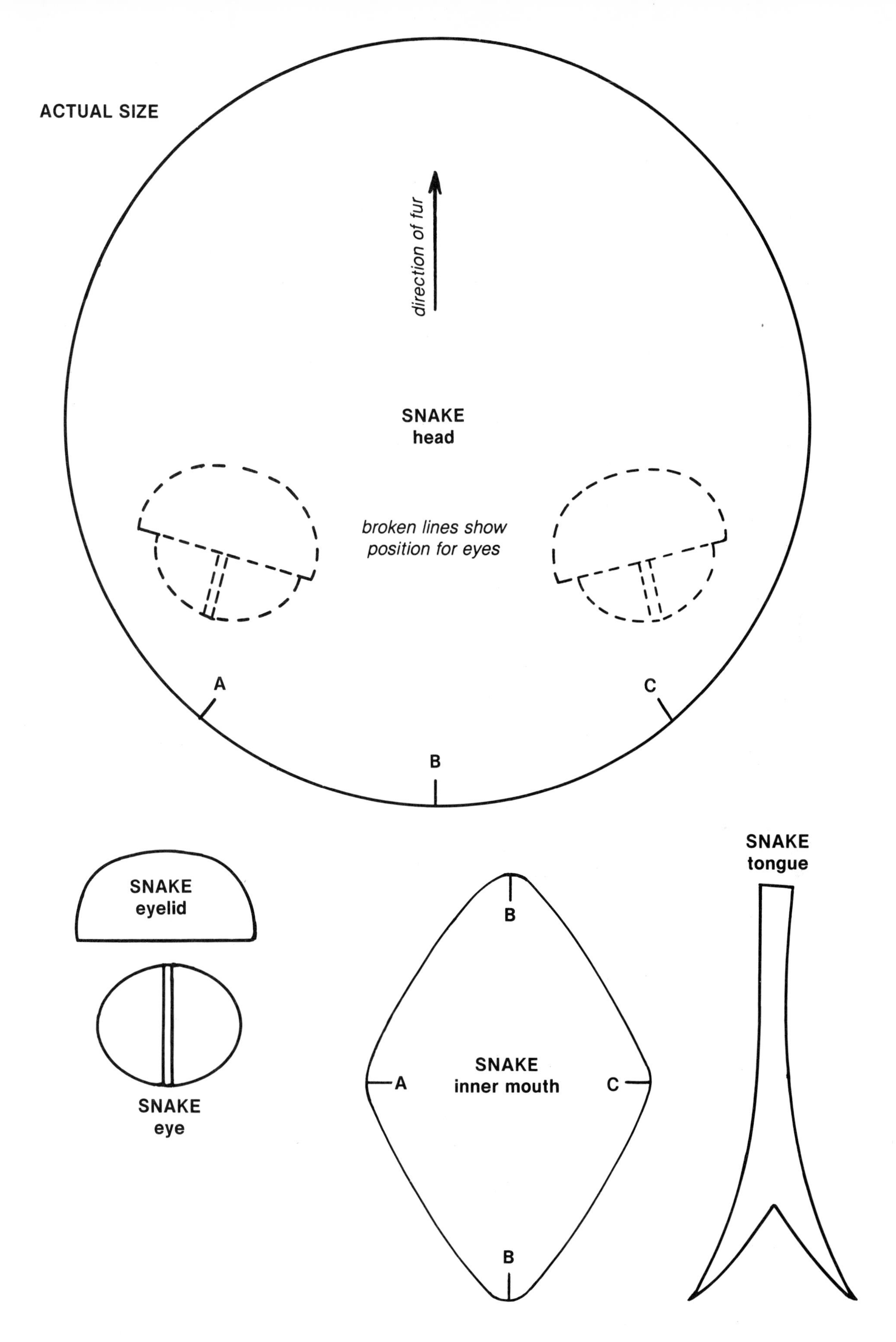
ACTUAL SIZE
direction of fur
SNAKE
head
broken lines show
position for eyes
A
B
C
SNAKE
eyelid
SNAKE
eye
B
A
SNAKE
inner mouth
C
B
SNAKE
tongue

Dolls

Here's a group of soft dolls to delight your favorite youngsters. There's a Baby Doll, a Girl and Boy, Mom and Grandma, and Dad and Grandpa. The men are dressed in overalls, ready to work with the animals on our fantasy farm.

Use polyester doubleknit fabric for the doll bodies, and felt for the shoes. Long-pile fur fabric makes great hair—you can style it in a variety of ways with a stiff brush. Embroider the faces, then fill in the eyes with satin stitches, or cut eye centers from felt and stitch them in place.

Directions for dresses, shirts and overalls call for elastic so that garments can easily be put on and removed. However, you can omit the elastic and sew the clothes onto the dolls. Simply run a gathering thread around the neck of a dress or a shirt, or around the waist of pants or overalls. Put the garment on the doll, pull the thread so the garment fits closely, and secure the thread. Then the doll is permanently dressed.

BABY DOLL

(color photo, page 32)

This 6" doll snuggles inside a flannel or velour bunting, ready to go visiting.

MATERIALS (for one doll)

skin color polyester doubleknit, 9x13", for body
flannel or velour, 11x14", for bunting
transparent or matching thread, for all stitching
polyester fiberfill, for stuffing
black embroidery thread, for embroidering face
felt scraps and matching thread, for eyes (optional)
12½" narrow, ruffled lace, for trim
2 small pompons or 9" narrow ribbon, for trimming bunting

DIRECTIONS

For tips on tracing patterns and working with fabric, see *Helpful Guides*, page 1.

Make pattern pieces

1. Trace pattern for doll body (inner line), page 59. Choose mouth line you wish, using full circle for round mouth or half circle for smiling mouth. Trace pattern for bunting (outer line), and mark face opening.
2. Cut out pattern pieces, and cut out face opening on bunting.

Assemble and stuff doll

1. Fold doubleknit fabric to make two layers, right side inside. On top layer, pin or trace pattern for doll body. By machine, straight-stitch around pattern; leave opening at head for turning (Fig. I).
2. Cut out body ¼" from pattern line. Slash inside curves at neck and in V areas under arms and between legs. Turn doll to right side.
3. Work seam to edge and pin flat around head. Position pattern on front of doll and transfer lines for face. (Punch a sharp pencil through pattern to make a line of dots. Remove pattern and use pencil to connect dots.)

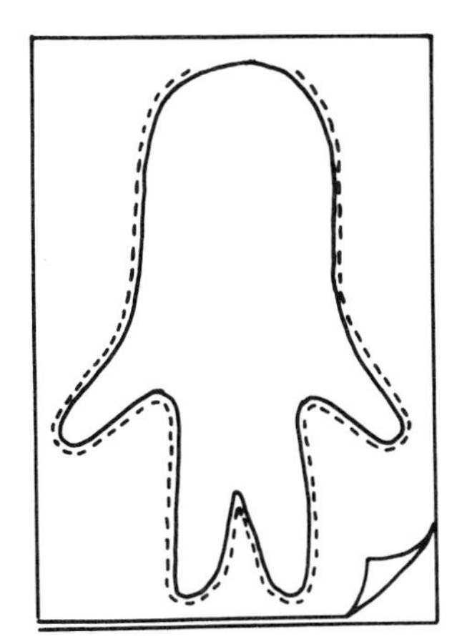

Fig. 1 *Stitching around pattern before cutting*

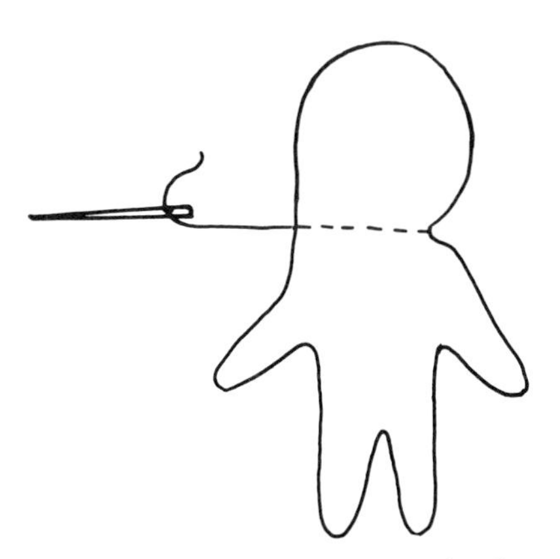

Fig. 2 *Gathering neck of Baby doll*

4. Stuff doll lightly with fiberfill, keeping doll rather flat. Close opening with invisible stitches.

5. Sew a gathering thread around neck and pull to make neck about 1¾" wide (Fig. 2).

6. Embroider face with black embroidery thread. Use a stem stitch (Fig. 18, page 6) to outline mouth and eyes, and make one straight stitch for the nose. Use a satin stitch (Fig. 17, page 6) to fill in centers of eyes, or cut centers from felt and sew in place.

Cut and make bunting

1. Fold flannel or velour to make two layers, right side inside. On top, pin or trace pattern for bunting; trace outline for face opening. Cut out fabric on outside line; ¼" seam allowance is included. *On top layer only*, cut out face opening. (This layer will be the front.)

2. Turn raw edge of face opening ⅛" to wrong side and stitch by hand.

3. Pin lace around face opening, with wrong side of lace against right side of bunting. Attach lace by hand or with a zigzag machine stitch.

Note: You can begin and end lace trim along center front, about 1½" below opening, or you can stitch lace around opening only.

4. Pin bunting front to back, right sides together, and straight-stitch a ¼" seam by machine; do not catch lace in seam. Slash seam allowance to stitching in V areas under arms and at neck. Turn to right side through face opening.

5. By hand, gather bottom edge of bunting.

Finish doll

1. Tuck Baby doll into bunting through face opening.

2. Hand-stitch a gathering thread around face opening, and pull so bunting fits close to face.

3. Hand-stitch a gathering thread around neck of bunting, and pull so bunting fits close to doll.

4. Attach pompons or ribbon bow to trim bunting.

GIRL

(color photo, page 33)

Yellow felt shoes match the felt heart on this doll's dress.

MATERIALS

skin color polyester doubleknit, 11x23", for body
cotton print, 8½x23", for dress and hair bow
yellow felt, 5½x10", for shoes and heart trim
yellow long-pile fur fabric, 5x6½", for hair (pile should run along the 6½" length)
transparent or matching thread, for all stitching
polyester fiberfill, for stuffing
black embroidery thread, for embroidering face
felt scraps and matching thread, for eyes (optional)
5½" elastic, ¼" wide, for dress
bobby pin, for fastening bow in hair

DIRECTIONS

For tips on tracing patterns and working with fabric, see *Helpful Guides*, page 1.

Make pattern pieces

1. Trace pattern for body, page 60, joining sections on broken lines. Also trace patterns for shoe, page 60, and for base, hair, dress and heart trim, page 61.

2. Cut out full pattern pieces.

Assemble doll

1. Fold doubleknit fabric to make two layers, right side inside. On top layer, pin or trace pattern for doll body. By machine, straight-stitch around pattern, leaving bottom open.

2. Cut out body ¼" from stitching; along bottom edge, cut on pattern line.

3. On one layer of doubleknit fabric, trace 1 base and cut out on traced line. Pin and stitch base to doll body (Fig. 3), making ¼" seams and leaving a small opening for turning.

Fig. 3 *Adding base to Girl doll*

4. Slash seam allowance to stitching along inside curves on arms and in V areas at neck, under arms and between fingers. Turn doll to right side.

5. Work seam to edge and pin flat around head. Position pattern on front of doll and transfer lines for face. (Punch a sharp pencil through pattern to make a line of dots. Remove pattern and use pencil to connect dots.)

Stuff and finish

1. Stuff doll with fiberfill and close opening with invisible stitches.

2. Embroider face with black embroidery thread. Use a stem stitch (Fig. 18, page 6) for lines. Use a satin stitch (Fig. 17, page 6) to fill centers of eyes, or cut eye centers from felt and sew in place with matching thread.

3. For hair, trace pattern on back of fur fabric, making sure fur is running in correct direction. Cut out.

Make a running stitch along front edge and gather so that hair fits on doll's forehead, overlapping seam at top of head. Pin hair on doll, with back edge just above doll's neck and side edges running along head seam. Gather back edge of hair to fit head.

Sew hair to doll with overcast stitches. Style hair with a stiff brush.

4. To make shoes, fold felt to make two layers. On top, trace shoe pattern twice. By machine, straight-stitch along pattern line, leaving a small opening for turning. Cut out fabric, ⅛" from stitching.

Turn shoes to right side, stuff lightly and close openings with invisible stitches. Position shoes on base, toes extending beyond body, and attach by hand.

Cut and make dress

1. Cut 1½x8½" strip from one edge of print fabric and set aside for hair bow.

2. Fold remaining fabric to make two layers, right side inside. On top, pin or trace dress pattern and cut out fabric.

3. By machine, straight-stitch ¼" side seams, leaving armholes open.

4. Press seams open. Use a zigzag stitch to catch opened seam allowances to garment, from neck edge to below armhole openings. (This finishes the armholes.)

5. To make casing for elastic, fold neck edge ⅛" to wrong side and press. Make a second fold ½" to wrong side and pin. By machine, straight-stitch along inner fold, leaving a small opening for inserting elastic.

6. Fasten a small safety pin to one end of the elastic and work it through the casing. Overlap elastic ends by ¼" and stitch by hand. Complete machine stitching along casing.

7. Slip dress on doll, pulling it over the head, and pin hem to desired length. Stitch hem by hand or machine.

8. Trace small heart pattern on yellow felt and cut out. Sew heart to front of dress.

9. To make hair bow, fold fabric strip in half lengthwise, right side inside. Stitch a ¼" lengthwise seam. Turn to right side, tuck raw edges to inside and close openings by hand.

Tie strip into a bow. Use a bobby pin to fasten bow in hair.

BOY

(color photo, page 33)

Most of these dolls have shoes, but the Boy is barefoot—so this pattern has a special foot construction.

MATERIALS

skin color polyester doubleknit, 14x22", for body
blue cotton, 10x16", for pants
print cotton, 6x30", for shirt
brown long-pile fur fabric, 5½x6", for hair (pile should run along the 6" length)
transparent or matching thread, for all stitching
polyester fiberfill, for stuffing
black embroidery thread, for embroidering face
black felt scraps, for eyes (optional)
5½" elastic, ¼" wide, for shirt
8½" elastic, ¼" wide, for pants

DIRECTIONS

For tips on tracing patterns and working with fabric, see *Helpful Guides*, page 1.

Make pattern pieces

1. Trace pattern for body, page 62, joining sections on broken lines. Also trace patterns for sole of foot and hair. Trace pattern for shirt, page 65, and for pants, page 66, using lines for small sizes.

2. Cut out full pattern pieces.

Assemble doll

1. Fold doubleknit fabric to make two layers, right side inside. On top layer, pin or trace pattern for doll body. By machine, straight-stitch around pattern; leave opening at head and foot (end stitching at broken line on leg).

2. Cut out body ¼" from pattern line. *On top layer only*, cut off tip of each foot ¼" below broken line (Fig. 4). Cut layer will be the back of doll.

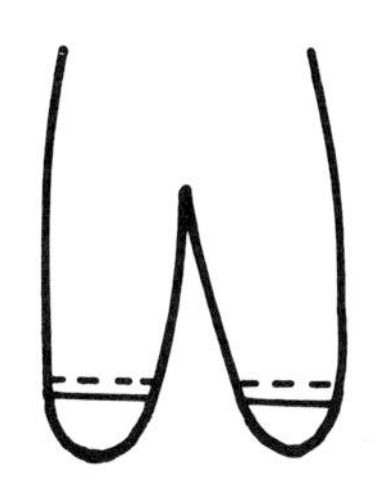

Fig. 4 *Cutting off ends of legs on top layer of Boy doll*

3. On doubleknit fabric, trace 2 soles and cut out on traced lines. Pin a sole to each leg, matching points A (toe) and B (heel) and distributing fullness. By hand, stitch together in two steps, making ¼" seams. Work from one leg seam to the other, first stitching toe area and then heel area (Fig. 5). You may want to do a final stitching by machine.

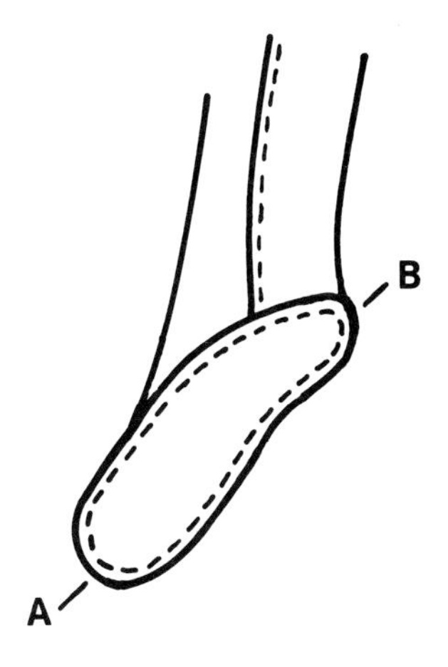

Fig. 5 *Adding sole of foot to Boy doll*

4. Slash seam allowance to stitching along inside curves on arms and in V areas at neck, under arms and between fingers and legs. Turn doll to right side.

5. Work seam to edge and pin flat around head. Position pattern on front of doll and transfer lines for face. (Punch a sharp pencil through pattern to make a line of dots. Remove pattern and use pencil to connect dots.)

Stuff and finish

1. Stuff each toe lightly, then bend foot into standing position and stuff leg. Finish stuffing doll, and close opening with invisible stitches.

2. Embroider face and attach hair; see Girl doll, *Stuff and finish*, Steps 2 and 3, page 54. On hair, sideburns will be in front of head seam.

Cut and make clothes

1. To make shirt, follow *Directions for shirt or dress with sleeves*, page 58.

2. To make pants, follow *Directions for pants and overalls*, page 58.

MOM & GRANDMA

(color photo, pages 32, 33)

You can use the same pattern to make two different dolls. Just cut Grandma's hair from white or gray fur fabric, and omit the long eyelashes on Grandma's face.

Each doll has a scarf. Mom's covers her head, while Grandma's is worn as a shawl. Mom also wears an apron.

The dress hems are trimmed with lace, and Mom's dress also has lace at the neck and sleeves. For dolls in the photograph, blue felt was used for shoes and for the centers of the dolls' eyes.

MATERIALS
(for each doll)

skin color polyester doubleknit, 14½x23", for body
cotton print, 44" wide: ½ yd. for Mom's dress and scarf; ⅓ yd. for Grandma's dress and shawl
white cotton, 5x10", for Mom's apron, plus a 2x27" strip, for apron band and ties
felt in color to match dress, 6½x10", for shoes
long-pile fur fabric, 5½x7½", for hair (pile should run along the 7½" length)
transparent or matching thread, for all stitching
polyester fiberfill, for stuffing
black embroidery thread, for embroidering face
blue felt scraps and matching thread, for eyes (optional)
6" elastic, ¼" wide, for dress
1⅓ yd. narrow, ruffled lace, for trimming clothes

DIRECTIONS

For tips on tracing patterns and working with fabric, see *Helpful Guides*, page 1.

Make pattern pieces

1. Trace pattern for body, page 63, joining sections on broken lines. Trace patterns for base, hair and shoe, page 63, and for dress, page 65.

Draft a pattern for Mom's scarf and apron or for Grandma's shawl; see dimensions on page 65.

2. Cut out full pattern pieces.

Assemble and finish doll

Follow directions for Girl doll; see *Assemble doll* and *Stuff and finish*, page 54.

Cut and make clothes

1. To make dress, follow *Directions for shirt or dress with sleeves*, page 58.

2. To make scarf or shawl, pin or trace pattern on wrong side of print fabric. Cut out on pattern line.

Turn all raw edges ⅛" to wrong side. Make a second turn, press and stitch. To finish Grandma's shawl, pin lace along the two short edges. Stitch in place by hand or machine.

3. To make Mom's apron, first stitch a narrow hem on three sides of the white cotton piece (leave one 10" edge unhemmed). To make the band and ties, fold the 2x27" strip of white cotton in half lengthwise, right side inside. Stitch a ¼" lengthwise seam, and turn to right side. Fold in raw ends and topstitch.

Sew a gathering thread along the unhemmed edge of apron, and pull thread to make edge 5" wide. Center apron band over right side of gathered edge and machine-stitch pieces together.

DAD & GRANDPA

(color photo, pages 32, 33)

Dad has a full head of hair, but Grandpa has only a fringe at the back to go with his long beard. Otherwise, you can use the same pattern pieces to make these two dolls.

Dress the dolls in shirts and bib overalls. For extra color, you could make a narrow red scarf to tie around Dad's neck.

To copy dolls in the photograph, outline the eyes with black embroidery thread, then add eye centers cut from black felt.

MATERIALS
(for each doll)

skin color polyester doubleknit, 15x23", for body
blue cotton, 10x23", for overalls
cotton print or check, 7x32", for shirt
long-pile fur fabric, 6x6½", for hair (pile should run along the 6½" length)
dark felt, 7x10", for shoes
transparent or matching thread, for all stitching
polyester fiberfill, for stuffing
black embroidery thread, for embroidering face
dark felt scraps and matching thread, for eyes (optional)
6½" elastic, ¼" wide, for shirt
9½" elastic, ¼" wide, for overalls
2 buttons, ¼" diameter, for overalls

DIRECTIONS

For tips on tracing patterns and working with fabric, see *Helpful Guides,* page 1.

Make pattern pieces

1. Trace pattern for body, page 64, joining sections on broken lines. Also trace pattern for shoe.

For Dad, trace hair, page 64; for Grandpa, trace hair and mustache/beard, page 66.

Trace pattern for shirt, page 65, using lines for large size. Trace pattern pieces for pants and for overalls bib, page 66, using lines for large size.

2. Cut out full pattern pieces.

Assemble doll

1. Fold doubleknit fabric to make two layers, right side inside. On top layer, pin or trace pattern for doll body. By machine, straight-stitch around pattern, leaving opening at head for turning.

2. Cut out body ¼" from pattern line. Slash seam allowance to stitching along inside curves on arms, and in V areas at neck, under arms and between legs and fingers. Turn doll to right side.

3. Work seam to edge and pin flat around head. Position pattern on front of doll and transfer lines for face. (Punch a sharp pencil through pattern to make a line of dots. Remove pattern and use pencil to connect dots.)

Note: For Grandpa's face, mark eyes and nose. Then position mustache/beard on face and mark a mouth line in center of opening.

Stuff and finish

1. Stuff doll, embroider face and add hair (for Dad); see Girl, *Stuff and finish,* Steps 1-3, page 54. On Dad's hair, sideburns will be in front of head seam.

For Grandpa's hair, sew small hair piece to back of head, and sew mustache/beard to face just below nose.

Style hair and mustache/beard with a stiff brush.

2. To make shoes, fold felt to make two layers. On top, trace shoe pattern twice. By machine, straight-stitch along pattern line, leaving a small opening for turning. Cut out fabric ⅛" from stitching.

Turn shoes to right side, stuff lightly and close openings with invisible stitches.

Position each shoe with dotted line on shoe pattern against bottom curve of leg seam. By hand, stitch shoe to leg, letting back of shoe curve up against leg.

Cut and make clothes

1. To make shirt, follow *Directions for shirt or dress with sleeves*, below.
2. To make overalls, follow *Directions for pants and overalls*, this page.

DIRECTIONS FOR SHIRT OR DRESS WITH SLEEVES

1. Fold print fabric to make two layers, right side inside. On top layer, pin or trace pattern for shirt or dress. Cut out fabric on pattern line; ¼" seam allowances are included.
2. To assemble, pin layers with right sides together. By machine, straight-stitch ¼" seams at sides and shoulders.
3. Slash seam allowances to stitching along curves under arms. Also slash to stitching at curve, 1⅛" below neck edge. Press seams open for the 1⅛", then use a zigzag stitch to catch the opened seam allowances to garment.
4. To make casing for elastic, fold neck edge ⅛" to wrong side and press. Make a second fold ½" to wrong side and pin. By machine, straight-stitch along inner fold, leaving a small opening for inserting elastic.

For Mom's dress, hand-stitch lace around neckline. Take stitches directly over stitching on casing, and leave lace free ½" on each side of casing opening. After elastic is added and casing finished (Step 5), finish sewing lace in place.

5. Fasten a small safety pin to one end of the elastic and work it through the casing. Overlap elastic ends by ¼" and stitch by hand. Complete machine stitching along casing.
6. Finish the hems.

For shirt, turn up a narrow hem at the bottom edge and stitch by hand or machine. Slip shirt on doll, turn up sleeves to desired length and finish hems by hand. (If sleeves are to be rolled up, as shown on Dad, finish raw seams with a zigzag machine stitch and use a narrow hem on each sleeve.)

For dress, slip garment on doll and turn up bottom edge and sleeves to desired lengths. Finish hems by hand or machine. Hand-stitch lace to bottom edge of dress. On Mom's dress, also stitch lace to edges of finished sleeves.

DIRECTIONS FOR PANTS AND OVERALLS

1. From longest edge of fabric, cut a 2x14½" strip for straps.
2. Fold remaining fabric to make two layers, right side inside (leave enough to cut a bib for Dad's or Grandpa's overalls). On top, pin or trace pants piece. Cut out the fabric on pattern line.

If bib is used, pin or trace bib piece on single layer of fabric and cut out.

3. To assemble, pin the two pants pieces, right sides together. By machine, straight-stitch ¼" leg seams. Slash seam allowance to stitching in V area between legs.
4. Press side seams open. Use a zigzag stitch to catch opened seam allowances to garment, from waist edge down at least 1⅛".
5. To make casing for elastic, fold waist edge ⅛" to wrong side and press. Make a second fold ½" to wrong side and pin. By machine, straight-stitch along inner fold; leave an opening at the back for inserting elastic.
6. To make bib (on Dad's or Grandpa's overalls), fold bib fabric in half, right side inside, to make it 1⅞x3¼". Straight-stitch side seams, then turn bib to right side. Finish raw edge with a zigzag stitch.

Center bib at front of pants, with raw edge inside and just below stitching on casing. From right side, machine-stitch directly over stitching on casing, catching bib in place. By hand, stitch top fold of casing to bib.

7. Fasten a small safety pin to one end of the elastic and work it through the casing. Overlap elastic ends by ¼" and stitch by hand. Complete machine stitching along casing.
8. To make straps, first cut fabric strip in half to make two 2x7¼" strips. Fold each strip in half lengthwise, right side inside, and straight-stitch a ¼" lengthwise seam. Turn to right side, tuck in raw ends and close openings by hand.
9. Slip overalls on doll. Pin one end of each strap to front of pants or bib. Cross straps in back and pin to pants. Stitch straps in place by hand.
10. Finish legs. To make a regular hem, turn raw edges to inside at desired length and finish by hand.

For rolled-up legs, finish raw edges and seam allowances with zigzag machine stitches.

11. For bib overalls, sew buttons to front of bib where straps are attached.

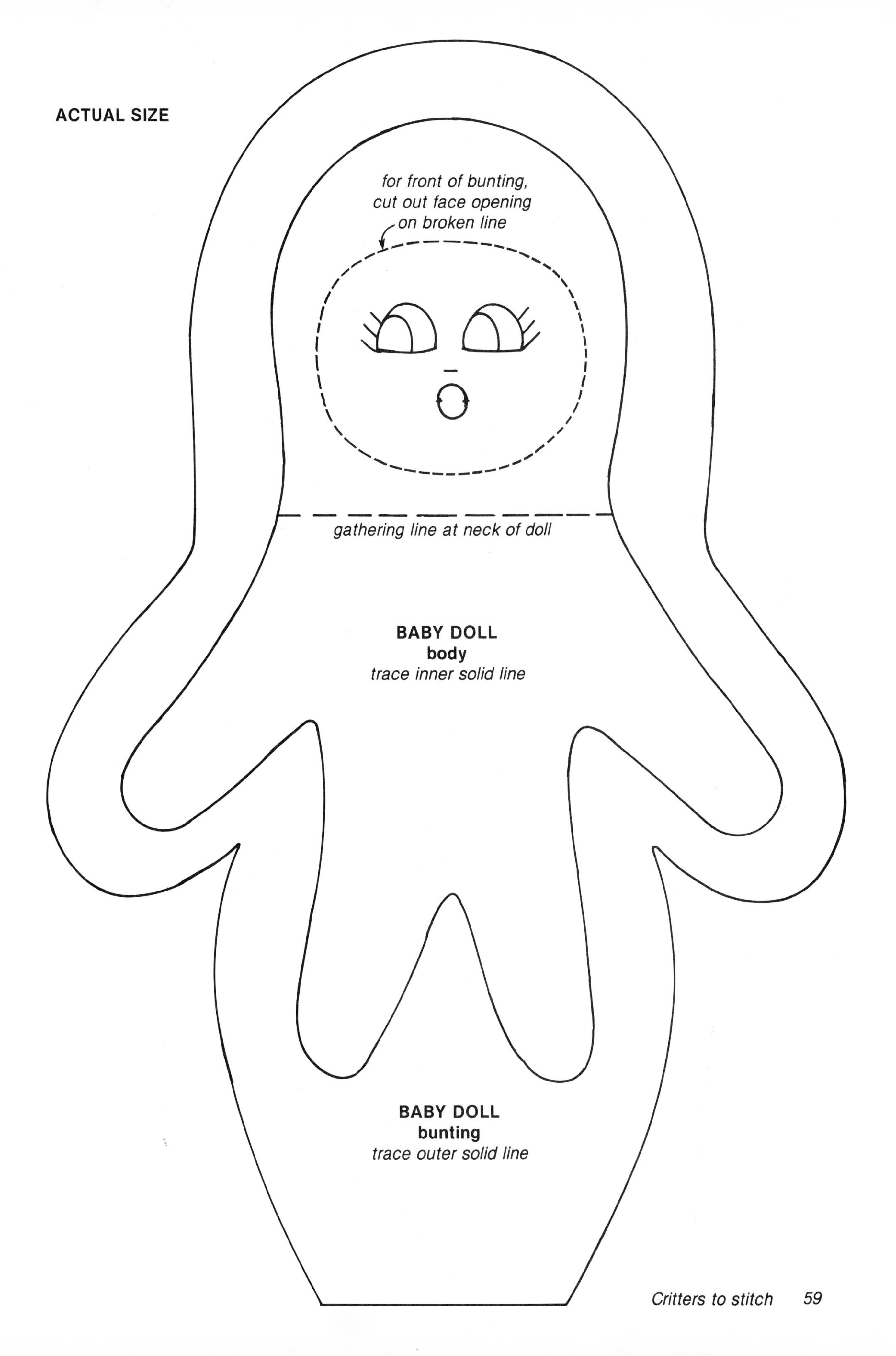
ACTUAL SIZE
for front of bunting,
cut out face opening
on broken line
gathering line at neck of doll
BABY DOLL
body
trace inner solid line
BABY DOLL
bunting
trace outer solid line

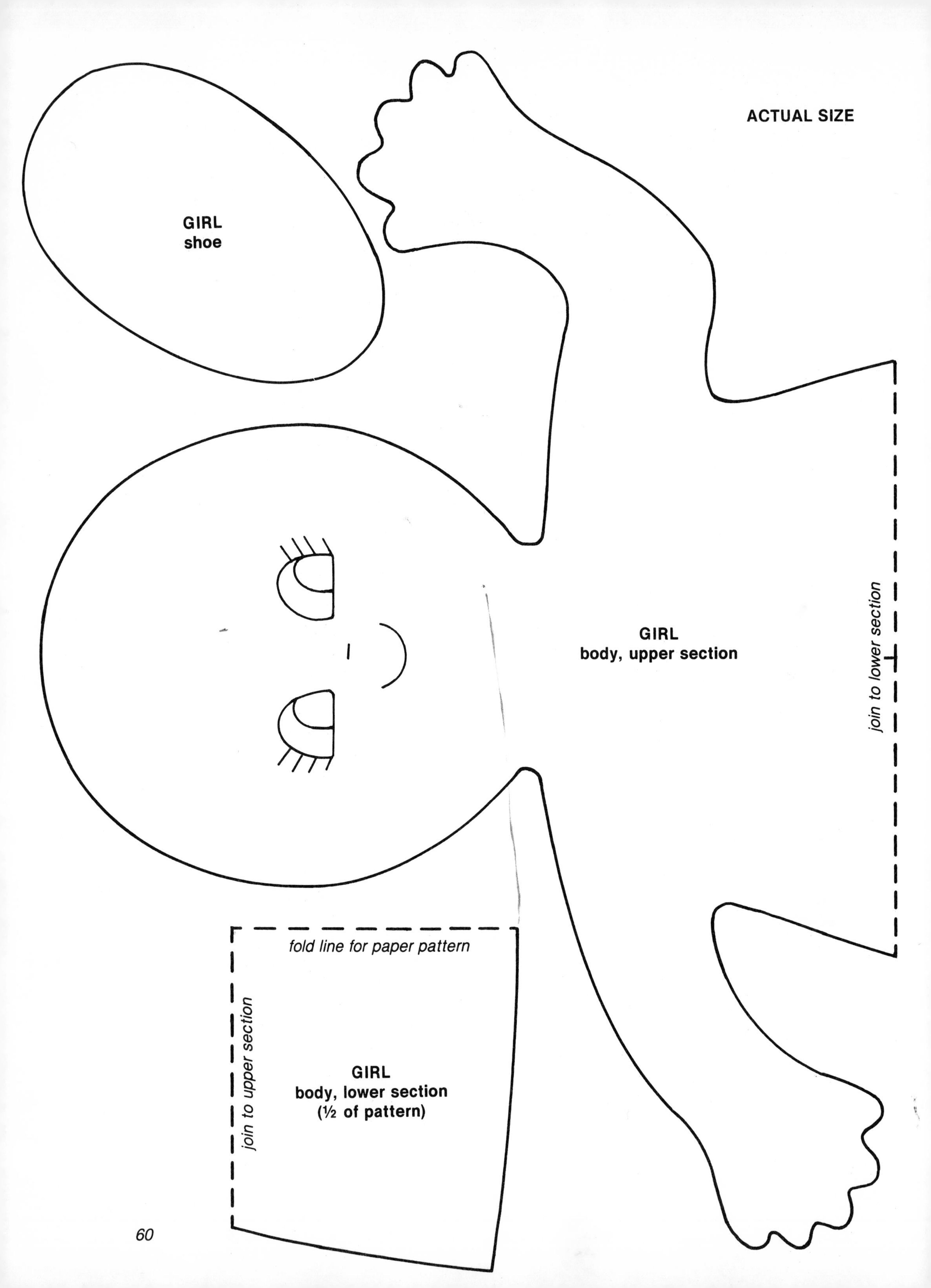
ACTUAL SIZE
GIRL
shoe
GIRL
body, upper section
join to lower section
fold line for paper pattern
join to upper section
GIRL
body, lower section
(½ of pattern)

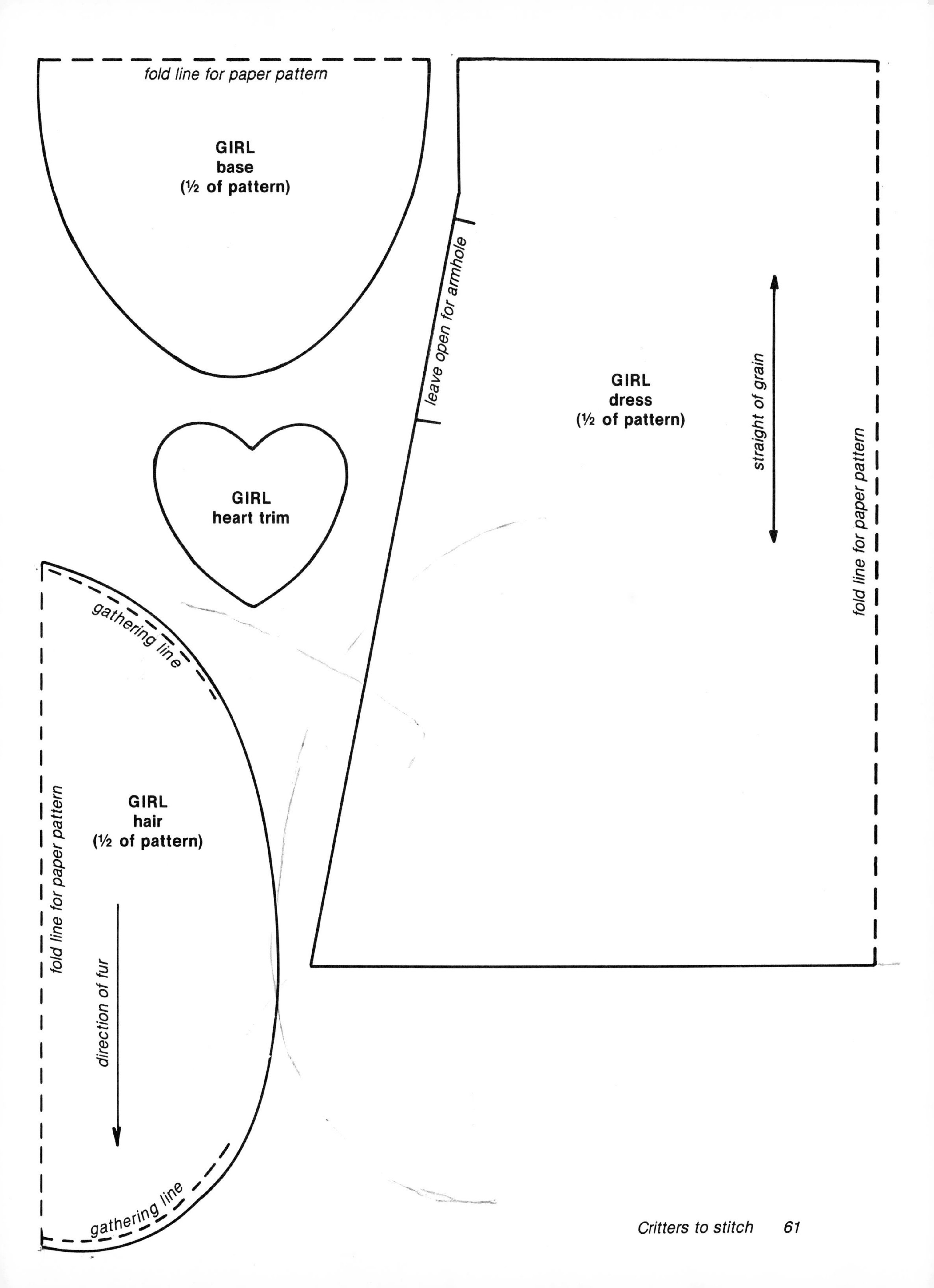
fold line for paper pattern
GIRL
base
(½ of pattern)
leave open for armhole
GIRL
heart trim
GIRL
dress
(½ of pattern)
straight of grain
fold line for paper pattern
gathering line
GIRL
hair
(½ of pattern)
fold line for paper pattern
direction of fur
gathering line

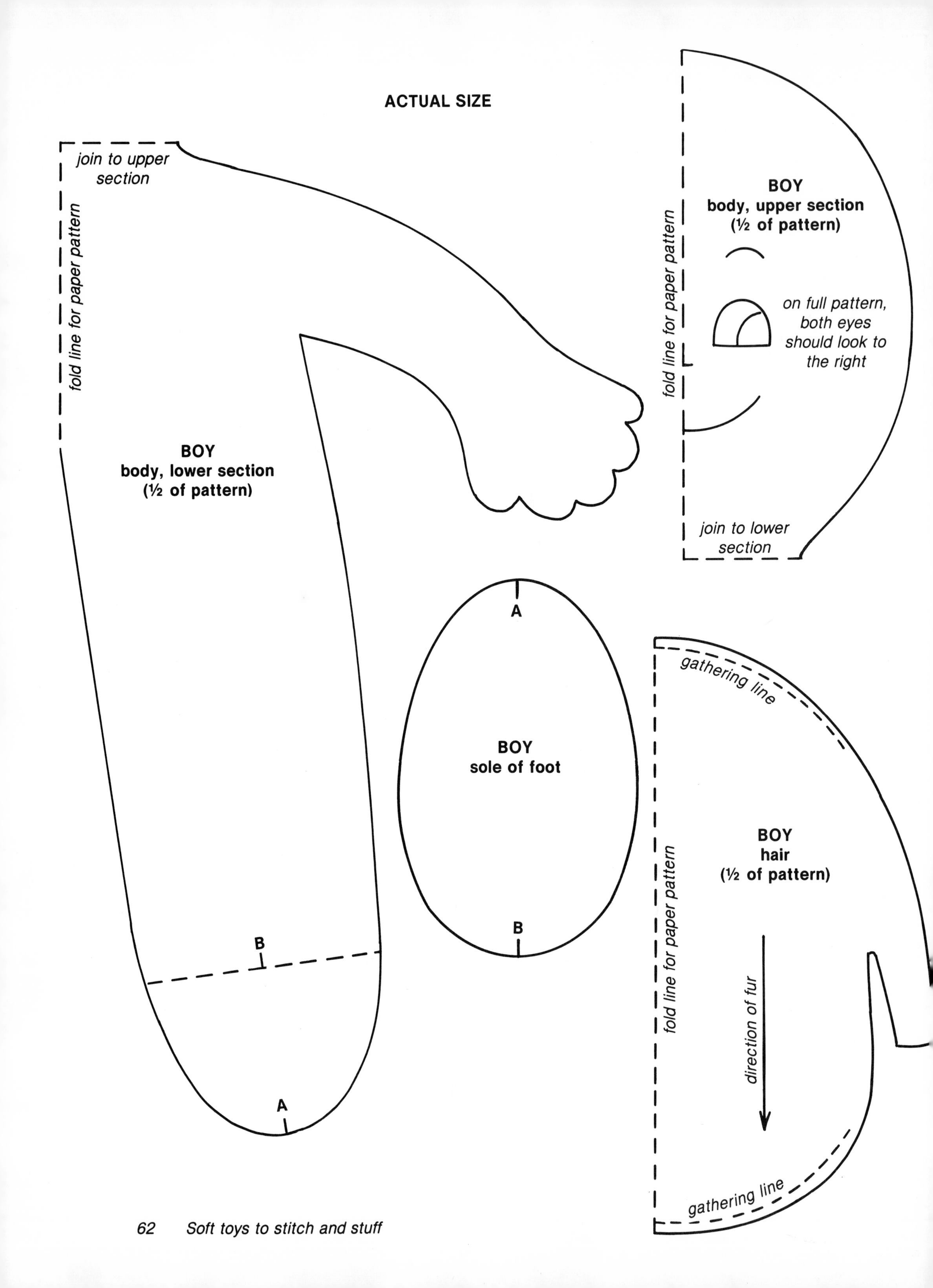

ACTUAL SIZE
join to upper section
fold line for paper pattern
BOY
body, lower section
(½ of pattern)
B
A
BOY
body, upper section
(½ of pattern)
on full pattern, both eyes should look to the right
fold line for paper pattern
join to lower section
A
BOY
sole of foot
B
gathering line
BOY
hair
(½ of pattern)
fold line for paper pattern
direction of fur
gathering line

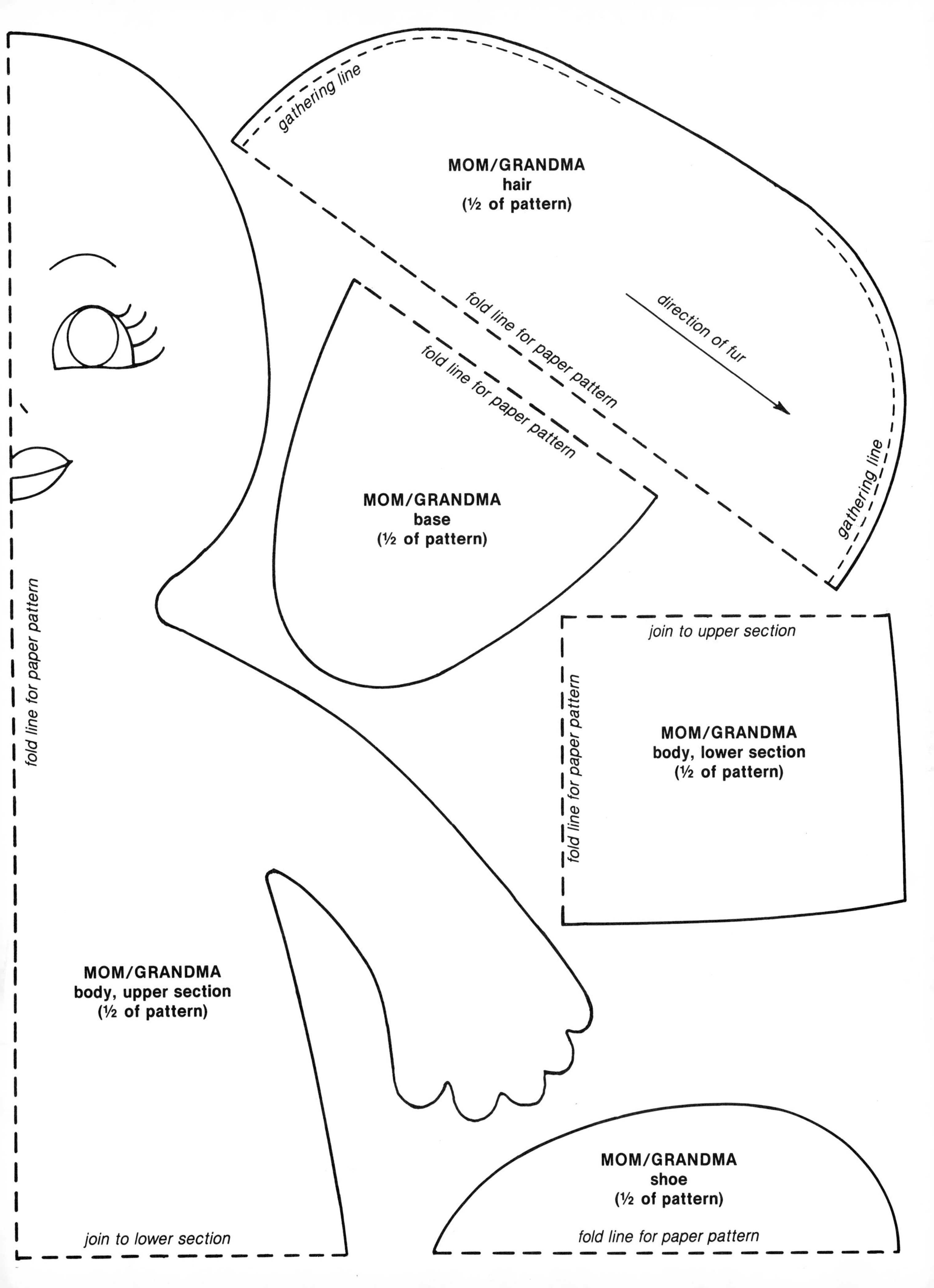
gathering line
MOM/GRANDMA
hair
(½ of pattern)
fold line for paper pattern
direction of fur
gathering line
fold line for paper pattern
MOM/GRANDMA
base
(½ of pattern)
fold line for paper pattern
join to upper section
fold line for paper pattern
MOM/GRANDMA
body, lower section
(½ of pattern)
MOM/GRANDMA
body, upper section
(½ of pattern)
join to lower section
MOM/GRANDMA
shoe
(½ of pattern)
fold line for paper pattern

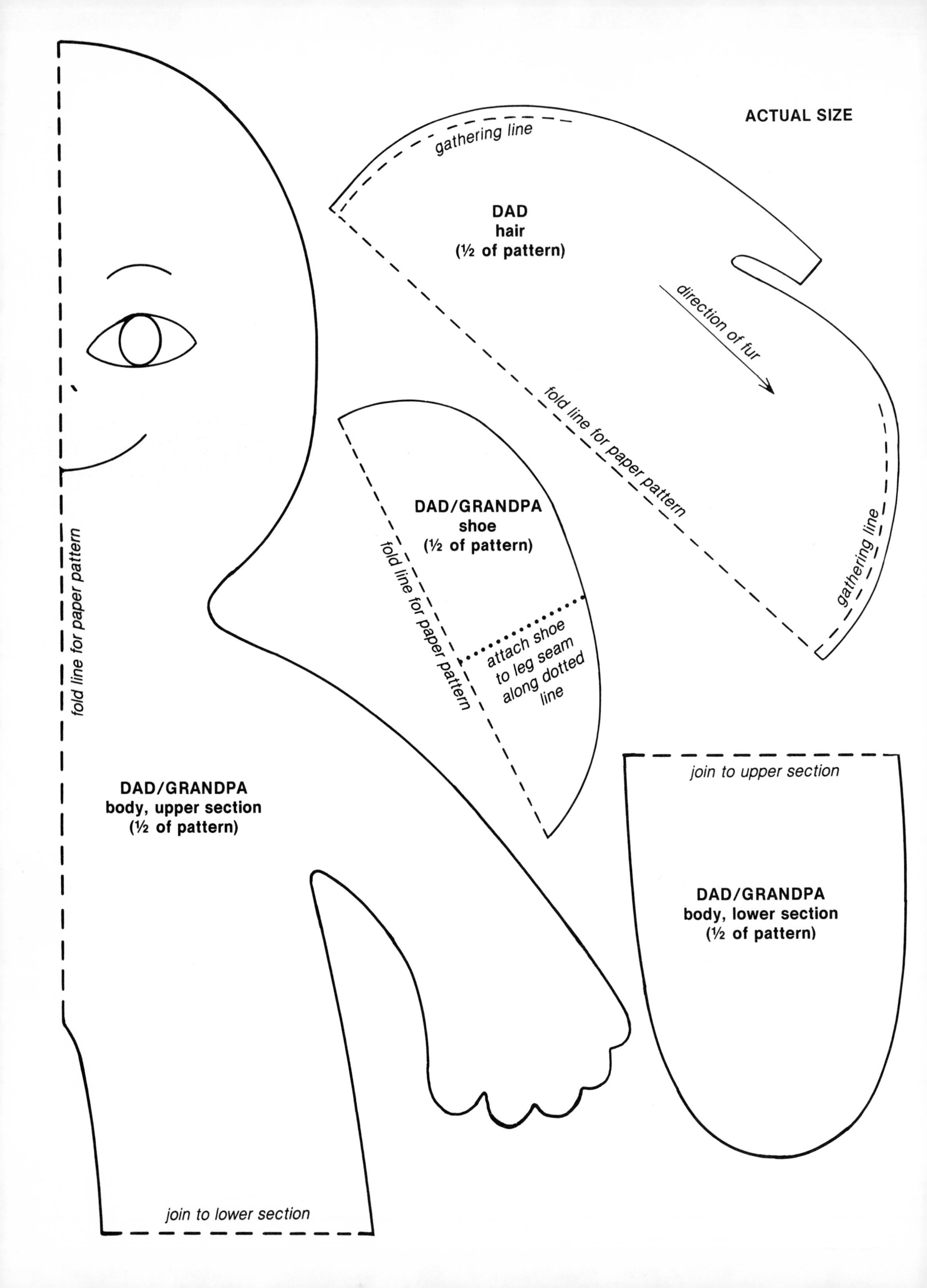
ACTUAL SIZE
gathering line
DAD
hair
(½ of pattern)
direction of fur
fold line for paper pattern
gathering line
DAD/GRANDPA
shoe
(½ of pattern)
fold line for paper pattern
attach shoe
to leg seam
along dotted
line
fold line for paper pattern
DAD/GRANDPA
body, upper section
(½ of pattern)
join to lower section
join to upper section
DAD/GRANDPA
body, lower section
(½ of pattern)

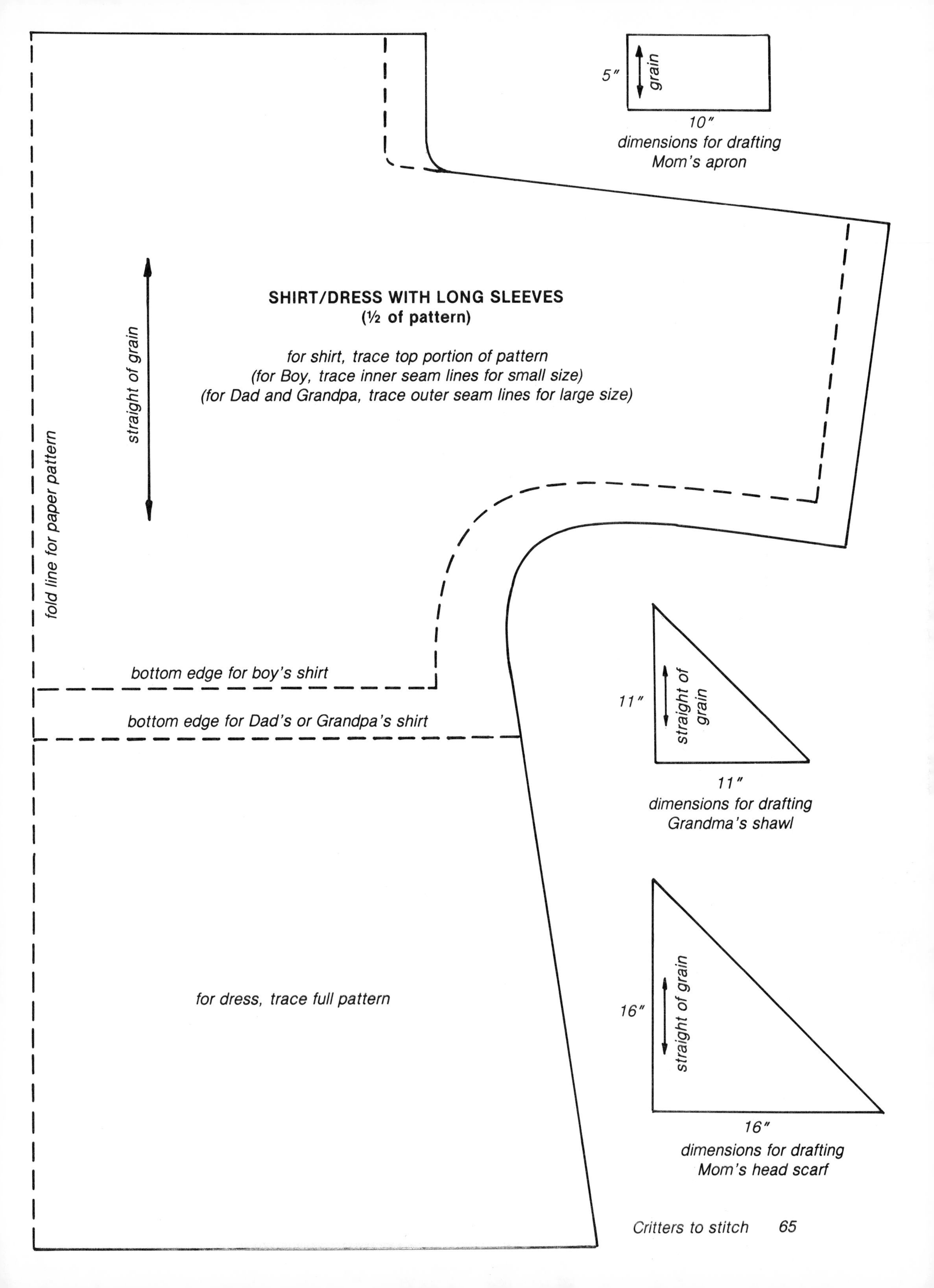
5″
grain
10″
dimensions for drafting
Mom's apron
SHIRT/DRESS WITH LONG SLEEVES
(½ of pattern)
for shirt, trace top portion of pattern
(for Boy, trace inner seam lines for small size)
(for Dad and Grandpa, trace outer seam lines for large size)
straight of grain
fold line for paper pattern
bottom edge for boy's shirt
bottom edge for Dad's or Grandpa's shirt
11″
straight of grain
11″
dimensions for drafting
Grandma's shawl
for dress, trace full pattern
16″
straight of grain
16″
dimensions for drafting
Mom's head scarf

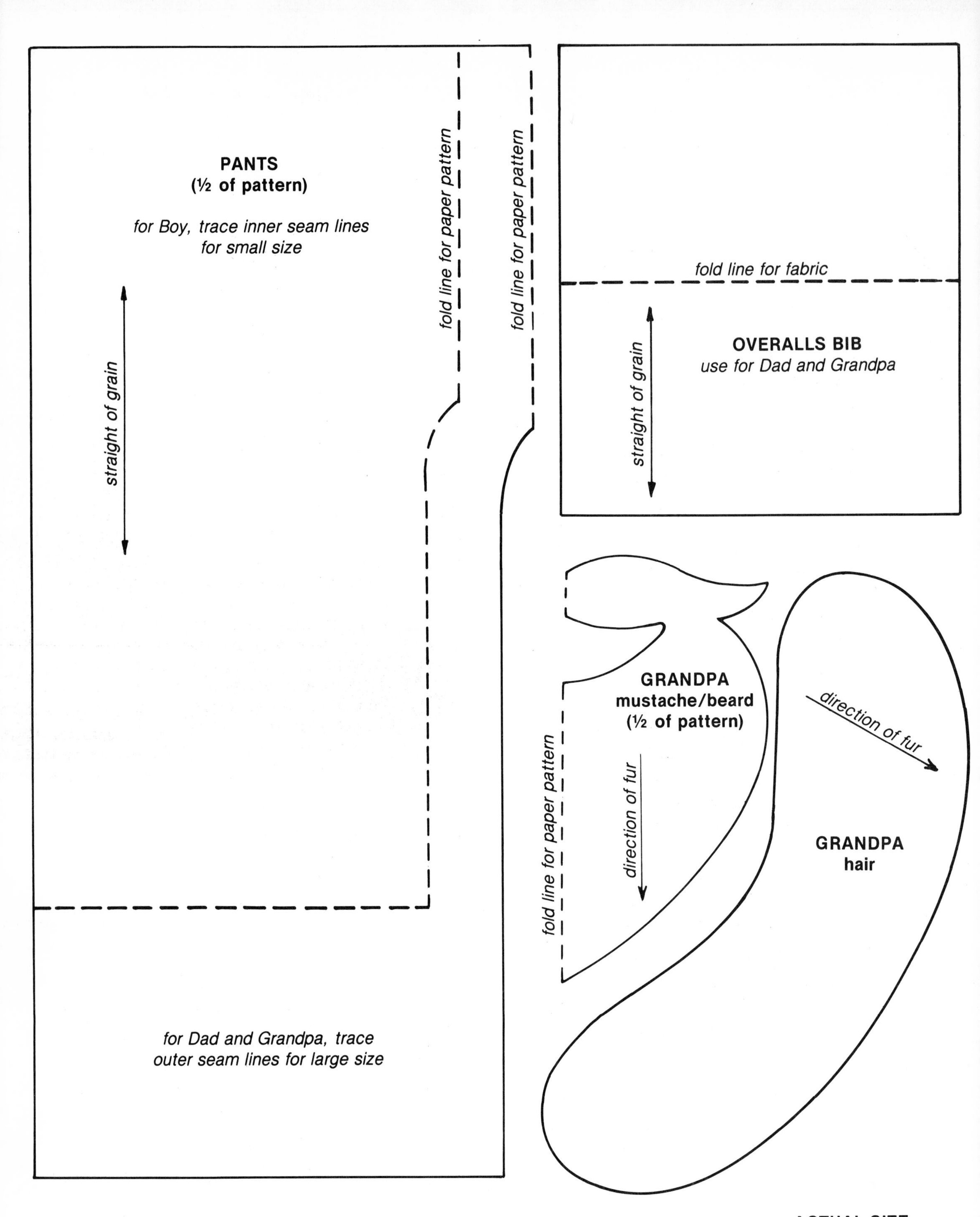
PANTS
(½ of pattern)
for Boy, trace inner seam lines
for small size
straight of grain
fold line for paper pattern
fold line for paper pattern
for Dad and Grandpa, trace
outer seam lines for large size
fold line for fabric
OVERALLS BIB
use for Dad and Grandpa
straight of grain
GRANDPA
mustache/beard
(½ of pattern)
fold line for paper pattern
direction of fur
direction of fur
GRANDPA
hair

ACTUAL SIZE

White crepe fabric and bulky yarn create this soft Unicorn (page 111), shown reclining on a mound of pillows.

Circles of fur fabrics are the main ingredients used to make the Robin, left, the Duck and the Chick (page 30).

The Pony & Friends, below, begin with one basic pattern. Use it to create a brown Pony (page 109), a plush Stick Pony (page 112), or a long-eared Burro (page 111). Follow the directions for adding an inner wire support if you want the long-legged critters to stand upright.

A variety of simple trims can turn basic slippers (page 86) into the critters pictured at right. You can have Puppies; Chicks, shown with a Hen Pajama Bag (page 82); or Rabbits.

Big felt eyelids give the Snake (page 50) a lazy look. He's pictured below right with a black and white Pig (page 15) that also could be made in one color. The fence unit (page 136) is two feet long and hooks to other units.

Hand puppets can rest on dowel supports "between acts." There's a sly Fox made of long-pile fabric (page 75), a big-mouthed Frog (opposite page) whose heavy eyelashes are optional, and a Parrot with a yellow felt beak (page 78).

Hand puppets

FROG

(color photo, opposite page)

(This pattern also may be used to make a stuffed toy.)

In the spring, every country pond vibrates with the song of the frog, and you can animate this hand puppet to make it talk or even sing. If you don't want a puppet, stuff the body, close the bottom seam and turn it into a floppy toy.

I used ready-made plastic eyes with a half-ball shape, but you could make the eyes from felt. The black felt eyelashes are optional.

MATERIALS

green plush fabric, 17x30" (pile should run along the 17" length)
red plush fabric or felt, 6x6", for inner mouth
green felt, 8x10", for front feet
plastic frog eyes with posts, 1½" diameter (available at craft shops); or white, green and black felt scraps, for felt eyes
black felt scraps, for eyelashes (optional)
transparent thread, for machine stitching
button-and-carpet thread, for handwork
polyester fiberfill, for stuffing
plastic lid and glue (if you make felt eyes)

DIRECTIONS

For tips on tracing patterns and working with fur fabric, see *Helpful guides*, page 1.

Make pattern pieces

1. Trace patterns for body front, body back, face and inner mouth, page 74. Trace front foot, hind foot, eyelid and eyelash (optional), page 73. If making felt eyes, also trace pattern for eye.

2. Cut out full pattern pieces.

Cut fabric

1. Lay pattern pieces on back of fur fabric, making sure fur is running in correct direction. On green plush, trace 1 body front, 1 body back, 1 face, 2 eyelids and 4 hind feet (2 reversed). Also mark 2 strips for hind legs, 3½x11½" each, and 2 strips for front legs, 3½x7½" each; have direction of fur running down longest measurements.

On red plush or felt, trace 1 inner mouth.

2. Cut out fabric on traced lines; ¼" seam allowances are included.

Assemble

Use ¼" seams and a zigzag machine stitch.

1. Pin inner mouth to face along lower curve, right sides together. Stitch from one corner of mouth to the other (Fig. 1).

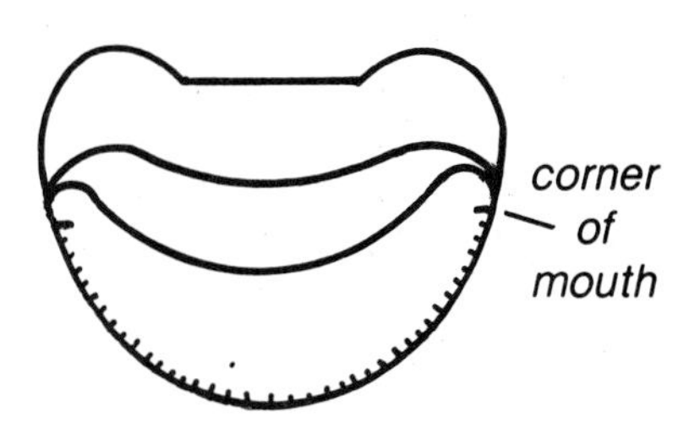

Fig. 1 *Stitching inner mouth to face along lower curve*

2. Pin top edge of face to body back, right sides together. Stitch from one corner of mouth, over eye humps, to other corner of mouth (Fig. 2).

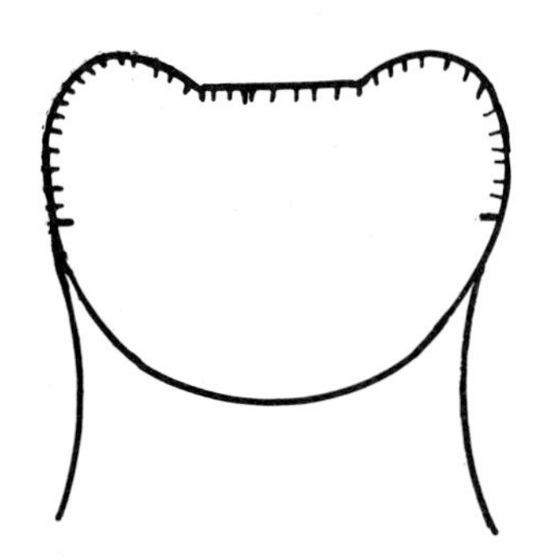

Fig. 2 *Stitching top edge of face to back*

3. Pin body front to free edge of inner mouth, right sides together (Fig. 3). Stitch from one corner of mouth to the other.

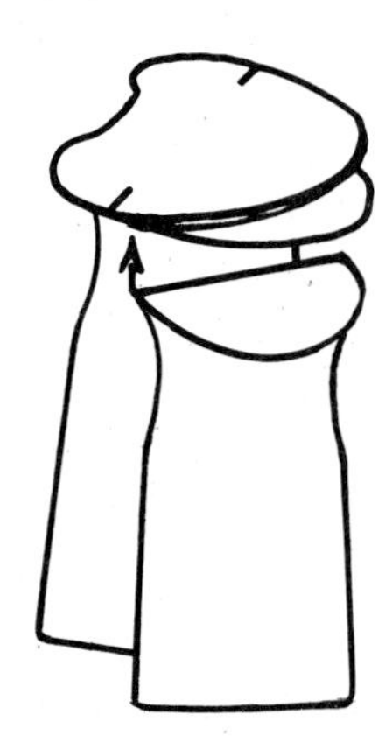

Fig. 3 *Joining upper curve of body front to inner mouth*

4. Pin body front to back along each side, and stitch from corner of mouth to bottom of body.

To secure seams at corners of mouth, use hand stitches if necessary. (Fabric may be too thick at corners to complete seams by machine.) Turn to right side.

5. Fold each leg in half lengthwise, with fur inside. Pin and stitch down the length to form a tube. Turn to right side.

Stuff and finish

1. Add eyes.

If you use plastic eyes, install at points indicated on the pattern.

To prepare eyelid for each plastic eye (Fig. 4), first fold eyelid ½" to wrong side along straight edge. Lay folded edge over plastic eye dome and fasten each end to face fabric. By hand, sew a running stitch

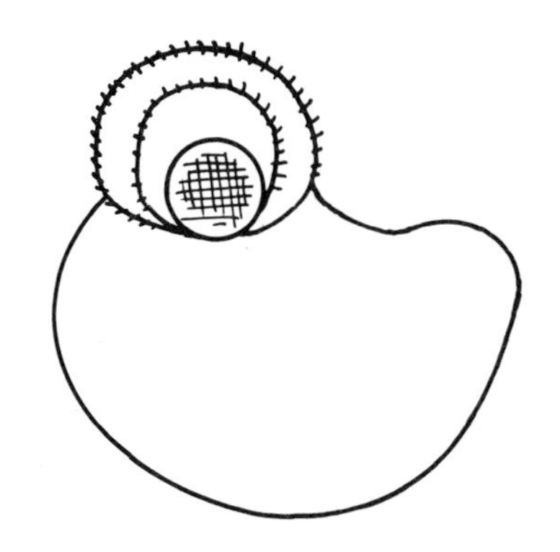

Fig. 4 *Adding eyelid to cover top of plastic eye*

around back curve of eyelid and gather to fit dome. Stitch gathered edge to head (eye hump will be inside eyelid).

If you use felt eyes, see *To make a felt eye*, page 5. For each eye, cut the large circle from the plastic lid and cover it with white felt. Glue on a middle-size green circle, then add a small black circle.

Lay each felt eye on face so that it is centered over eye position indicated on pattern. By hand, stitch bottom edge of eye to face for about ¼" (eye should stand up on face when finished).

To prepare eyelid for each felt eye, fold eyelid ½" to wrong side along straight edge. Fit folded edge around edge of eye and sew in place. By hand, sew a running stitch around back curve of eyelid (Fig. 5) and gather tightly. Roll up a wad of stuffing and insert to form eye bulge. Then stitch gathered edge to head (eye hump will be inside eyelid).

Fig. 5 *Stitching gathering line along curve of eyelid*

2. *Add eyelashes* (optional). Cut two eyelashes from black felt. Stitch one to the fold of each eyelid, framing top of eye.

3. Finish bottom edge of body.

For hand puppet, turn edge ½" to wrong side and hem. Stuff a small ball of fiberfill into head, leaving enough room for your hand to fit into mouth. Attach with a few stitches.

For toy, stuff body loosely and close bottom seam with invisible stitches.

4. To make each front foot, pin or trace pattern on double thickness of green felt. Straight-stitch around shape by machine, leaving straight edge open. Cut out shape along straight edge, and ⅛" from stitching. Do not turn. Stuff tiny wads of stuffing into toes and foot (a knitting needle helps).

5. Attach each front foot to the end of a front leg, using invisible stitches; have fur on leg running downward toward foot.

6. Stuff front legs very lightly (or leave unstuffed so they are limp). Attach to body at side

ACTUAL SIZE

seams, about 2" below corners of mouth. Use invisible stitches, and keep edges of each leg close together so legs will hang down at side.

7. To make each hind foot, pin matching foot pieces right sides together. Stitch, leaving short edge open. Turn to right side and stuff lightly or leave unstuffed.

8. Attach a hind foot to each hind leg, using invisible stitches; have fur on leg running downward toward foot.

Fig. 6 *Adding leg to front of body*

9. Stuff hind legs lightly (or leave unstuffed so they are limp). Attach to bottom edge of body front, just inside side seams (Fig. 6). Next, take a few stitches to catch each leg to body about ½" above bottom edge. This gives leg an upward lift.

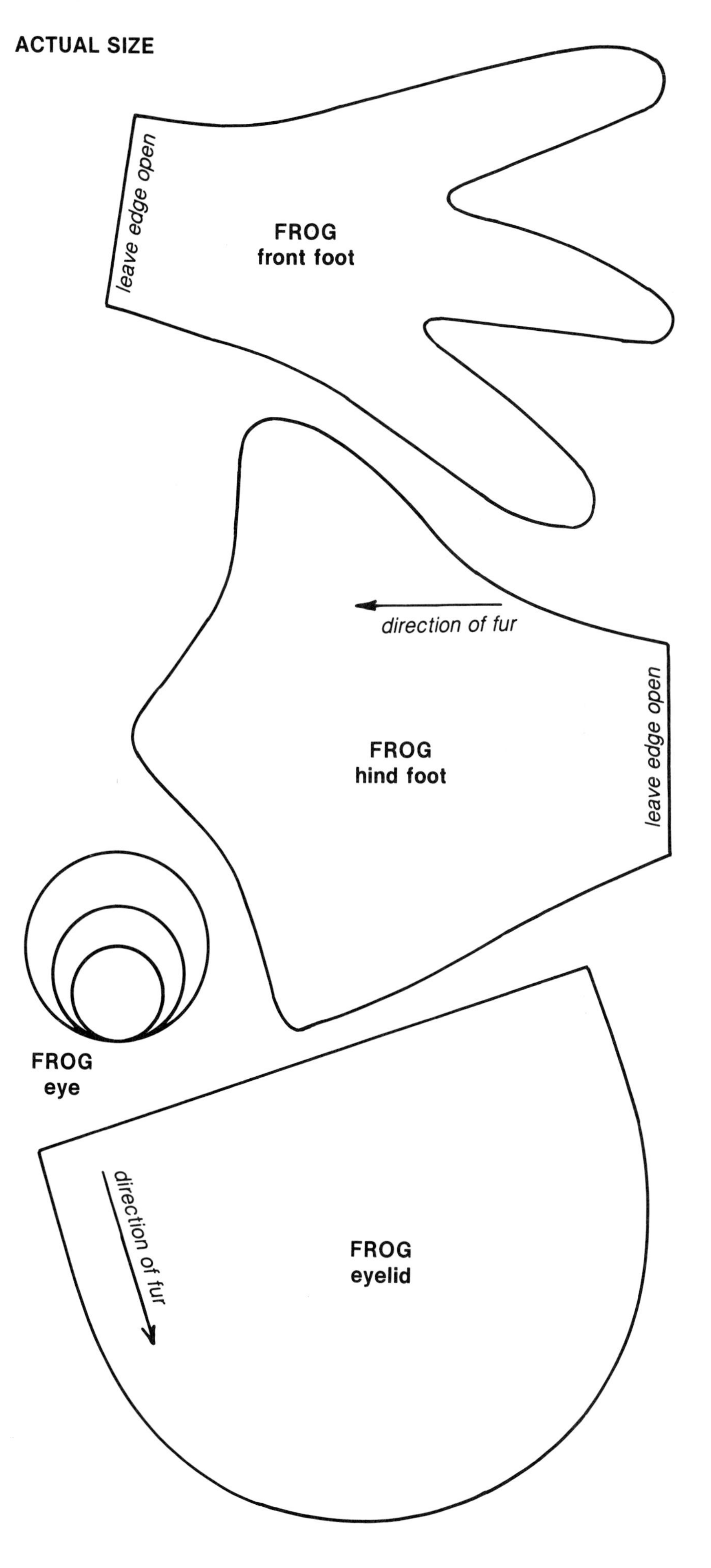

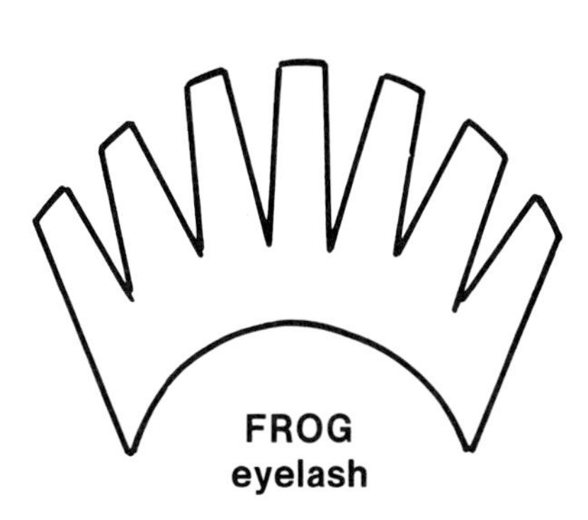

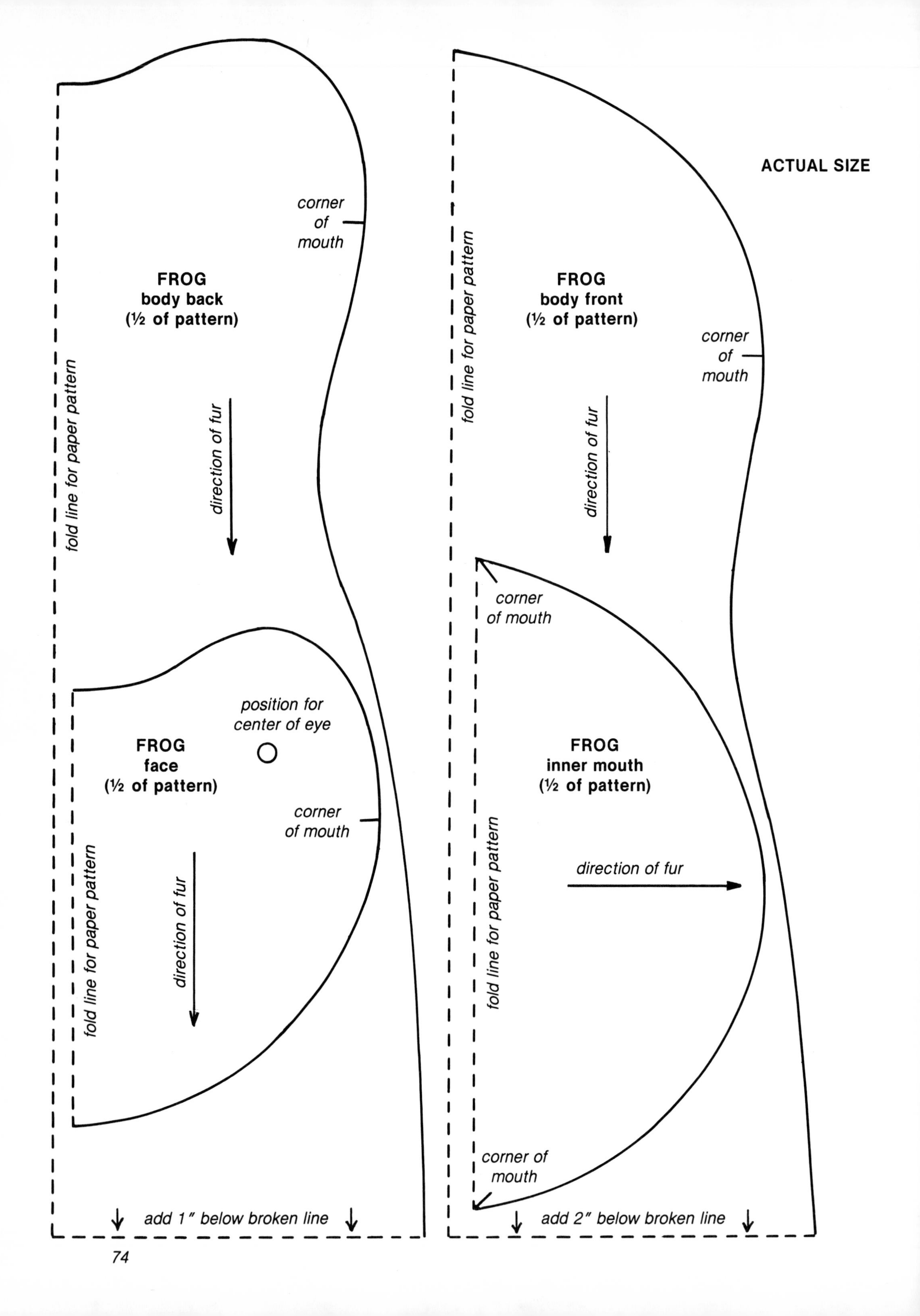
ACTUAL SIZE
FROG
body back
(½ of pattern)
corner
of
mouth
direction of fur
fold line for paper pattern
FROG
face
(½ of pattern)
position for
center of eye
corner
of mouth
direction of fur
fold line for paper pattern
add 1″ below broken line
FROG
body front
(½ of pattern)
corner
of
mouth
direction of fur
fold line for paper pattern
corner
of mouth
FROG
inner mouth
(½ of pattern)
direction of fur
fold line for paper pattern
corner of
mouth
add 2″ below broken line

FOX

(color photo, page 70)

The feisty fox can still be seen in the woodland and meadows in the country. Because of his reputation for being wise and sly, he should make a witty puppet character.

MATERIALS

rust long-pile fur fabric, 18x24" (pile should run along the 18" length)
muslin or other smooth fabric, 10x11", for head liner
red felt, 4x11", for inner mouth and tongue
brown felt, 7x9", for inner ears
black and green felt scraps, for nose and eyes
transparent thread, for machine stitching
button-and-carpet thread, for handwork
polyester fiberfill, for stuffing
plastic lid, for eyes
glue

DIRECTIONS

For tips on tracing patterns and working with fur fabric, see *Helpful Guides*, page 1.

Make pattern pieces

1. Trace pattern for head, pages 76-77, joining sections on broken lines. Trace patterns for head liner (top of head), eye, nose, tongue and tooth, page 76. Trace ear and inner mouth, page 77.
2. Cut out full pattern pieces. On head piece, slash along line at mouth as indicated on pattern.

Cut fabric

1. Lay pattern pieces on back of fur fabric, making sure fur is running in correct direction. Trace 2 heads (1 reversed) and 2 ears.
2. On wrong side of muslin, trace 2 head liner pieces (1 reversed).
3. On brown felt, trace 2 ears. On red felt, trace 1 inner mouth and 1 tongue.
4. Cut out fabric on traced lines; ¼" seam allowances are included. Slash head pieces at mouth.

Assemble and finish

Use ¼" seams and a zigzag machine stitch.

1. Pin head pieces right sides together. Stitch from mouth slash around top of head to bottom edge. Stitch from mouth slash down neck to bottom edge. Leave bottom edge open.
2. For fangs, fold white felt to make two layers.

Trace tooth pattern twice. Straight-stitch on top of traced lines, then cut out close to stitching. (*Or* glue the two felt layers together and let dry. Then trace and cut out two teeth.)

3. Pin a tooth to each side of upper mouth slash, right sides together; keep short edge of tooth even with edge of mouth. Stitch to hold tooth in place.
4. Pin inner mouth to mouth slash, right sides together, matching points A, B and C. Baste layers together. Stitch by hand or machine, tapering seam at points.
5. Gather straight edge of tongue and stitch to center of inner mouth.
6. Make and attach eyes; see *To make a felt eye*, page 5. Cut the large crescent from the plastic lid and cover it with green felt. Glue on a black felt pupil.
7. Cut nose from black felt. By hand, sew a running stitch around the outside, put a small wad of stuffing in center of circle and pull thread tightly. Stitch nose to head.
8. To make each ear, pin a brown felt piece to a fur piece, right sides together. Stitch along curved edges, leaving straight edge open for turning. Turn to right side.

Fold ear along the straight edge, bringing outside edges to meet at center; felt is inside. Stitch ear to head.

9. Turn up bottom edge ½" to wrong side and hem by hand (or leave unfinished).
10. Clip pile around mouth and between nose and eyes to make it about ⅝" long.
11. To make head liner, pin the two muslin pieces right sides together. Join with a straight machine stitch, leaving a small opening for turning. Turn to right side, stuff firmly and close opening by hand.

Insert liner in head, and attach with a few stitches.

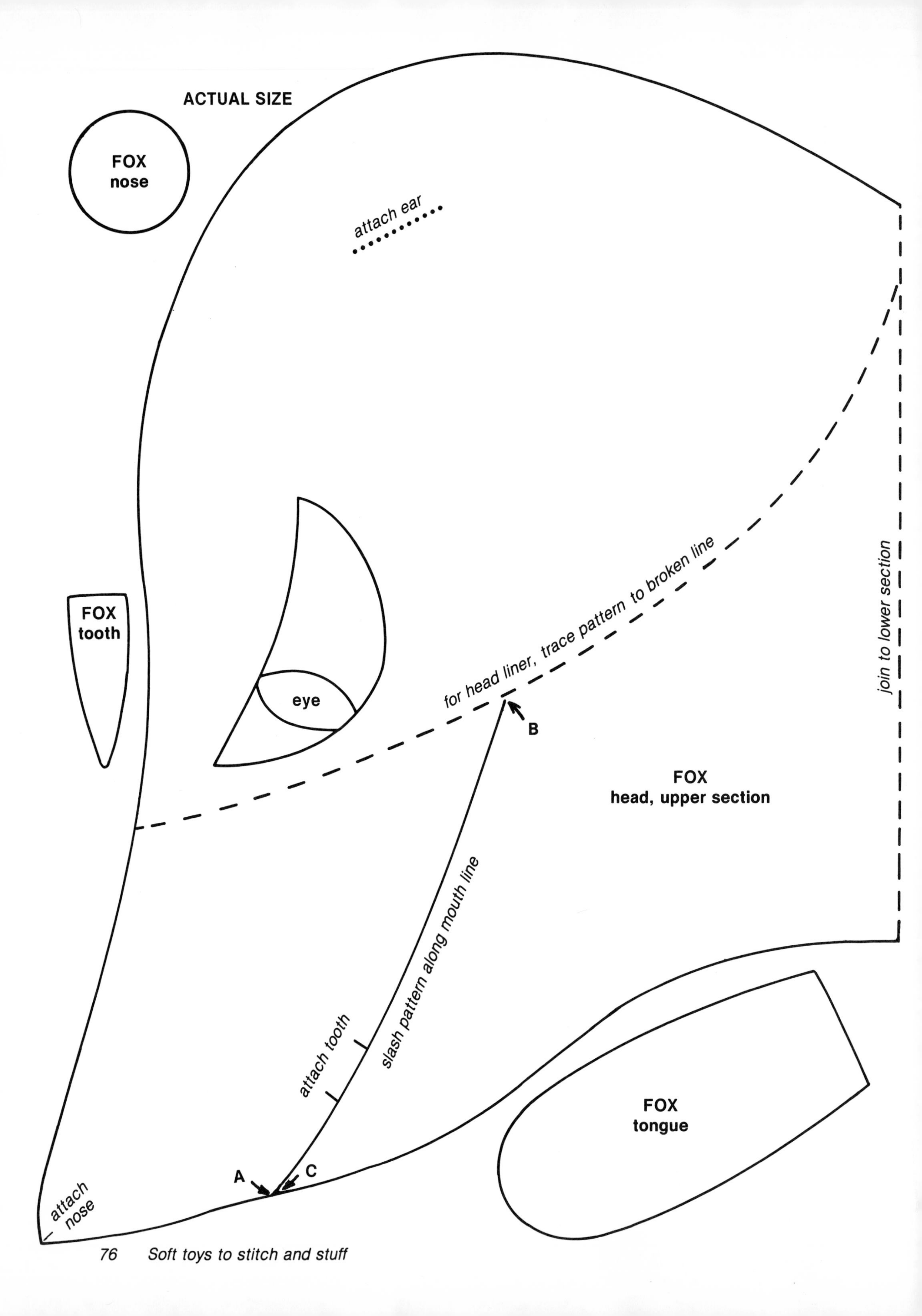
ACTUAL SIZE
FOX
nose
attach ear
FOX
tooth
eye
for head liner, trace pattern to broken line
B
FOX
head, upper section
join to lower section
slash pattern along mouth line
attach tooth
A
C
attach
nose
FOX
tongue

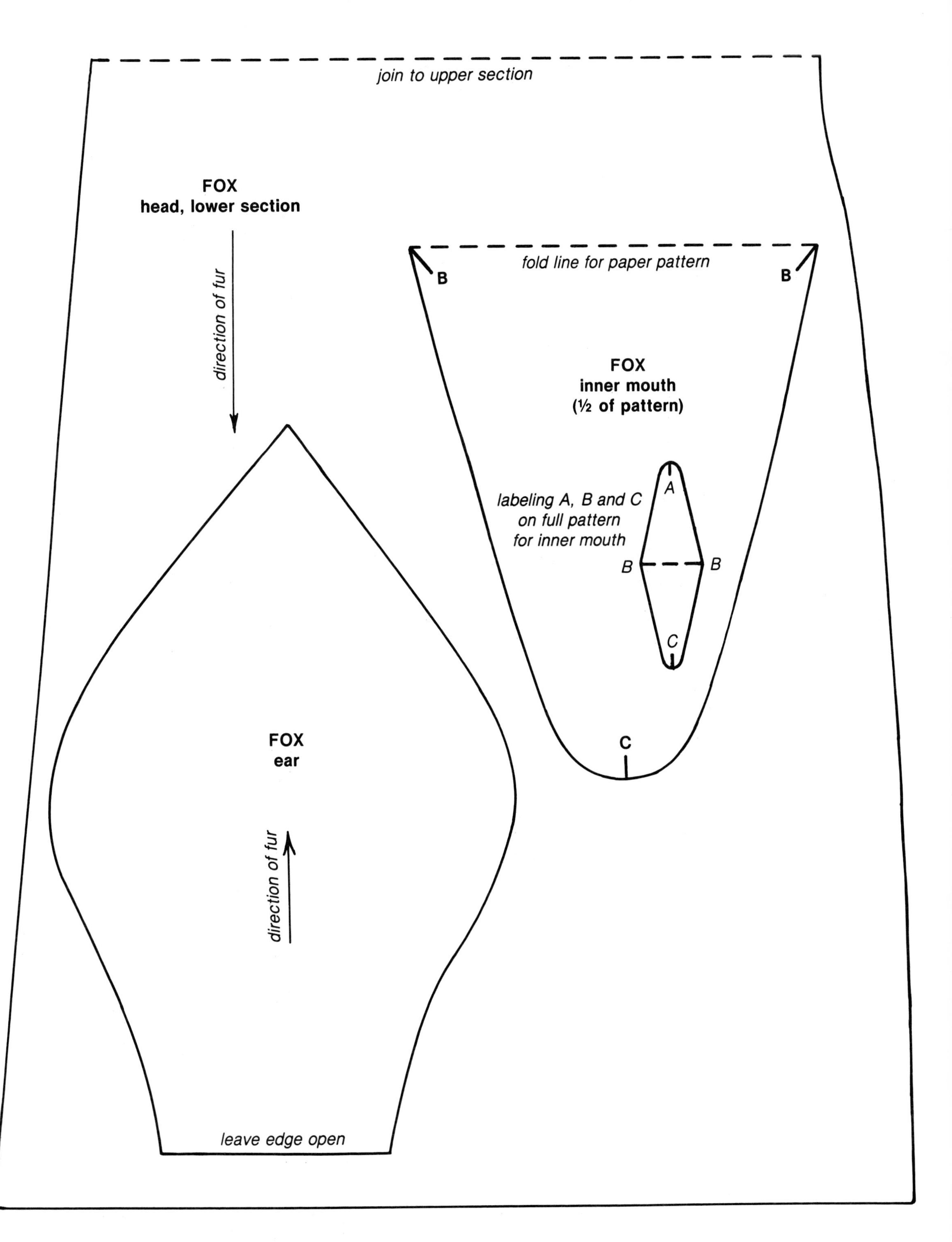
join to upper section
FOX
head, lower section
direction of fur
fold line for paper pattern
B
B
FOX
inner mouth
(½ of pattern)
labeling A, B and C
on full pattern
for inner mouth
A
B
B
C
C
FOX
ear
direction of fur
leave edge open

PARROT

(color photo, page 70)

I've never had much luck trying to teach a real bird to talk, but here's one I can handle. This Polly will talk any time I want to strike up a conversation.

My puppet is made of green, yellow and red plush fur fabric. Since the plumage of real parrots covers a wide range of brilliant colors, you can use almost any color combination and still not be far from reality.

MATERIALS

green plush fabric, 15x36", for body, wings and short tail feather (pile should run along the 15" length)
yellow plush fabric, 2½x11", for front gusset (pile should run along the 11" length)
red plush fabric, 10x15", for long tail feather (pile should run along the 15" length)
yellow felt, 6½x6½", for beak and eyes
red and black felt scraps, for eyes
transparent thread, for machine stitching
button-and-carpet thread, for handwork
polyester fiberfill, for stuffing
plastic lid, for eyes
glue

DIRECTIONS

For tips on tracing patterns and working with fur fabric, see *Helpful Guides*, page 1.

Make pattern pieces

1. Trace pattern for body, page 80, joining upper and lower sections on broken lines. Trace patterns for eye, page 80; for wing and top beak, page 79; and for front gusset and inner beak, page 81. Trace separate patterns for long and short tail feathers, page 81, joining sections on broken lines.
2. Cut out full pattern pieces.

Cut fabric

1. Lay pattern pieces on back of fur fabric, making sure fur is running in correct direction. On green plush, trace 2 body pieces (1 reversed), 4 wings (2 reversed) and 2 short tail feathers. On yellow plush, trace 1 front gusset. On red plush, trace 2 long tail feathers.
2. On yellow felt, trace 2 top beaks (1 reversed) and 1 inner beak.
3. Cut out fabric on traced lines; ¼" seam allowances are included.

Assemble

Use ¼" seams and a zigzag machine stitch, unless otherwise noted.

1. Pin green body pieces right sides together. Stitch from A over head to B at bottom of bird.
2. Pin inner beak to end of front gusset, right sides together. Match points D-E-D and machine-stitch between points.
3. Pin front gusset to each body piece, right sides together, from D to bottom of bird (see Fig. 1). Stitch by machine.

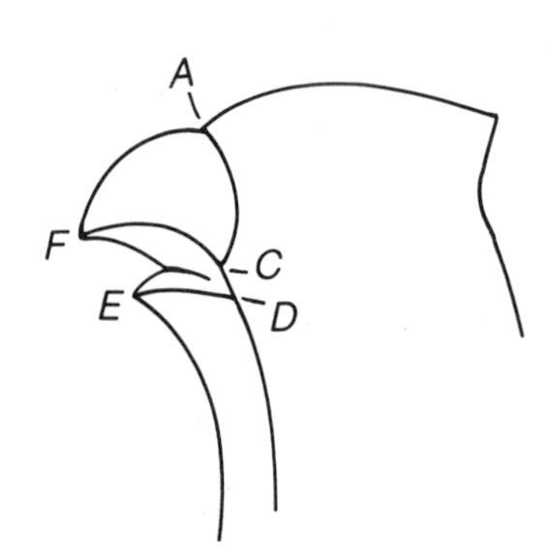

Fig. 1 *Stitching beak to body*

4. Pin top beak pieces together along top curve. Straight-stitch from A to F.
5. Pin each side of top beak to body, right sides together, from A to C. Stitch by hand, then stitch by machine.
6. Pin inner beak to top beak at F, right sides together. Pin along each side of top beak, from F to C, and along body, from C to D. Stitch by hand, then stitch by machine. Turn to right side.
7. Pin red tail-feather pieces right sides together. Stitch around curve, leaving straight edge open for turning. Turn to right side.

Repeat step to make green tail feather.

8. Center short green tail feather over back seam of body, right sides together; have all raw edges even. Stitch to bird by hand with overcast stitches.

Center red tail feather over green tail feather, with edges even. Pin and stitch to body.

9. To make each wing, pin matching pieces right sides together. Stitch, leaving small opening for turning. Turn to right side and close opening with invisible stitches.
10. Center a wing on each side of parrot, with bottom tip of wing about 1" above bottom of bird. Gather top of each

wing slightly between points G and H, then sew wing to bird along gathered edge.

Stuff and finish

1. Stuff a ball of fiberfill into top of Parrot's head and top beak. Leave room to insert your hand so you can manipulate beak, and attach fiberfill with a few stitches.

2. Turn bottom edge of bird ½″ to inside and hem by hand (or leave unfinished).

3. Make and attach eyes; see *To make a felt eye*, page 5. Cut the large circle from the plastic lid and cover it with red felt. Glue on a yellow felt circle and then a smaller black felt circle.

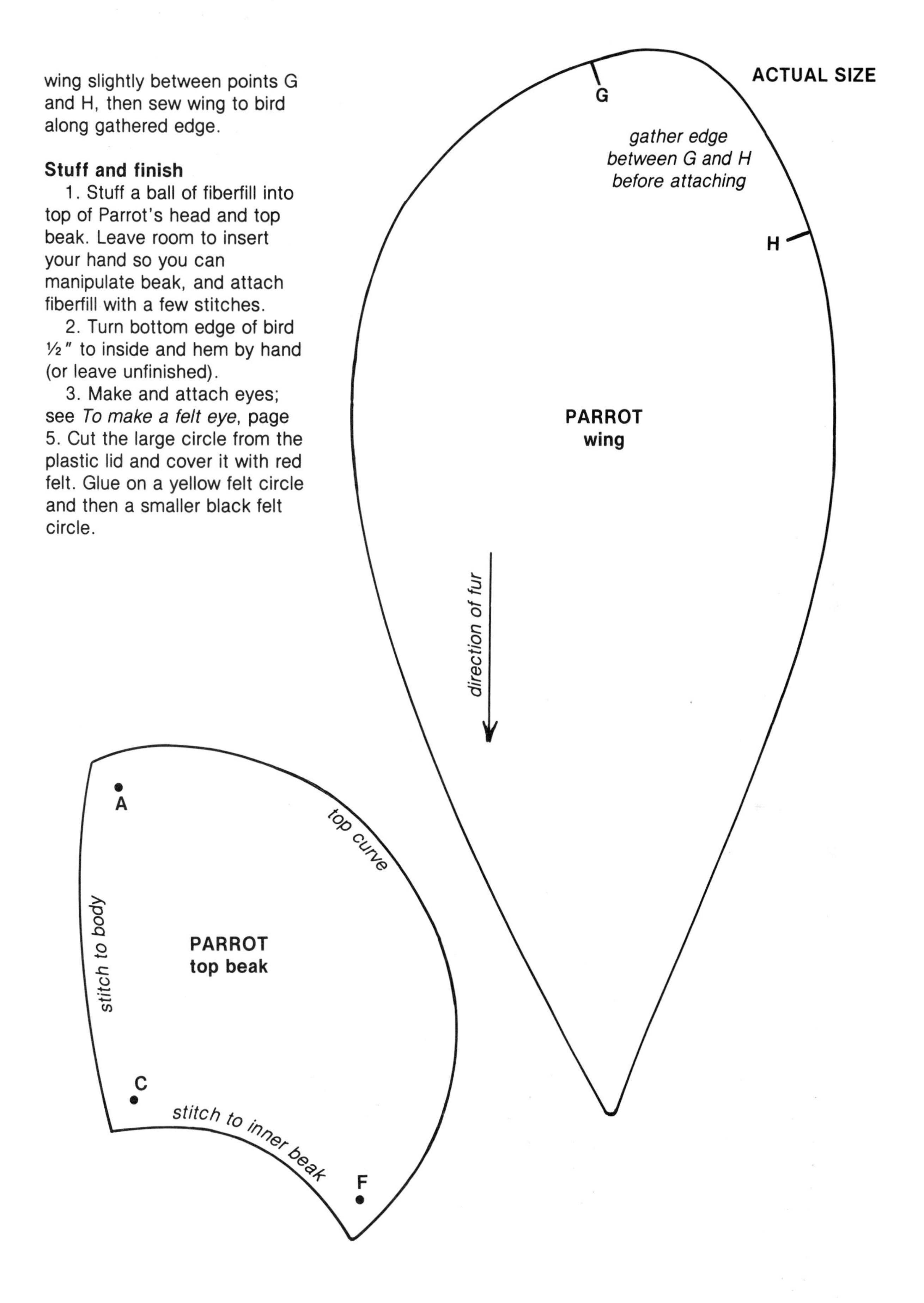

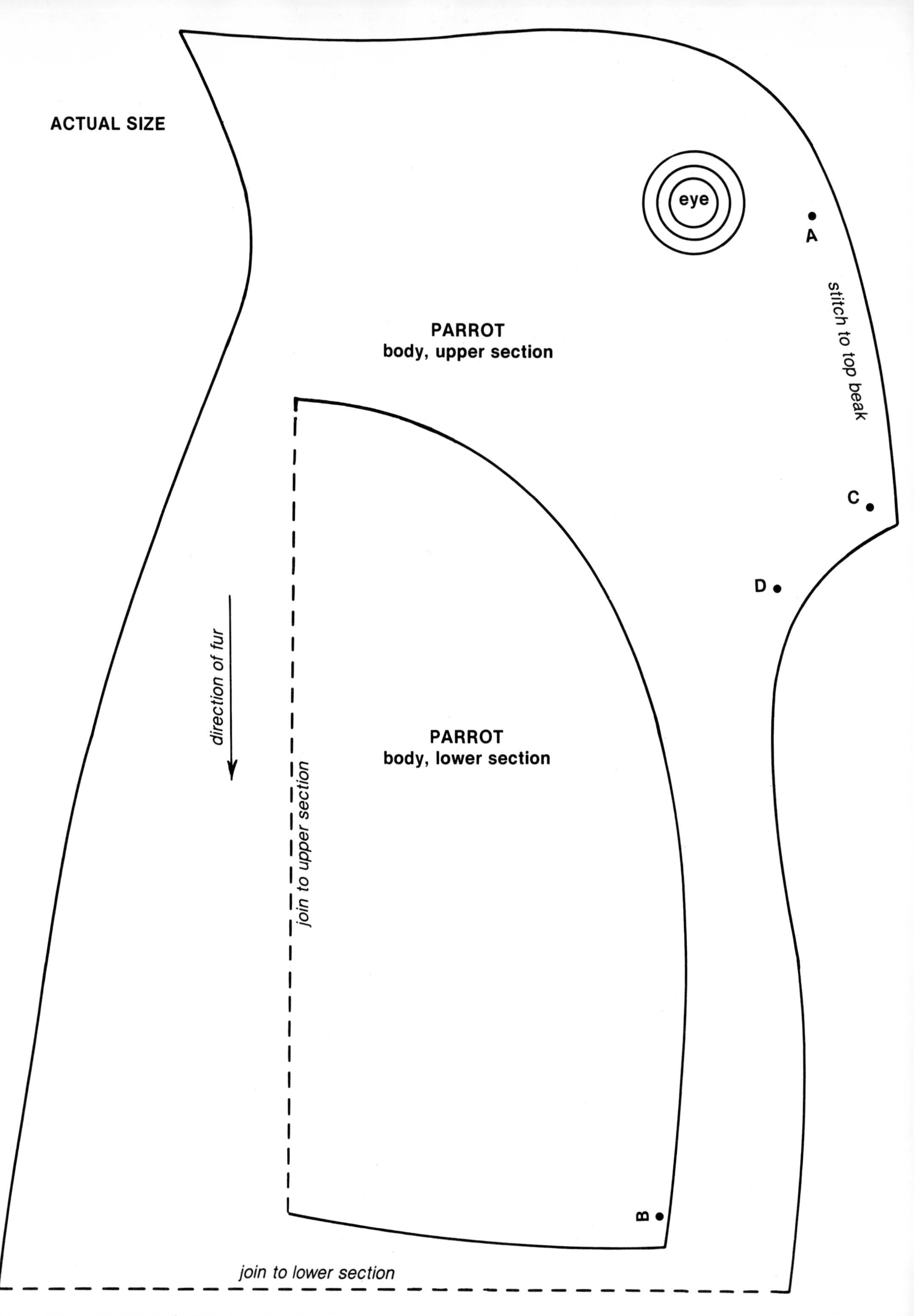
ACTUAL SIZE
eye
A
stitch to top beak
PARROT
body, upper section
C
D
direction of fur
PARROT
body, lower section
join to upper section
B
join to lower section

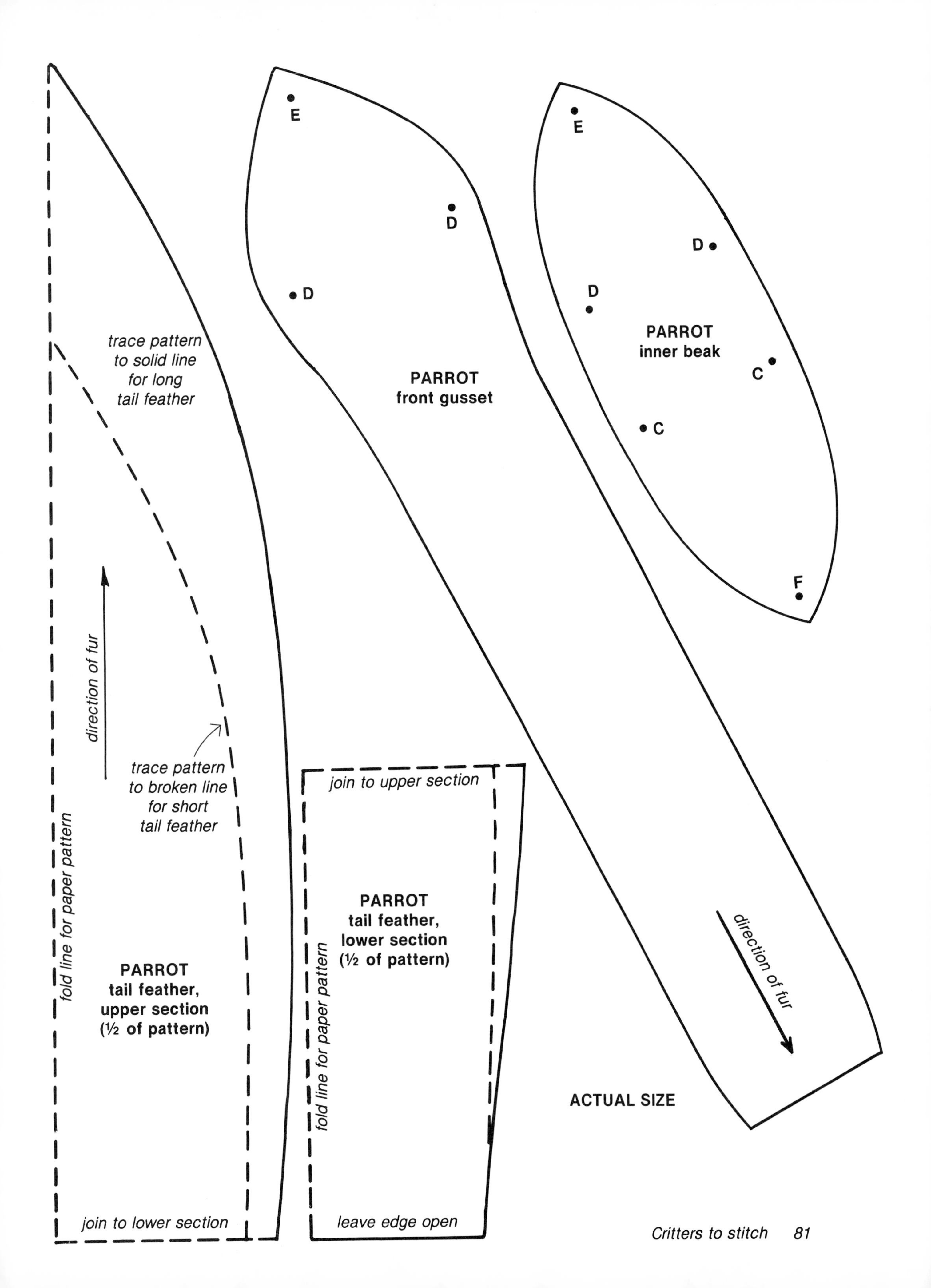
E
D
D
PARROT
front gusset
E
D
D
PARROT
inner beak
C
C
F
trace pattern
to solid line
for long
tail feather
direction of fur
trace pattern
to broken line
for short
tail feather
fold line for paper pattern
PARROT
tail feather,
upper section
(½ of pattern)
join to lower section
join to upper section
PARROT
tail feather,
lower section
(½ of pattern)
fold line for paper pattern
leave edge open
direction of fur
ACTUAL SIZE

Hen pajama bag & slippers

HEN PAJAMA BAG

(color photo, page 69)

(Hen may also be made into a stuffed toy or pillow.)

In the farmyard, a mother hen keeps busy scratching for food and tending her chicks. This mother Hen sits on the bed and tends pajamas (stuffed inside) by day. Her two Chicks, shown snuggled under her wings on page 69, are really slippers designed to keep little feet warm.

To make the Hen into a toy or pillow, stuff the body with fiberfill and close the seam.

Directions for slippers follow on page 86. You can make Chick slippers to go with the Hen, or change the trim to create a pair of Bunny or Puppy slippers.

MATERIALS

white long-pile fur fabric, 18x30" (pile should run along the 18" length)
red and white cotton check or print fabric, 9x25", for comb and to line head and wings
white, black and blue felt scraps, for eyes
yellow felt scrap, for beak
transparent thread, for machine stitching
button-and-carpet thread, for handwork
9" white zipper
polyester fiberfill, for stuffing head
plastic lid, for eyes
glue

DIRECTIONS

For tips on tracing and enlarging patterns, and working with fur fabric, see *Helpful Guides*, page 1.

Make pattern pieces

1. Use a 16x18" sheet of paper (marked in 2" squares) to enlarge patterns for body and wing on opposite page. Use another sheet of paper to trace enlarged wing (this gives you a separate wing pattern).
2. Trace patterns for beak, eye, comb, head liner top and head liner bottom, page 84.
3. Cut out pattern pieces.

Cut fabric

1. Lay pattern pieces on back of fur fabric, making sure fur is running in correct direction. Trace 2 body pieces (1 reversed) and 2 wings (1 reversed).
2. On wrong side of red and white fabric, trace 2 wings (1 reversed), 2 combs, 2 head liner top pieces (1 reversed), and 1 head liner bottom piece.
3. On yellow felt, trace 2 beaks.
4. Cut out fabric on traced lines; ¼" seam allowances are included.

Assemble

Use ¼" seams, with a zigzag machine stitch on fur fabric and a straight stitch on felt and woven fabrics.

1. Pin body pieces right sides together, and stitch; leave 9" open at bottom for zipper.
2. Open zipper a short way. Pin edges of zipper tape to edge of opening, right sides together. Machine-stitch along edges, and turn to right side through zipper opening.
3. To make each wing, pin lining to fur piece, right sides together. Stitch, leaving a small opening for turning. Turn to right side, and close opening with invisible stitches.

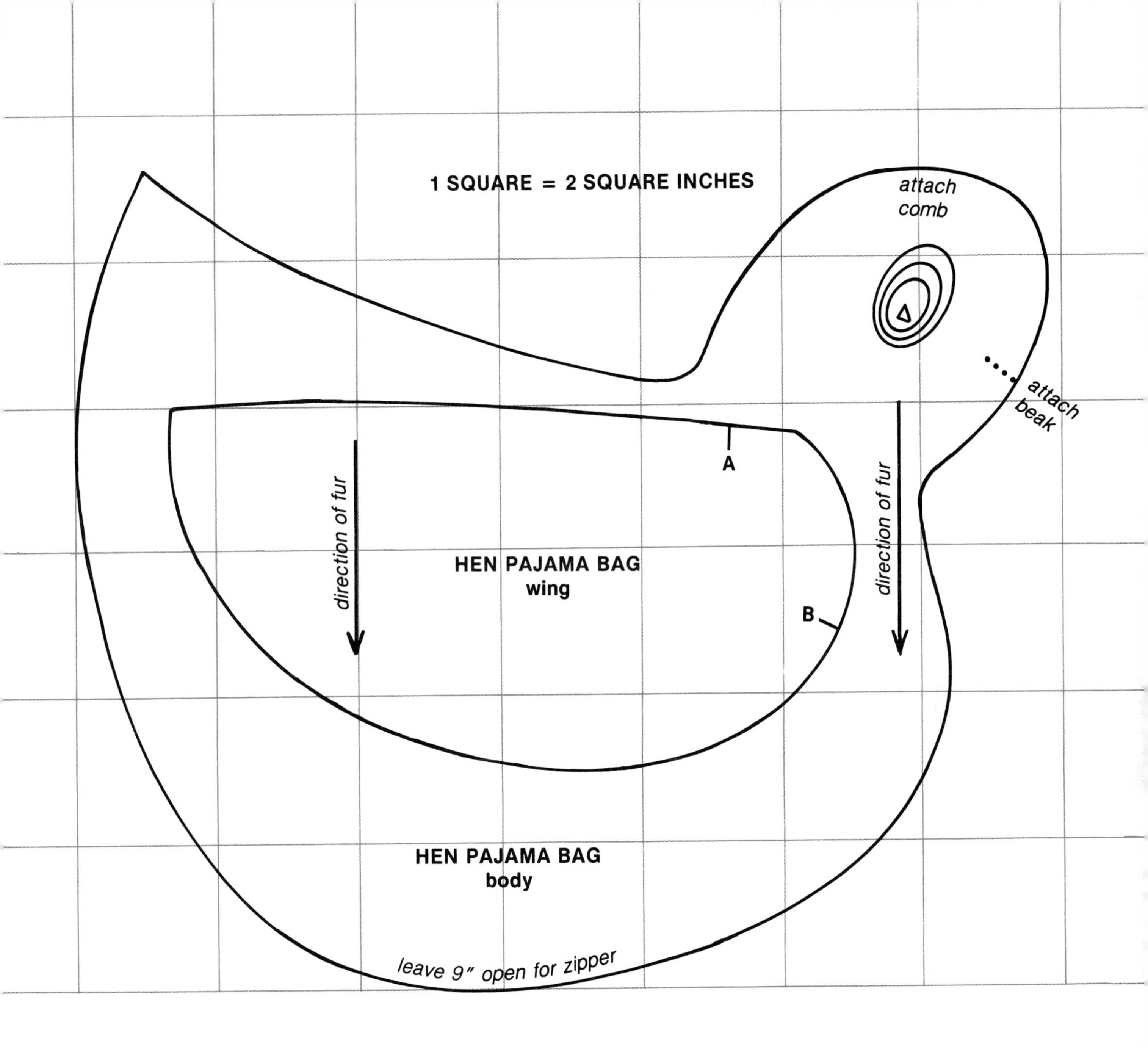

4. Attach wings to body by hand, stitching along front curve from A to B.

5. To make a separate liner unit for head, pin liner top pieces right sides together. Straight-stitch from C over head curve to D.

Pin bottom piece to top pieces, right sides together, matching points C and D. Stitch, leaving a small opening for turning. Slash seam allowance to stitching along neck curve, and turn liner to right side.

Stuff and finish

1. Stuff head liner and close opening with invisible stitches.

2. Insert liner in body and attach with a few hand stitches.

3. To make comb, pin the two cotton pieces right sides together. Stitch around the small curves, leaving bottom curve open. Slash seam allowance to stitching in V areas, turn to right side, and stuff lightly. Turn raw edges to the inside and close opening with invisible stitches.

Position comb on head and sew in place.

4. To make beak, machine-stitch the two yellow felt pieces together; leave a small opening for turning. Turn to right side, stuff lightly, and close opening with invisible stitches.

Fold beak across center and stitch to body along fold.

5. Make and attach eyes; see *To make a felt eye*, page 5. Cut the large oval from the plastic lid and cover it with white felt. Glue on a blue felt oval, a smaller black felt oval, and a white felt highlight.

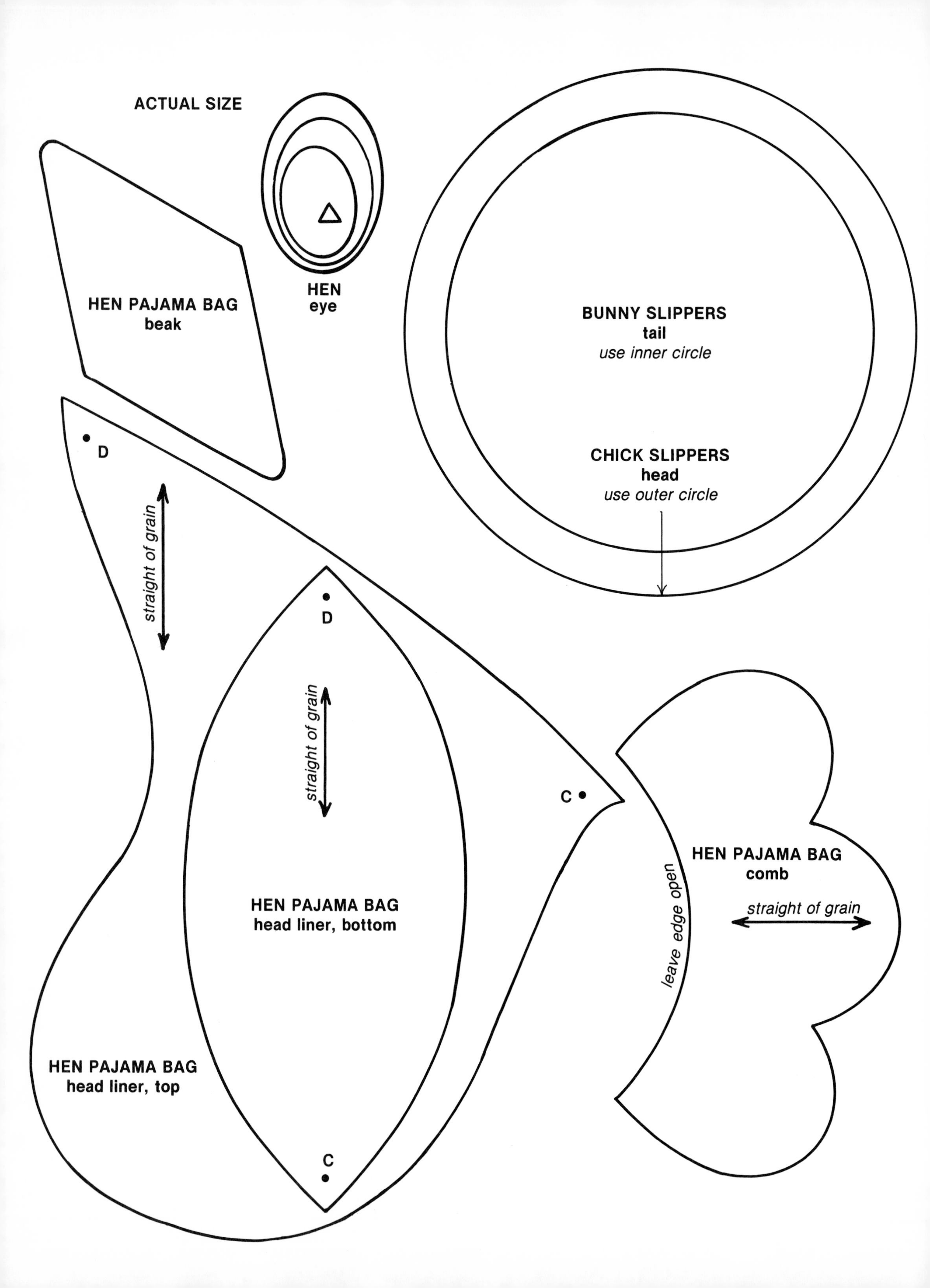
ACTUAL SIZE
HEN PAJAMA BAG
beak
HEN
eye
BUNNY SLIPPERS
tail
use inner circle
CHICK SLIPPERS
head
use outer circle
D
straight of grain
D
straight of grain
C
HEN PAJAMA BAG
head liner, bottom
HEN PAJAMA BAG
head liner, top
C
HEN PAJAMA BAG
comb
leave edge open
straight of grain

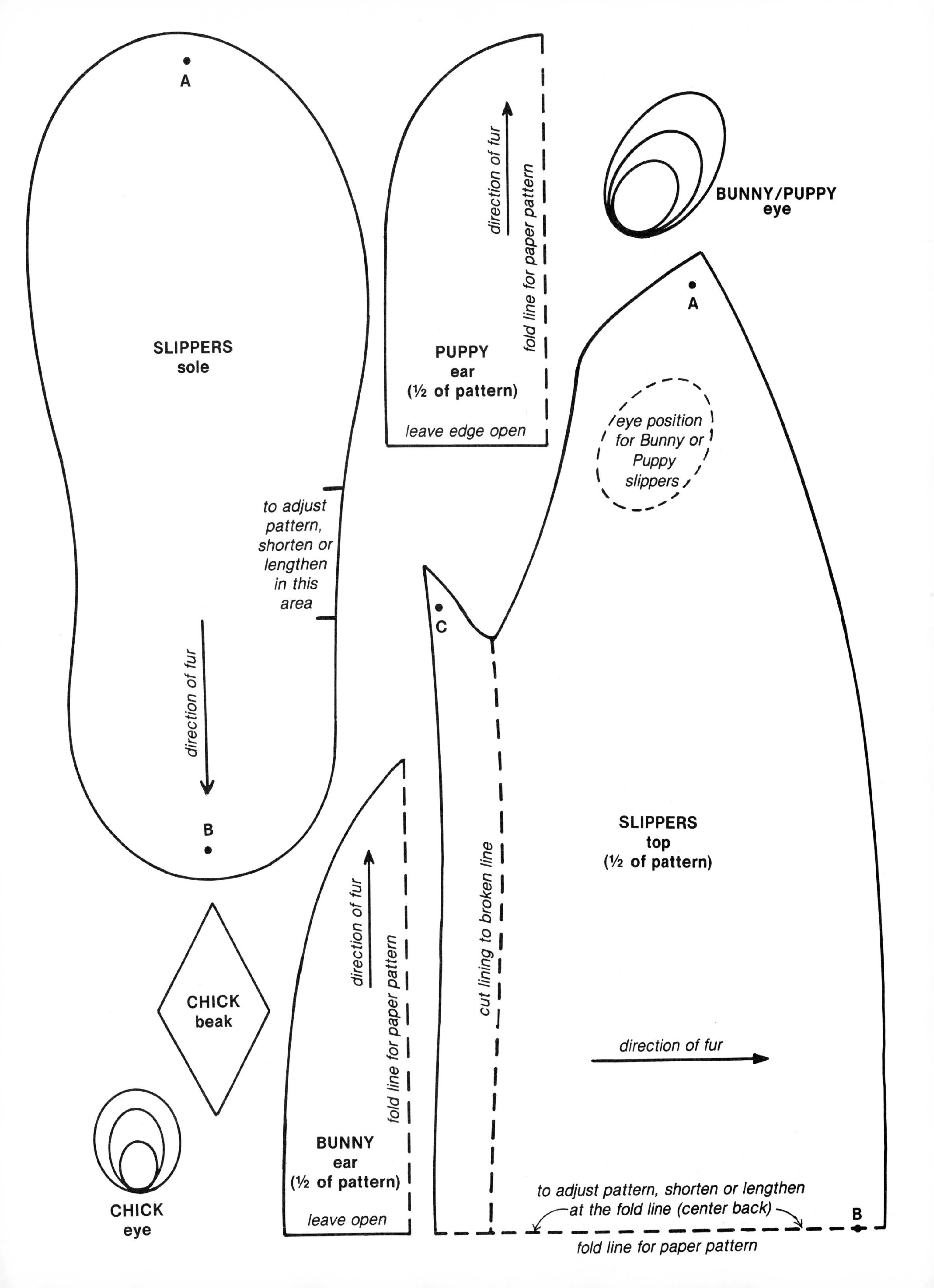

SLIPPERS
sole
A
B
direction of fur
to adjust
pattern,
shorten or
lengthen
in this
area
PUPPY
ear
(½ of pattern)
direction of fur
fold line for paper pattern
leave edge open
BUNNY/PUPPY
eye
eye position
for Bunny or
Puppy
slippers
A
C
SLIPPERS
top
(½ of pattern)
cut lining to broken line
direction of fur
to adjust pattern, shorten or lengthen
at the fold line (center back)
B
fold line for paper pattern
BUNNY
ear
(½ of pattern)
direction of fur
fold line for paper pattern
leave open
CHICK
beak
CHICK
eye

SLIPPERS

(color photo, page 69)

(color photo, page 69)

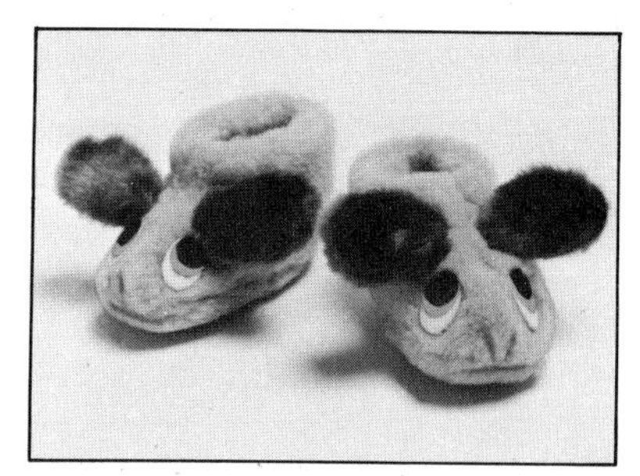

(color photo, page 69)

Directions are given for a basic slipper, along with variations for trims that turn the slippers into Chicks, Bunnies or Puppies.

MATERIALS

plush or other fur fabric, about 9x30", for slippers (yellow for Chicks, pink for Bunnies, or beige for Puppies); pile should run along the 9" length
soft knit or woven fabric in coordinating color, about 9x26", for lining
felt scraps, for eyes (white, black and blue for Chicks or Bunnies; white, black and brown for Puppies)
muslin or other scrap fabric (for testing pattern)
transparent thread, for machine stitching
button-and-carpet thread, for handwork
plastic lid, for eyes
glue

ADDITIONAL MATERIALS

for Chicks: yellow felt scrap, for beaks; polyester fiberfill, for heads
for Bunnies: white fur fabric or felt, 7x8½", for tails and inner ears (pile should run along the 8½" length); polyester fiberfill, for tails
for Puppies: brown fur fabric, 7½x13", for ears (pile should run along the 7½" length)

DIRECTIONS

For tips on tracing patterns and working with fur fabric, see *Helpful Guides,* page 1.

Make pattern pieces

1. To determine slipper length needed, first trace around youngster's foot. Mark 1" beyond toes (for seams and ease), then measure from heel to mark.

2. Trace pattern for sole, page 85, making it longer or shorter according to slipper length needed.

3. Place tracing of sole pattern over tracing of foot, and correct pattern width if necessary. Allow 3/8" beyond heel and each side of foot (there will be more room at toe area). Cut out final sole pattern.

4. Trace pattern for slipper top, page 85, making it longer or shorter according to slipper length needed. Cut out a full pattern.

5. To be sure pattern pieces fit together, test them by cutting one sole and one slipper top from muslin. Pin and baste top to sole, beginning at center back and working to the front. The top piece should meet in a center front seam. Make any needed adjustment on the slipper top pattern.

6. Trace and cut out other needed patterns:

For Chicks, trace head, page 84, and eye and beak, page 85.

For Bunnies, trace tail, page 84, and eye and ear, page 85.

For Puppies, trace ear and eye, page 85.

Cut fabric

1. Lay pattern pieces on back of fur fabric, making sure fur is running in correct direction. On main color, trace 2 soles (1 reversed) and 2 slipper tops.

For Chicks, also trace 2 head circles.

For Bunnies, also trace 4 ears.

2. On back of contrasting fabric, trace any trims needed.

For Bunnies, trace 4 ears and 2 tails on white.

For Puppies, trace 8 ears on brown.

3. On wrong side of lining fabric, trace 2 soles (1 reversed) and 2 slipper tops (follow top edge for lining noted on pattern).

4. Cut out fabric on traced lines; ¼" seam allowances are included.

Assemble

Use ¼" seams, with a zigzag machine stitch on fur and knit fabrics, and a straight stitch on woven fabric.

1. Fold each slipper top in half, with fur inside, and pin from A to C. Stitch the seam (Fig. 1).

2. Pin each top to a sole, right sides together, matching points A at the toe and points

B at the heel. Stitch.

3. Complete slipper linings in the same manner, first closing the tops, then adding the soles.

4. Place each lining sole against the matching slipper sole, wrong sides together. Stitch seam allowances together by hand.

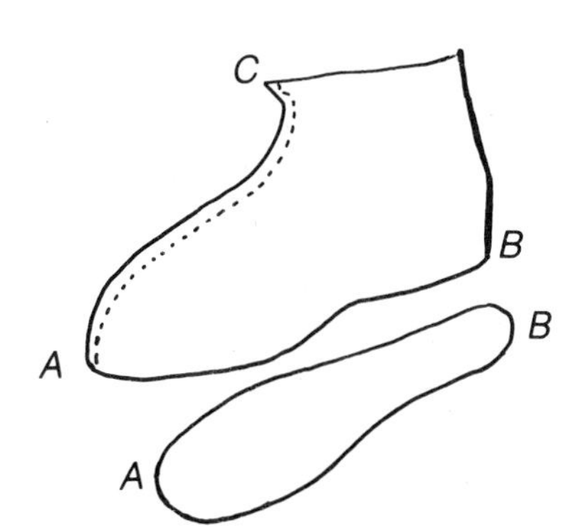

Fig. 1 *Stitching slipper top, positioning sole*

5. Turn each fur unit to the right side (lining will be inside). Fold raw edge of fur over lining ½" and pin. By hand, stitch raw edge to outside of slipper, catching lining in place (Fig. 2).

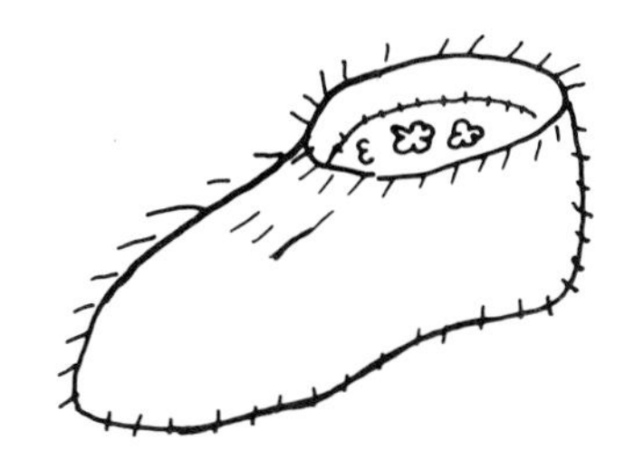

Fig. 2 *Hemming slipper top*

Finish Chicks

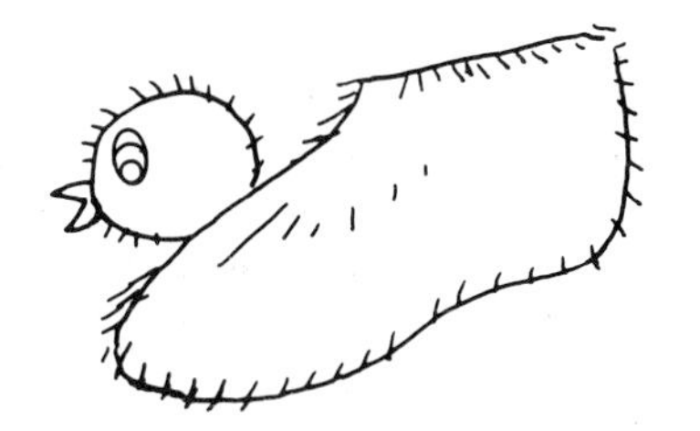

Fig. 3 *Adding head and trims for Chick slipper*

1. To make each head, sew a running stitch by hand around the edge of the circle. Pull thread to gather. Stuff a little fiberfill in the center of the circle, then pull thread tightly to make a ball and secure. Sew heads to slippers.

2. To make each beak, place pattern on top of a double layer of yellow felt and stitch around it. Cut out the beak, 1/8" from stitching. Fold beak in half and catch with hand stitches to hold. Attach beak to head, sewing along fold.

3. Make and attach eyes; see *To make a felt eye*, page 5. Cut the large oval from the plastic lid and cover it with white felt. Glue on a medium-size blue felt oval, then add a small black felt oval.

Finish Bunnies

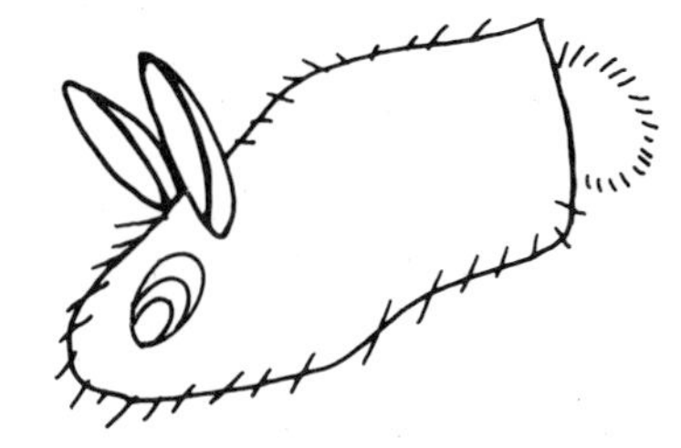

Fig. 4 *Adding tail and trims for Bunny slipper*

1. Make tails, following directions for making Chick head; see *Finish Chicks,* Step 1.

Stitch a tail to the back of each slipper.

2. To make each ear, pin one pink piece to a white piece, right sides together. Machine-stitch a narrow seam, leaving bottom edge open. Turn to right side.

Fold each ear down center, bringing curved edges forward. Stitch two ears to each slipper, with ears pointed upward.

3. Make and attach eyes; see *To make a felt eye*, page 5. Cut the large oval from the plastic lid and cover it with white felt. Glue on a medium-size blue felt oval, then add a small black felt oval.

Finish Puppies

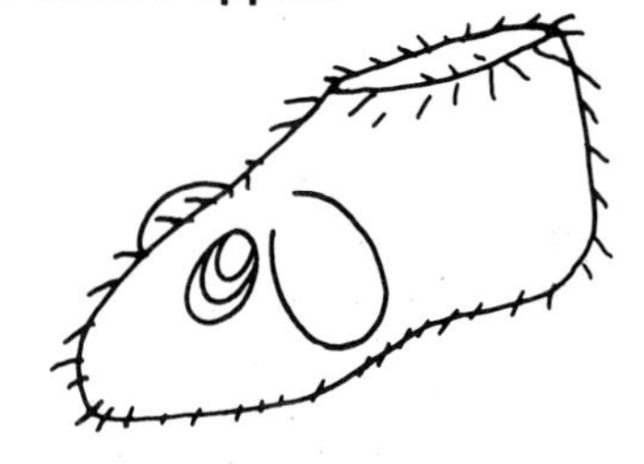

Fig. 5 *Adding trims to Puppy slipper*

1. To make each ear, pin two pieces right sides together. Machine-stitch a narrow seam, leaving straight edge open. Turn ear to right side.

Gather ears along the straight edges, and stitch two ears to each slipper.

2. Make and attach eyes; see *To make a felt eye*, page 5. Cut the large oval from the plastic lid and cover it with white felt. Glue on a medium-size brown felt oval, then add a small black felt oval.

Pets

SHAG DOG

(color photo, page 34)

This little Dog is very much like the puppy who came to our farm one rainy spring day. We found Muffy on the back steps, his fur matted and muddy, and his sad eyes looking for help.

"Can I keep him?" my young daughter asked as she scooped him up and brought him inside. She fed him, bathed him and hoped we couldn't find his owners. We did try to locate his home, but when no one claimed him, Muffy joined our growing family of critters.

Long-pile fur fabric gives this Dog a true shaggy look. I used a gray fabric with a frosted pile, then added a plastic nose and plastic eyes with lashes. If you want to satin-stitch the nose oı make felt eyes, refer to *Helpful Guides,* page 1.

MATERIALS

gray long-pile fur fabric, 18x31" (pile should run along the 18" length)
red felt scrap, for tongue
transparent thread, for machine stitching
button-and-carpet thread, for handwork
plastic nose and plastic eyes with posts (available at craft shops)
polyester fiberfill, for stuffing

DIRECTIONS

For tips on tracing patterns and working with fur fabric, see *Helpful Guides,* page 1.

Make pattern pieces

1. Trace separate patterns for body and inner legs, pages 89-90, joining sections on broken lines. Also trace patterns for ear and tongue, page 89.
2. Cut out full pattern pieces.

Cut fabric

1. Lay pattern pieces on back of fur fabric, making sure fur is running in correct direction. Trace 2 body pieces (1 reversed), 2 inner legs pieces (1 reversed) and 4 ears.
2. Cut out fabric on traced lines; ¼" seam allowances are included.

Assemble

Use ¼" seams and a zigzag machine stitch.

1. Pin each inner legs piece to matching body piece, right sides together. Machine-stitch around legs, tapering seam to make it narrower at each end; leave top curve of inner legs open.
2. Pin the two body units right sides together, first along the head and back, and then along inner legs. Stitch around body to join the two units, leaving a small opening between legs for turning. Turn to right side.

Stuff and finish

1. Install plastic eyes and nose.
2. Stuff head and legs firmly, making sure stuffing is packed tightly where legs join body. Stuff body firmly and close opening with invisible stitches.
3. To make each ear, pin two ear pieces right sides together. Stitch around the curved edges, leaving the straight edge open for turning. Turn to right side. Position ear on head and stitch in place.
4. To make tongue, trace pattern on red felt and cut out. Stitch to face below nose.

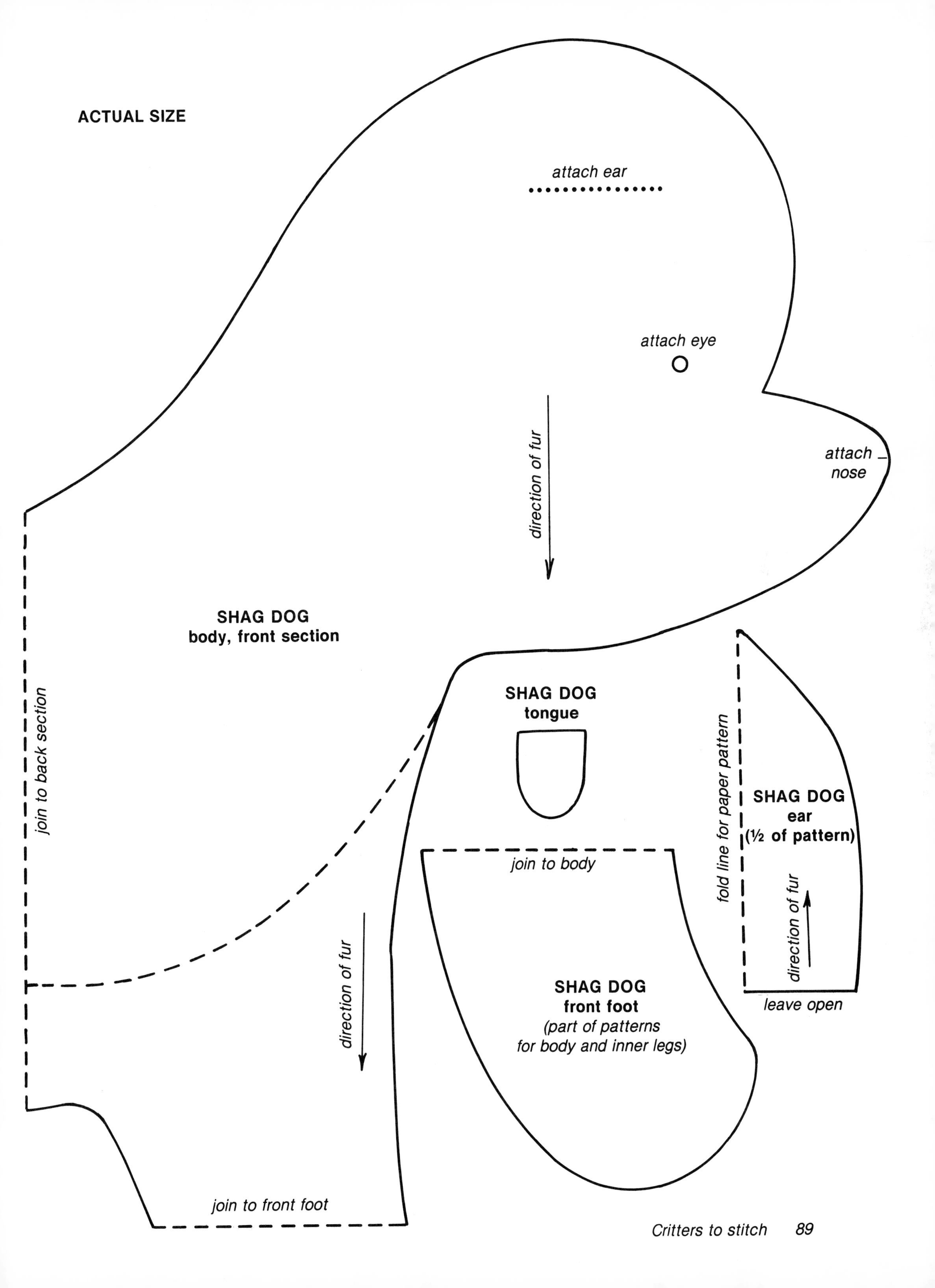
ACTUAL SIZE
attach ear
attach eye
attach nose
direction of fur
SHAG DOG
body, front section
join to back section
SHAG DOG
tongue
SHAG DOG
ear
(½ of pattern)
fold line for paper pattern
direction of fur
leave open
join to body
SHAG DOG
front foot
(part of patterns
for body and inner legs)
direction of fur
join to front foot

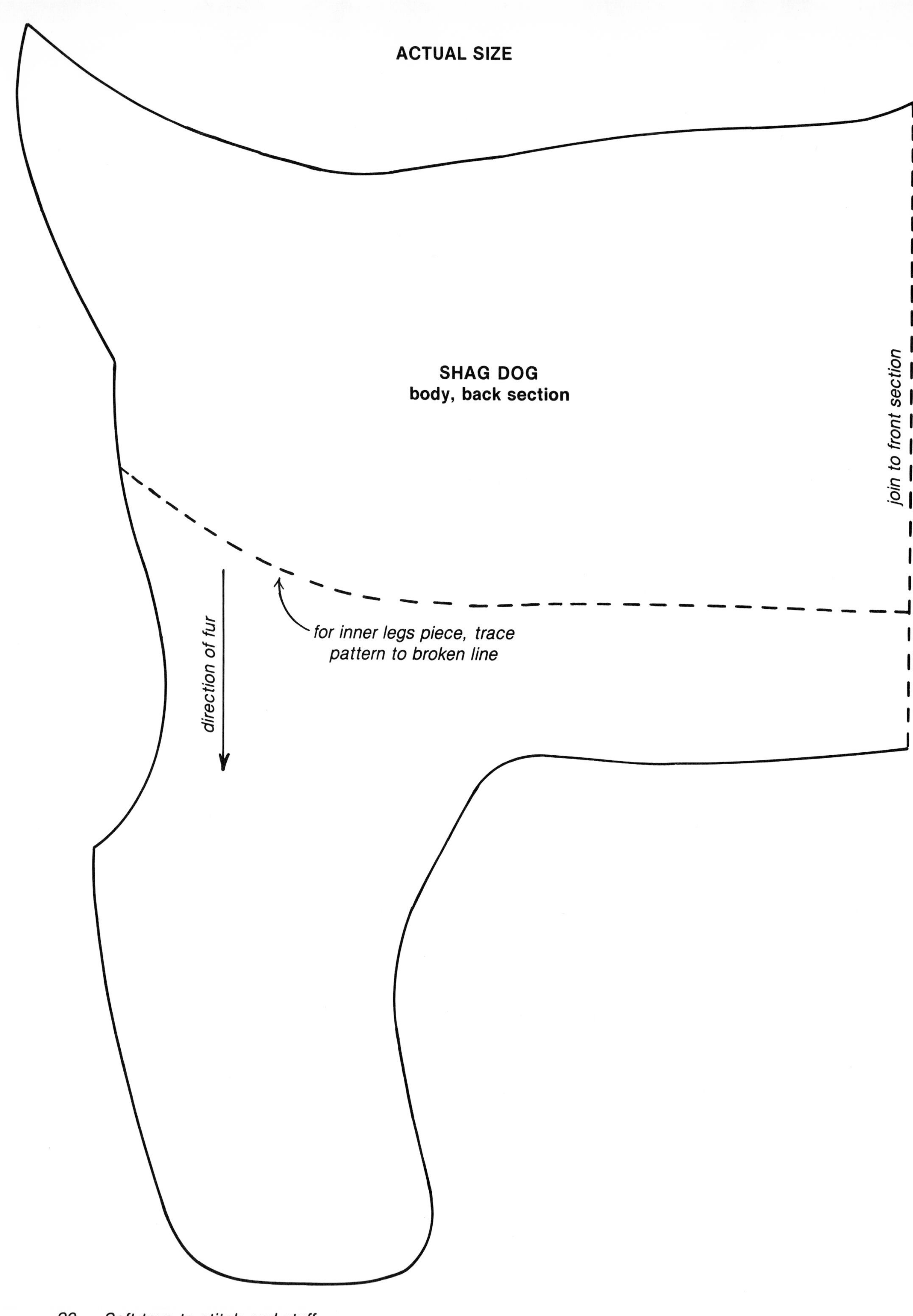
ACTUAL SIZE
SHAG DOG
body, back section
join to front section
direction of fur
for inner legs piece, trace
pattern to broken line

SIAMESE CAT

(color photo, page 31)

When I made my first Siamese cat, I was amazed at the reaction of my real Siamese. Honey usually ignores my critter creations, but that toy cat was different. Honey growled, arched her back and circled around it. Finally, she moved in to sniff and touch. Only when Honey was quite satisfied there was no threat to her kingdom did she lose interest.

This 17″-tall Cat is made of tan and black fur fabrics. For a different look, you can cut all pattern pieces from the same color fabric.

MATERIALS

tan short-pile fur fabric, 22x23″, for body (pile should run along the 22″ length)
black plush fabric, 9x21″, for legs, tail and muzzle (pile should run along the 9″ length)
black felt scrap, for inner ears
transparent thread, for machine stitching
button-and-carpet thread, for handwork
black button-and-carpet thread, for whiskers (optional)
tan yarn or embroidery thread, for nose and mouth
blue plastic cat eyes with posts (available at craft shops)
polyester fiberfill, for stuffing
glue, for adding nose and mouth (optional)

DIRECTIONS

For tips on tracing patterns and working with fur fabric, see *Helpful Guides,* page 1.

Make pattern pieces

1. Trace patterns for body, pages 93-94, and for front gusset, page 92, joining sections on broken lines. Trace separate pattern for inner haunch, page 94.

Also trace patterns for inner ear, page 93; for ear and hind leg, page 94; and for tail, front leg and muzzle, page 95.

2. Cut out full pattern pieces. On body piece, slash along line at haunch as indicated on pattern.

Cut fabric

1. Lay pattern pieces on back of fur fabric, making sure fur is running in correct direction. On tan, trace 2 body pieces (1 reversed), 2 inner haunch pieces (1 reversed) and 1 front gusset. On black, trace 4 front legs (2 reversed), 4 hind legs (2 reversed), 2 ears and 1 muzzle.

2. On black felt, trace 2 inner ears.

3. Cut out fabric on traced lines; ¼″ seam allowances are included. Slash body pieces at haunches.

Assemble

Use ¼″ seams and a zigzag machine stitch.

1. Position each inner haunch against matching body piece, right sides together, and pin along outside edge. Stitch outside edge, tapering seam to make it narrower at each end; leave top curve of inner haunch open (see Fig. 1, a).

2. On each body piece, lift cut edge above haunch (see Fig. 1, b). Pin edge to top curve of inner haunch, right sides together. Stitch, tapering seam at each end.

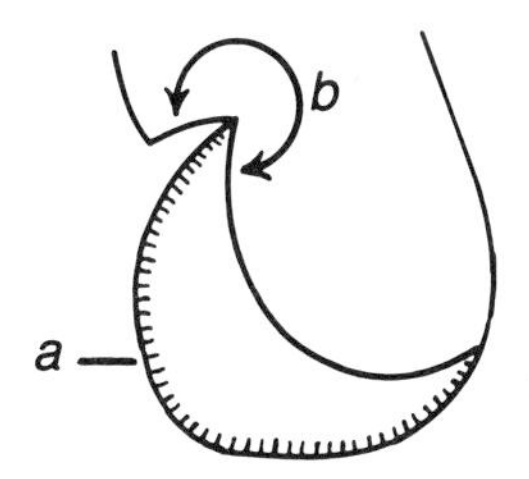

Fig. 1 *Stitching inner haunch to body (a), and matching cut edge to top of inner haunch (b)*

3. Pin front gusset to one body piece, right sides together, matching points A and B (on inner haunch). Stitch between points.

Pin and stitch front gusset to other body piece in the same manner.

4. Install plastic eyes.

5. Pin body pieces together down back and along inner haunches, from point A to B. Stitch, leaving 4″ open on back for turning. Turn to right side.

6. To make each front and hind leg, pin two matching pieces right sides together. Stitch, leaving top curve open. Turn to right side.

7. To make tail, pin the two matching pieces right sides together. Stitch, leaving straight edge open. Turn to right side.

Stuff and finish

1. Stuff body firmly and close opening with invisible stitches.
2. Stuff each front and hind leg firmly. Attach to body with a circular seam, using invisible stitches.
3. Stuff tail firmly. Position on body so tail rests on the floor and tip of tail turns up. Attach with a circular seam, using invisible stitches.
4. To make muzzle, pin the two straight edges right sides together. Stitch seam. Pad muzzle with a little fiberfill and sew to face with invisible stitches.
5. To make each ear, pin a felt inner ear to a fur ear piece, right sides together. Stitch two edges, leaving bottom open. Turn to right side. Fold each ear forward in a V shape, and stitch to head.
6. To finish face, position tan yarn on muzzle, following guide in Fig. 2. (Trim pile on muzzle if

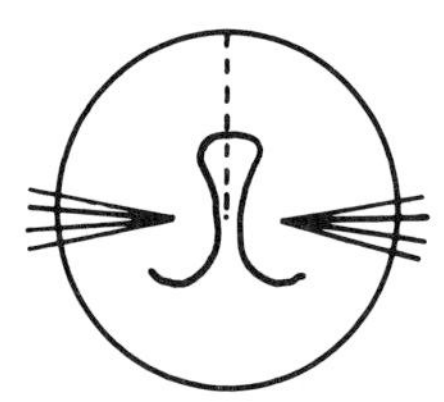

Fig. 2 *Positioning nose and mouth line on muzzle*

necessary.) Glue or stitch yarn in place.

If you prefer, embroider the line in a chain stitch (see Fig. 19, page 6), using yarn or six strands of embroidery thread.

7. For whiskers (optional), use black button-and-carpet thread. With doubled thread in needle, take a small stitch on each side of muzzle. Tie thread in a knot and cut off, leaving 1½" lengths.
8. Trim tan pile above muzzle and eyes, up to ears (optional).

ACTUAL SIZE

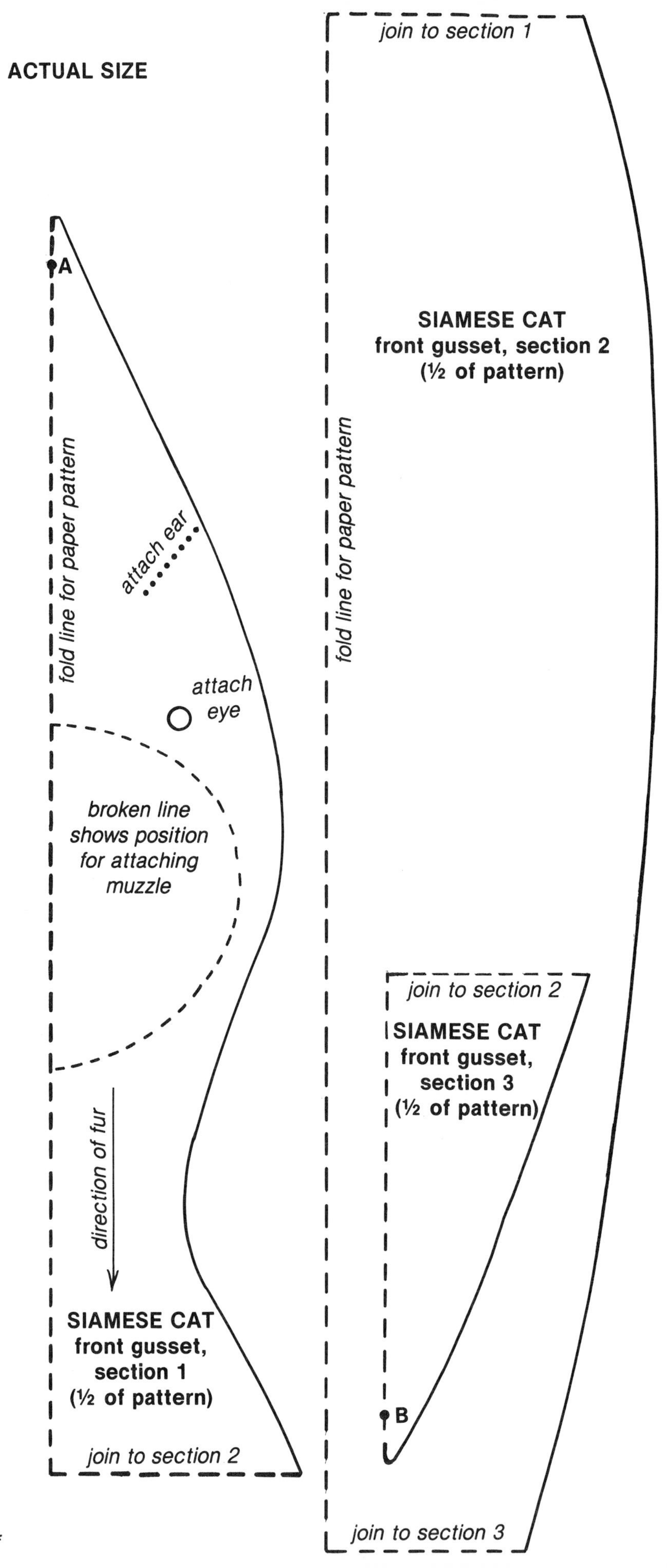

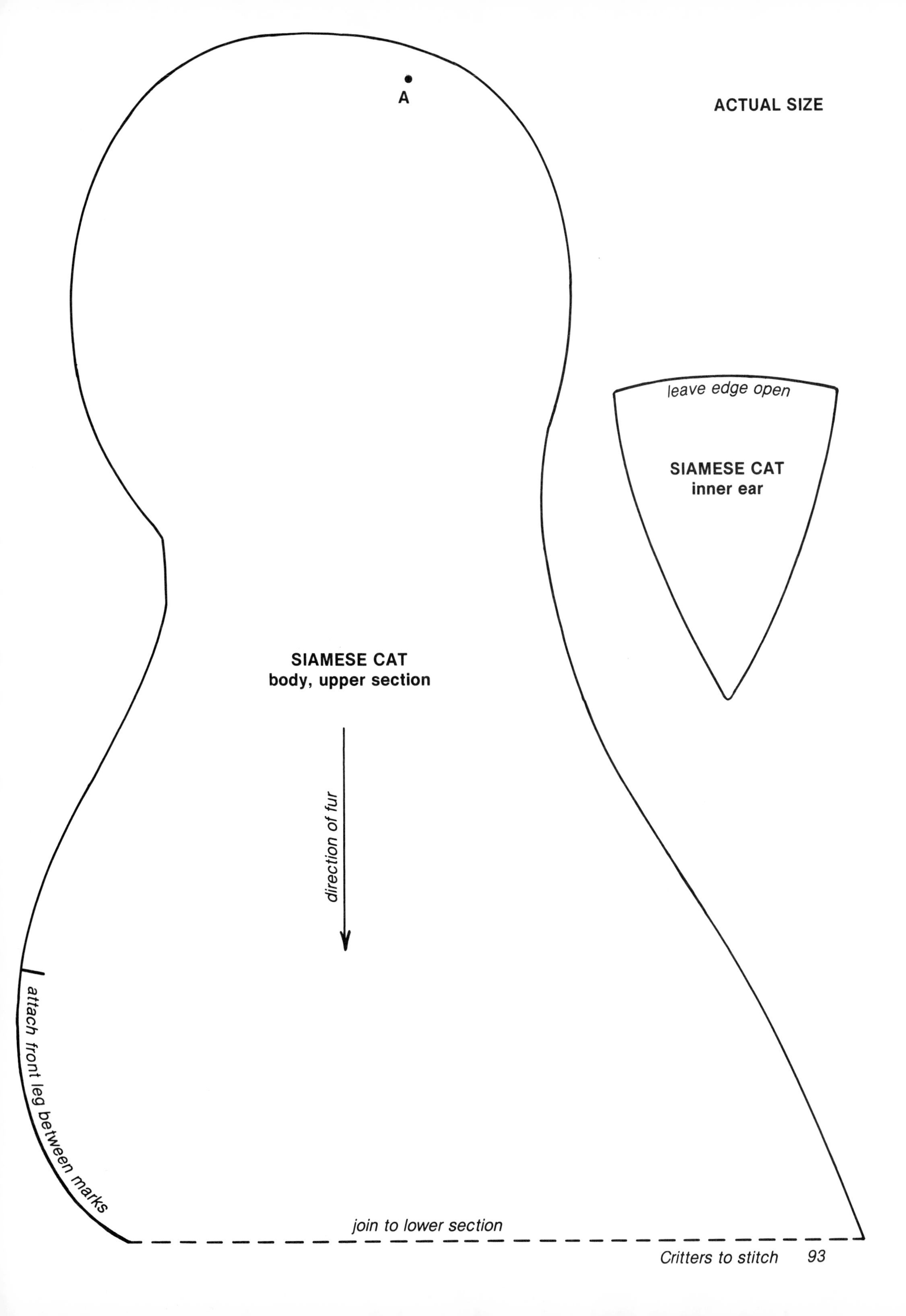
A
ACTUAL SIZE
leave edge open
SIAMESE CAT
inner ear
SIAMESE CAT
body, upper section
direction of fur
attach front leg between marks
join to lower section

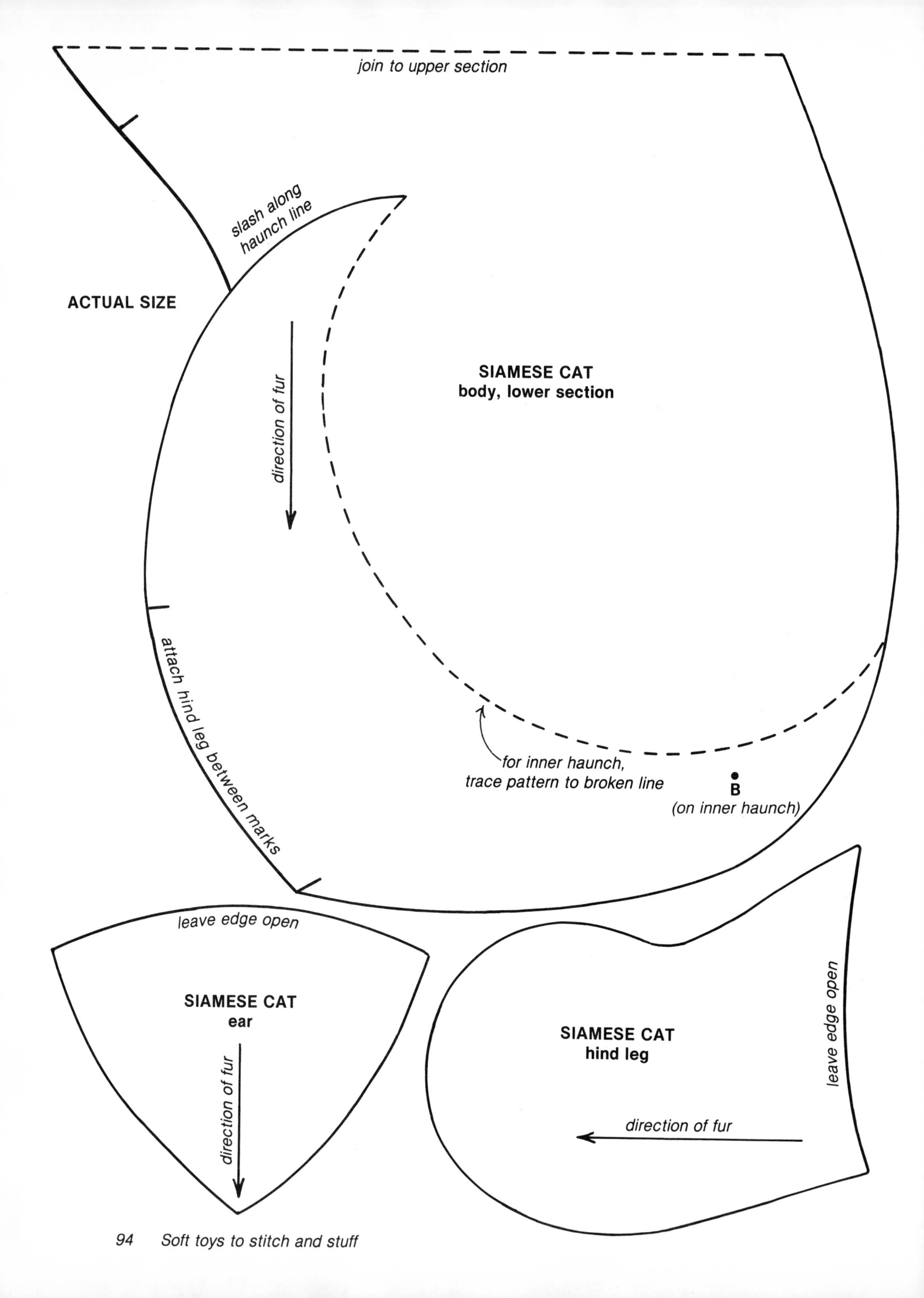
join to upper section
slash along haunch line
ACTUAL SIZE
SIAMESE CAT
body, lower section
direction of fur
attach hind leg between marks
for inner haunch, trace pattern to broken line
B
(on inner haunch)
leave edge open
SIAMESE CAT
ear
direction of fur
SIAMESE CAT
hind leg
leave edge open
direction of fur

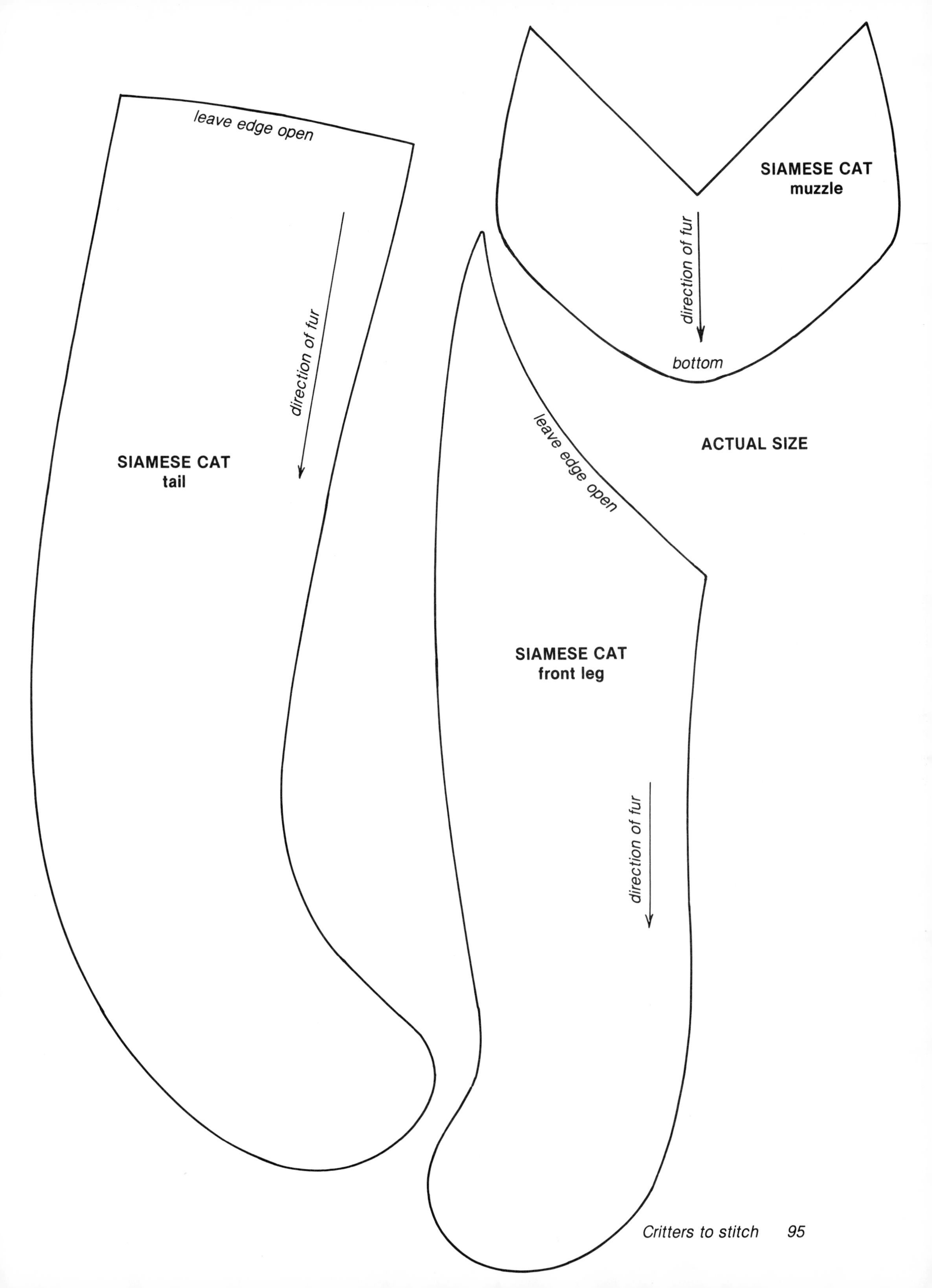
SIAMESE CAT
muzzle
direction of fur
bottom
leave edge open
direction of fur
SIAMESE CAT
tail
leave edge open
ACTUAL SIZE
SIAMESE CAT
front leg
direction of fur

MONKEY

(color photo, page 106)

On our real farm, we had a squirrel monkey named George—probably the most popular member of the family. Kids came by to see him. Neighbors and business associates would ask, ''How's George?''

At first, we carefully followed instructions, keeping him in a cage in the house where he would be warm and out of drafts. Soon, we set the cage outdoors in warm weather, and then we put George on a leash. Eventually, George had complete freedom in the yard and came inside only in freezing weather.

George was always where the action was—or he was the action. He ruled supreme over the cats, dogs, horses, cows, pigs and my flower garden, where he sorted through petals for insects.

Of course, George was my inspiration for this critter.

MATERIALS

black (or gold) long-pile fur fabric, 14x37" (pile should run along the 14" length)
1/8 yd. black (or gold) felt, 72" wide (or three 9x12" pieces), for mouth, ears, hands and feet
red felt, 3½x4", for inner mouth
white, brown and black felt scraps, for eyes
transparent thread, for machine stitching
button-and-carpet thread, for handwork
polyester fiberfill, for stuffing
plastic lid, for eyes
glue

DIRECTIONS

For tips on tracing patterns and working with fur fabric, see *Helpful Guides,* page 1.

Make pattern pieces

1. Trace separate patterns for hand, foot, mouth and inner mouth, page 97; for body, page 98; and for eye and ear, page 99. Also trace pattern for front gusset, page 99, joining sections on broken lines.
2. Cut out pattern pieces.

Cut fabric

1. On back of fur fabric, trace 2 body pieces (1 reversed) and 1 front gusset. Also mark 4 strips, 4x10" each, for arms and legs and 1 strip, 3x14", for tail; have fur running lengthwise on strips.
2. On wrong side of black (or gold) felt, trace 2 mouths. On red felt, trace 1 inner mouth.
3. Cut out fabric on traced lines; ¼" seam allowances are included.

Assemble

Use ¼" seams and a zigzag machine stitch on fur fabrics. Use 1/8" seams and a straight machine stitch on felt.

1. Pin front gusset to one body piece, matching points A and B. Stitch between points.

Pin and stitch front gusset to other body piece.

2. Pin body pieces together down the back. Stitch, leaving 3" open for turning. Turn to right side.
3. To make arms and legs, fold each strip lengthwise and pin edges together. Stitch a lengthwise seam to form a tube. Turn to right side.
4. Fold tail in half lengthwise and pin edges together. Stitch lengthwise, tapering to a point at end. Turn to right side.
5. To make mouth, pin a black (or gold) mouth piece to one end of the red inner mouth; match C and D points. Pin second mouth piece to other end of inner mouth. (Edges of mouth pieces will butt together at D points.)

Straight-stitch a 1/8" seam completely around inner mouth. Leave seam exposed.

Stuff and finish

1. Stuff body firmly. Close opening with invisible stitches.

2. Pin seam edges of mouth together at C (to keep mouth closed while stitching). Stuff upper and lower mouth and position mouth on front gusset. Turn free edge 1/8" to wrong side and pin in place.

Sew upper part of mouth to front gusset with invisible stitches, easing in fullness as you work. Stitch lower part of mouth to gusset in the same manner.

3. To make each ear, place pattern on double thickness of felt. Straight-stitch around curve, then mark straight edge with pencil or chalk. Cut out felt along straight edge and 1/8" from stitching.

Gather straight edge of ear, and stitch to head.

4. To make each hand and foot, place pattern on double thickness of felt. Stitch around pattern, leaving straight edge open for stuffing; mark straight edge with pencil or chalk. Cut out felt along straight edge and 1/8" from stitching.

5. Stuff hands and feet lightly, using small wads of fiberfill in fingers and toes.

6. Position a hand at the bottom of each arm and sew in place with invisible stitches; have fur running downward toward hand.

7. Add a foot to the end of each leg in the same manner.

8. Stuff arms and legs loosely, then stitch them to body so they hang at sides.

9. Stuff tail loosely and sew to body.

10. Make and attach eyes; see *To make a felt eye,* page 5. Cut large circle from the plastic lid and cover it with white felt. Glue on a brown felt circle, then a black felt circle.

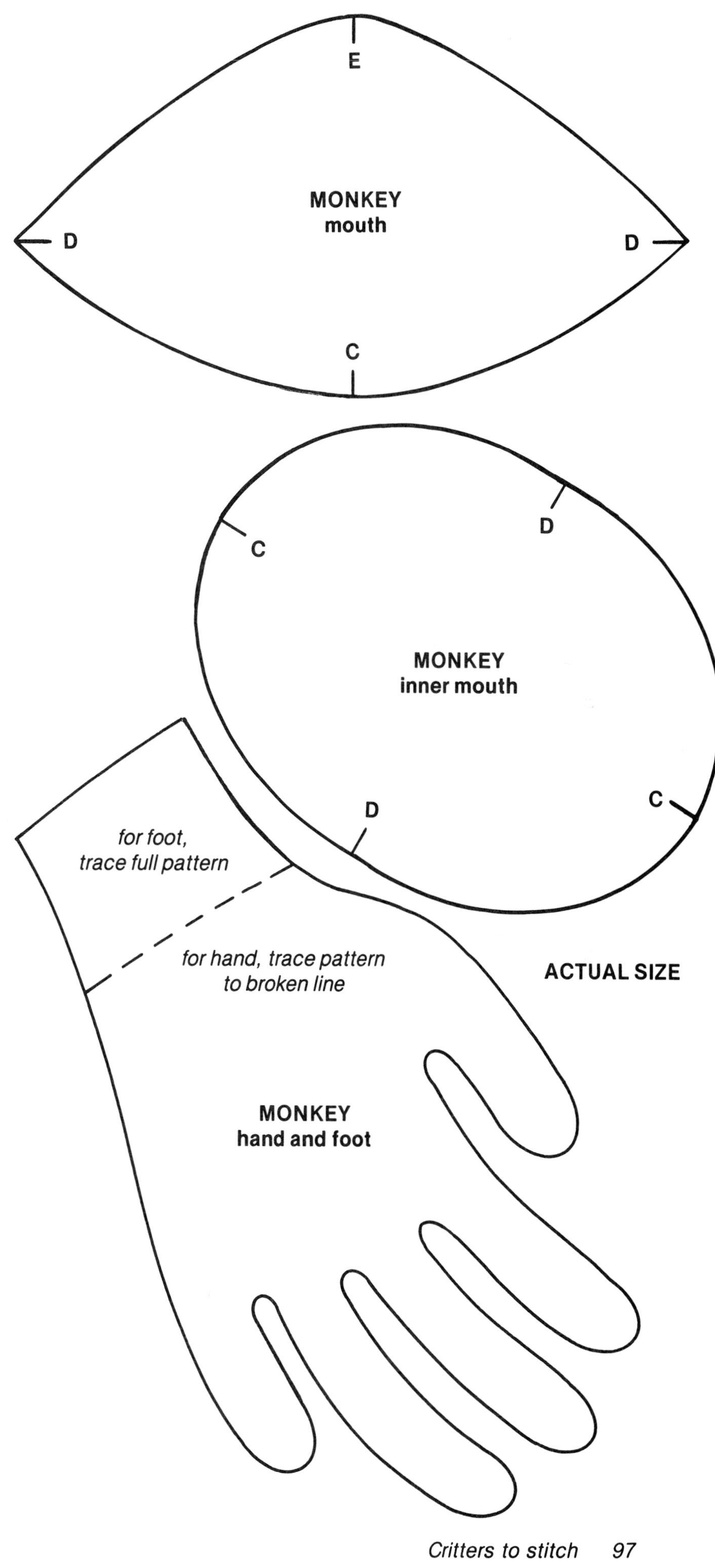

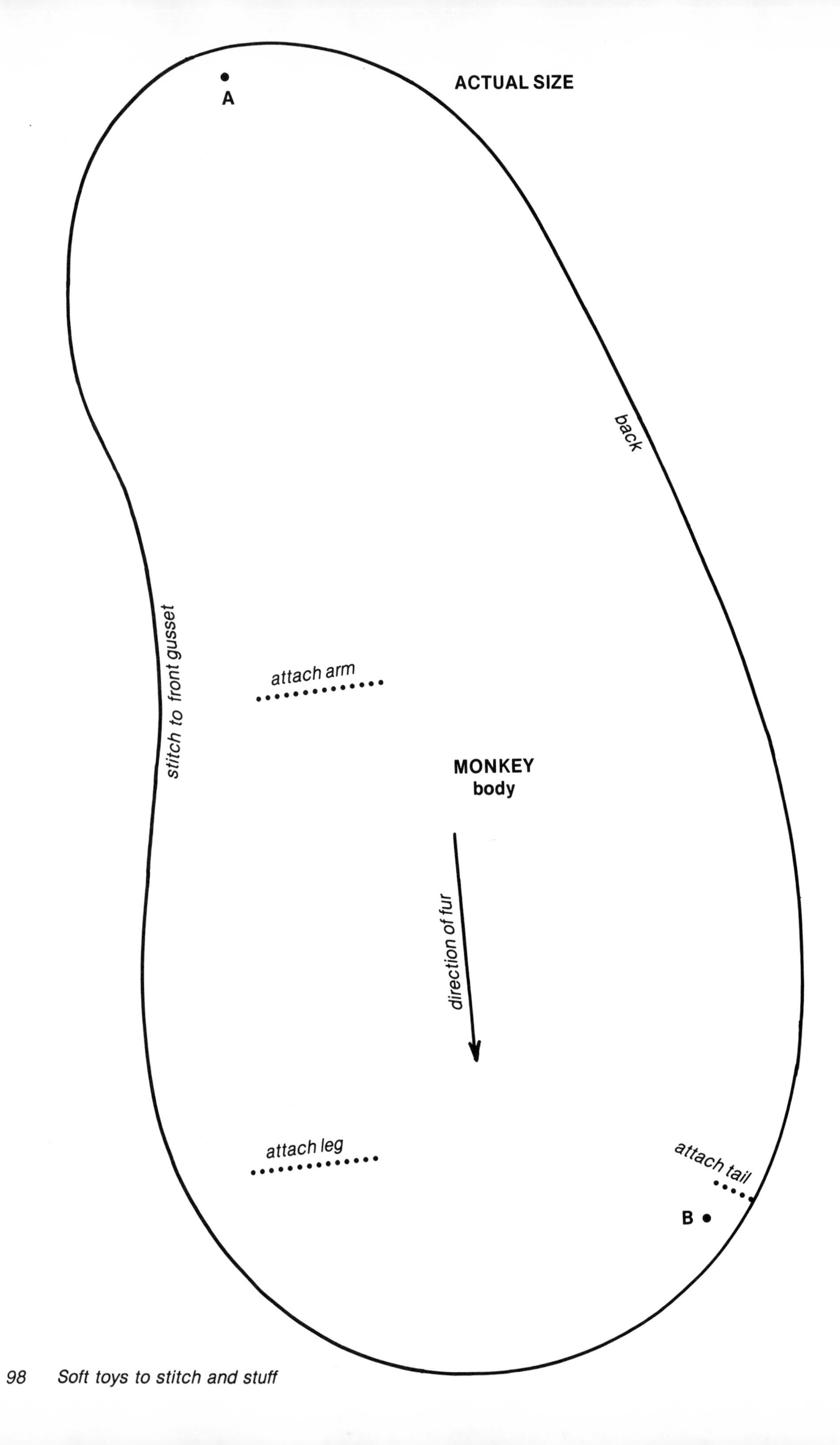
ACTUAL SIZE
A
back
stitch to front gusset
attach arm
MONKEY
body
direction of fur
attach leg
attach tail
B

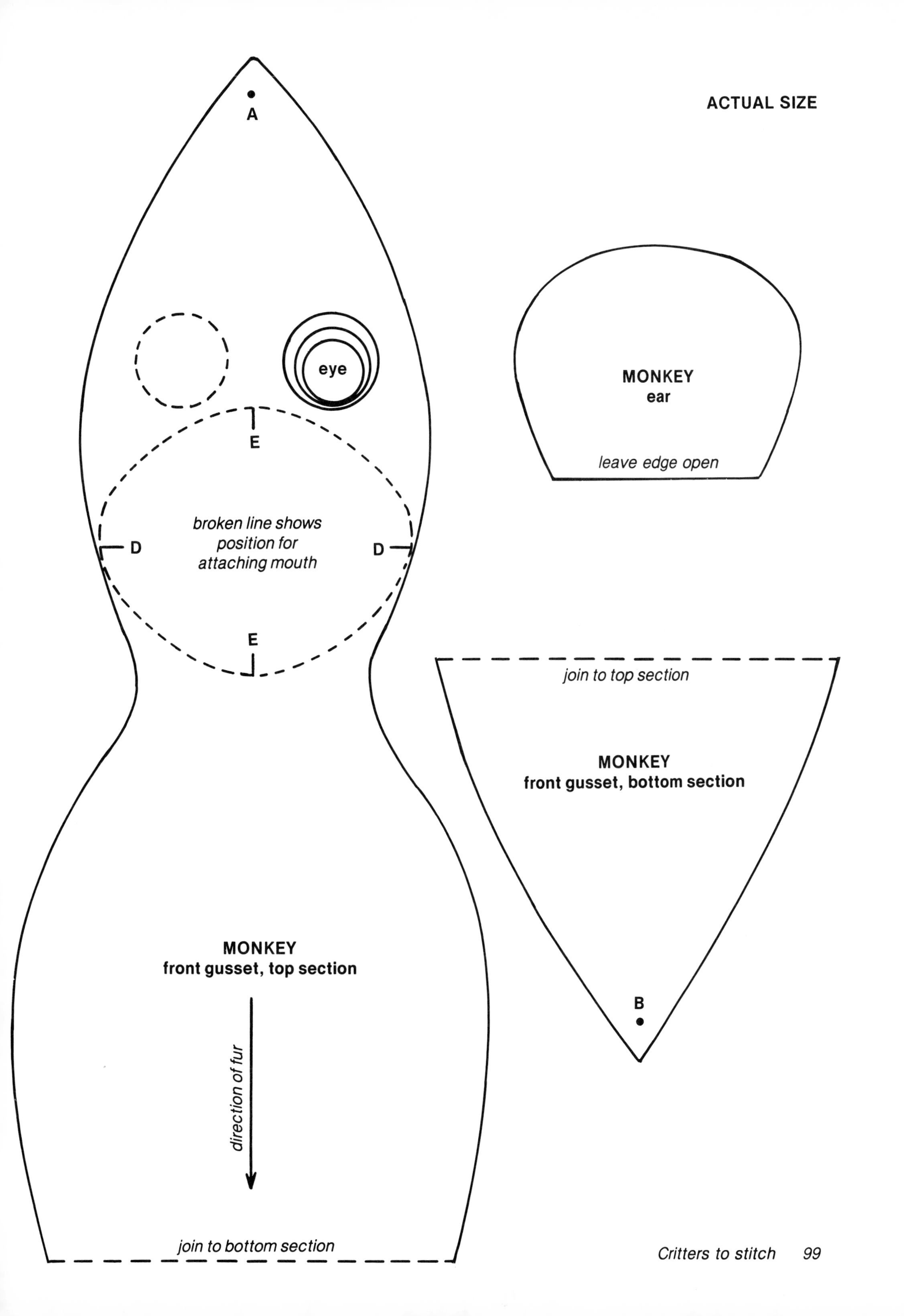
ACTUAL SIZE
A
eye
E
D
broken line shows
position for
attaching mouth
D
E
MONKEY
front gusset, top section
direction of fur
join to bottom section
MONKEY
ear
leave edge open
join to top section
MONKEY
front gusset, bottom section
B

Lovey bear

(color photo, page 103)

No toy collection would be complete without a teddy bear, and Lovey Bear is one of my favorites. You can use any kind of fur fabric in any color, and the Bear will turn out lovable every time. Stuff it loosely to make it cuddly.

To add variety, you might use a longer pile fabric for the forehead and tail of one Bear, and cut contrasting inner ears for another.

The mouth and nose are embroidered, and the eyes are made of felt. If you prefer to substitute a plastic nose and eyes, be sure to install them before you stuff the toy.

MATERIALS

¼ yd. fur fabric, 60″ wide
white, brown and black felt scraps, for eyes (or blue and black felt, for a white Bear)
transparent thread, for machine stitching
button-and-carpet thread, for handwork
black yarn or embroidery thread, for nose and mouth
polyester fiberfill, for stuffing
plastic lid, for eyes
glue

DIRECTIONS

For tips on tracing patterns and working with fur fabric, see *Helpful Guides*, page 1.

Make pattern pieces

1. Trace pattern for back, pages 107-108, joining body and foot sections on broken lines.

Trace a separate pattern for front, pages 107-108; front includes foot, and ends at broken (center front) line.

Trace patterns for forehead, ear and arm, page 102; for tail, page 107; and for face, eye and head back, page 108.

2. Cut out full pattern pieces.

Cut fabric

1. Lay pattern pieces on back of fur fabric, making sure fur is running in correct direction. Trace 2 back pieces (1 reversed), 2 front pieces (1 reversed), 2 face pieces (1 reversed), 1 forehead, 2 head back pieces (1 reversed), 2 arms, 4 ears and 1 tail.

2. Cut out fabric on traced lines; ¼″ seam allowances are included.

Assemble

Use ¼″ seams and a zigzag machine stitch.

1. Pin front pieces, right sides together, along center front seam. Stitch from point A to top of neck.

2. Pin each back piece to the matching front piece, right sides together. Stitch from point A around leg to top of neck (Fig. 1).

Fig. 1 *Stitching back pieces to front pieces*

3. Pin back pieces together along center back. Stitch from top of neck to A. Turn body to right side through the neck opening.

4. Arrange face and forehead pieces (Fig. 2). Pin face pieces right sides together, from B (nose) to neck. Stitch the seam.

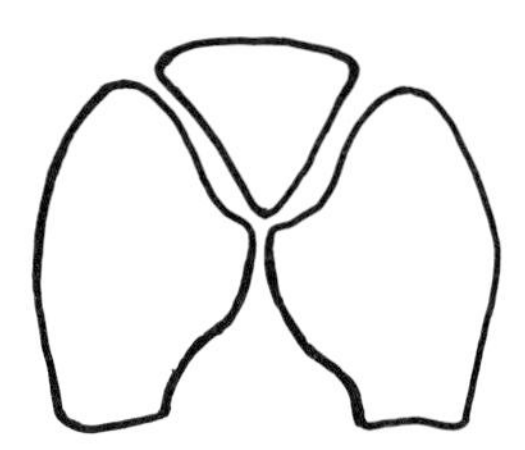

Fig. 2 *Arranging face pieces before stitching*

5. Pin forehead to one face piece, right sides together, from B to top of head. Stitch. Pin and stitch forehead to other face piece.

6. Pin head back pieces together along center back, and stitch.

7. Pin and stitch head front to head back. Turn head to right side.

8. Fold each arm piece down the center, with fur inside, and pin edges together. Stitch down lengthwise seam and around the bottom curve; leave short, straight edge open. Turn arm to right side.

Stuff and finish

1. To make the Bear cuddly, stuff body and head loosely. Use just enough stuffing to fill out the shape.

2. Gather edge of body opening to match size of head opening (do not close). Pin head to body, matching front and back seams, then side seams. Sew together in a circular seam, using invisible stitches. Add extra stuffing in neck area if needed before closing seam.

Arrange stuffing so Bear stays in a seated position.

3. Stuff each arm loosely, leaving the last inch free of stuffing. Lay arm flat on back piece about ½" from neck and 1½" behind side seam (Fig. 3). Sew each edge of arm separately, using invisible stitches; keep edges of arm close together so arms can move.

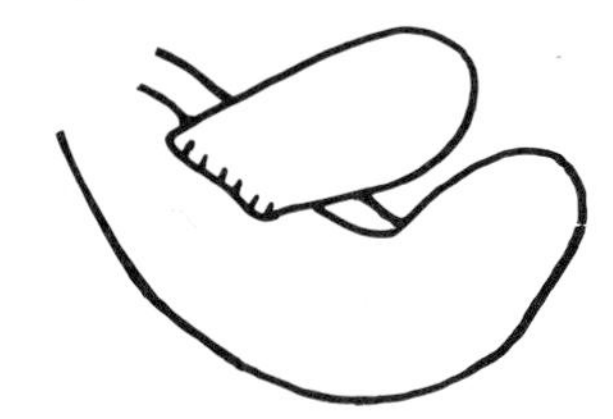

Fig. 3 *Stitching arm to body*

4. To make each ear, pin two pieces right sides together. Stitch, leaving bottom edge open. Turn ear to right side.

Position ear along head seam, centered at forehead/face seam (see Fig. 4). Attach with invisible stitches, gathering edge of ear so that it cups forward.

Fig. 4 *Positioning ears and features*

5. To make tail, fold fabric down center, with fur inside. Stitch around curve; leave an opening for turning.

Turn to right side. Position tail along back seam, about 1½" above A. Attach with invisible stitches.

6. Embroider a nose about ½" wide and ½" long (Fig. 5). Use yarn or six strands of black embroidery thread and a satin stitch (see Fig. 17, page 6).

Fig. 5 *Guide for embroidering nose and mouth*

7. Embroider mouth, using yarn or six strands of black embroidery thread and a chain stitch (see Fig. 19, page 6).

8. Make and attach felt eyes; see *To make a felt eye*, page 5. Cut the large eye shape from the plastic lid and cover it with white felt. Glue on a middle-size brown felt oval, then add a small black felt circle. (For a white Bear, cover the plastic oval with blue felt, then glue on a small black felt circle.)

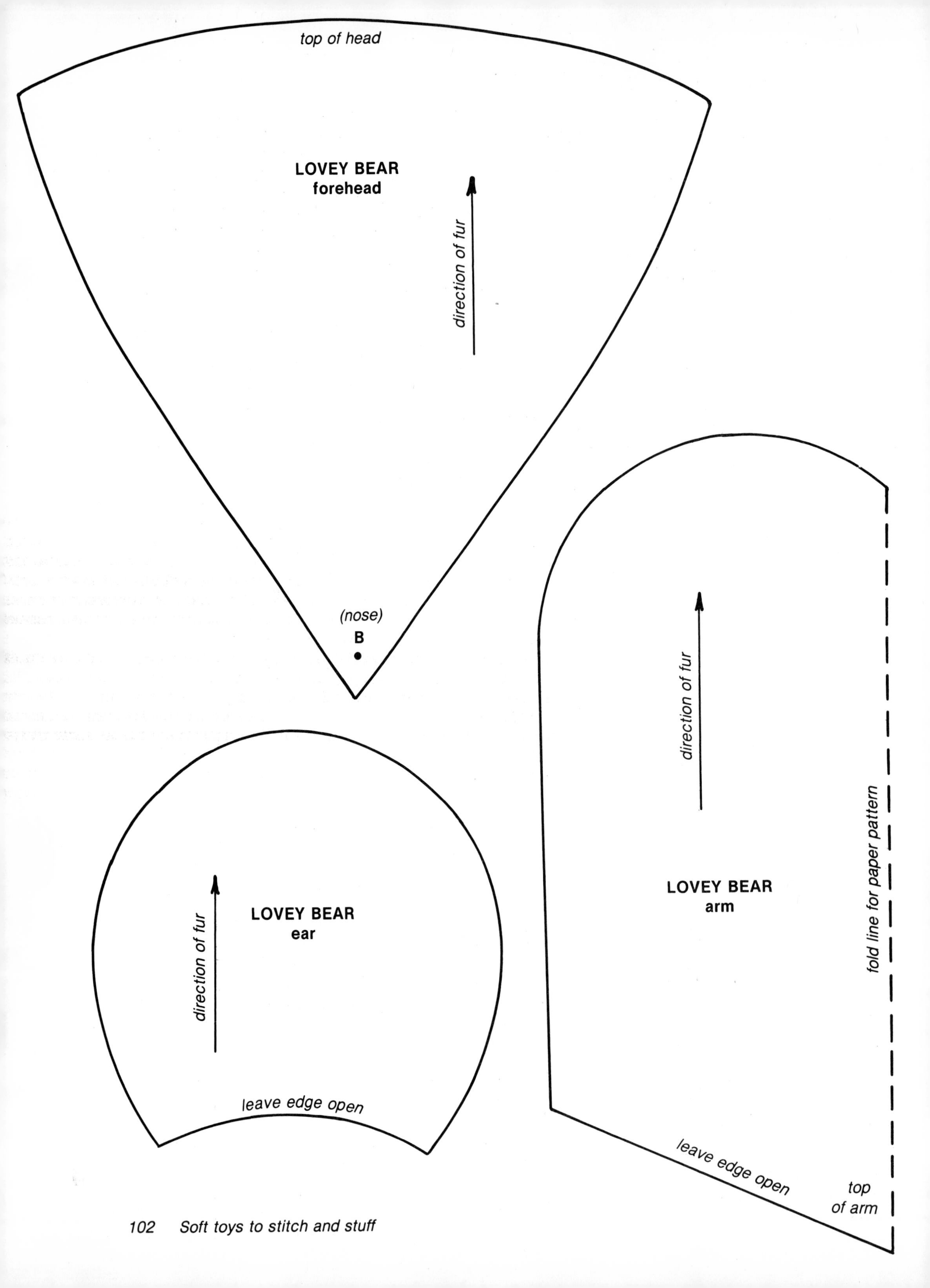
top of head
LOVEY BEAR
forehead
direction of fur
(nose)
B
LOVEY BEAR
ear
direction of fur
leave edge open
direction of fur
LOVEY BEAR
arm
fold line for paper pattern
leave edge open
top
of arm

A variety of colors and fur fabrics gives each of these Lovey Bears its own look (page 100). Trim with ribbon bows for extra color.

This red Barn toy box (page 135) has a pull-down door, and it can be used for play or toy storage.

At far left and far right are TV Horses (page 120) big enough to be "ridden" by small children. Other critters, left to right, are a Simple Circle Bluebird (page 30), a Squirrel that stands on its hind legs (page 26), and a Rooster with big yellow feet (page 7). A second Bluebird perches on the Barn.

Long-pile fur fabrics are the best choices for these jungle critters. The Ape (page 130) has long arms and flexible hands and feet, and the Monkeys (page 96) have loose-hanging arms, legs and tails. They're easy to drape over chairs or shelves.

ACTUAL SIZE

LOVEY BEAR
back

for back, trace full pattern to end of foot

center back

LOVEY BEAR
front

for front, trace pattern from broken (center front) line to end of foot

center front (on front piece)

direction of fur

join to foot section

• A

LOVEY BEAR
tail
(½ of pattern)

fold line for paper pattern

direction of fur

leave open

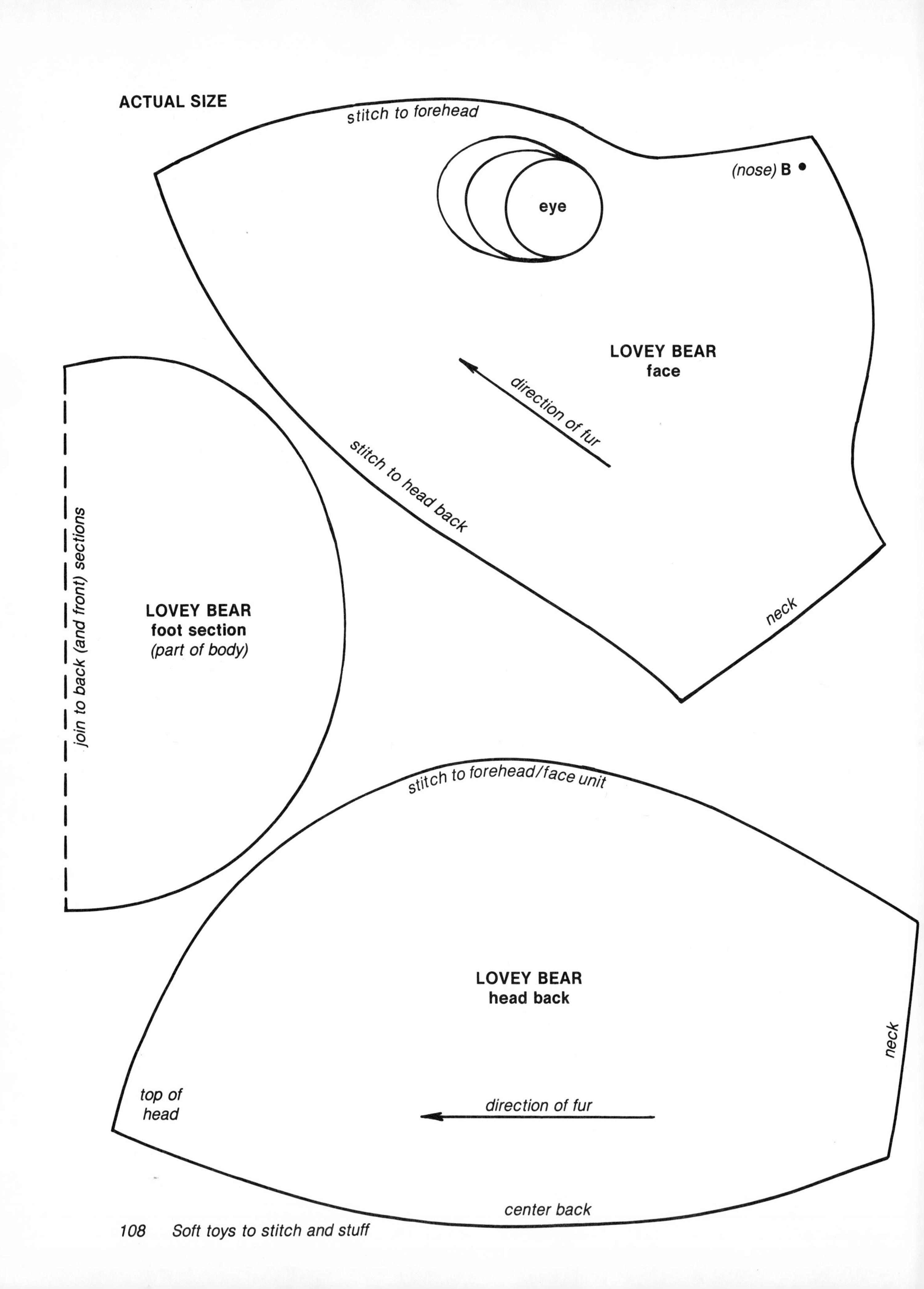
ACTUAL SIZE
stitch to forehead
eye
(nose) B
LOVEY BEAR
face
direction of fur
stitch to head back
neck
join to back (and front) sections
LOVEY BEAR
foot section
(part of body)
stitch to forehead/face unit
LOVEY BEAR
head back
neck
top of
head
direction of fur
center back

Pony & friends

You can make three different long-legged animals from one basic pattern—a Pony, a Burro and a Unicorn. By varying the fabrics, and by changing the ears, mane and tail, you give each critter its own special look. For the fourth version, a Stick Pony, you'll need pattern pieces for the head section only.

PONY

(color photo, page 68)

My grandchildren liked the big TV Horse I made for them, but they wanted him to stand up. So I straightened the legs and designed this smaller, 19"-high farm Pony.

If you stuff him entirely with fiberfill, he'll tend to slide down on his haunches, as he does in the photo. To keep him standing upright, add an inner support of wire.

MATERIALS

5/8 yd. brown short-pile fur fabric, 60" wide
beige long-pile fur fabric, 10x12", for mane and tail (pile should run along the 12" length)
brown, black and white felt scraps, for eyes
transparent thread, for machine stitching
button-and-carpet thread, for handwork
polyester fiberfill, for stuffing (about 1¼ lb.)
plastic lid, for eyes
glue
for inner support (optional): wire; tape; old nylons or strips of knit fabric

DIRECTIONS

For tips on tracing patterns, working with fur fabric and making an inner support of wire, see *Helpful Guides*, page 1.

Make pattern pieces

1. Trace pattern for body, pages 116-119, joining sections on broken lines (see sketch with pattern).
2. From full body pattern, trace separate patterns for inner front leg and inner hind leg.
3. Trace patterns for tail and ear, page 113, and for mane, face and chin gusset, page 114. Trace under gusset, page 115, joining sections on broken lines. Trace eye, page 116.
4. Cut out full pattern pieces. On body piece, slash along lines at chin and legs as indicated on pattern.

Cut fabric

1. Lay pattern pieces on back of fur fabric, making sure fur is running in correct direction. On short-pile fabric, trace 2 complete body pieces (1 reversed). Also trace 2 inner front legs (1 reversed), 2 inner hind legs (l reversed), 1 under gusset, 1 face, 1 chin gusset and 4 ears.
2. On long-pile fabric, trace 1 mane and 2 tails.
3. Cut out fabric on traced lines; ¼" seam allowances are included. Slash body pieces at chin and legs.

Assemble
Use ¼" seams and a zigzag machine stitch.

1. Pin each inner leg to matching body piece, right sides together (Fig. 1). Machine-stitch around leg, tapering seam to make it narrower at each end; leave top curve of inner leg open.

2. On each body piece, lift belly flap between legs. Pin front cut edge to top curve of inner front leg, right sides together (Fig. 2, a). Stitch; taper seam at each end, forming a dart at the slash end.

Pin back cut edge of belly flap to top curve of inner hind leg, right sides together (see Fig. 2, b). Stitch in the same manner.

3. Pin chin gusset to each body piece, matching points A and B (Fig. 3). Stitch, tapering seam at slash end (B).

4. Pin face to mane, matching points C and D (Fig. 4). Stitch in two steps, pivoting at center point D.

5. Sew face/mane unit to each body piece, beginning at mouth A (Fig. 5) and ending at E on back. (You may want to baste this first.)

6. Add under gusset to one body piece, right sides together, beginning at F. Pin along curve on inner front leg, along belly flap and along curve on inner hind leg to G. Stitch the seam.

Pin under gusset to other body piece and stitch, leaving about 7" open between front and hind legs for turning. (Leave a wider opening if using wire support.)

7. Pin body pieces together along front neck above F, and stitch.

8. Pin body pieces together along back and inner hind legs to G, and stitch. Turn to right side.

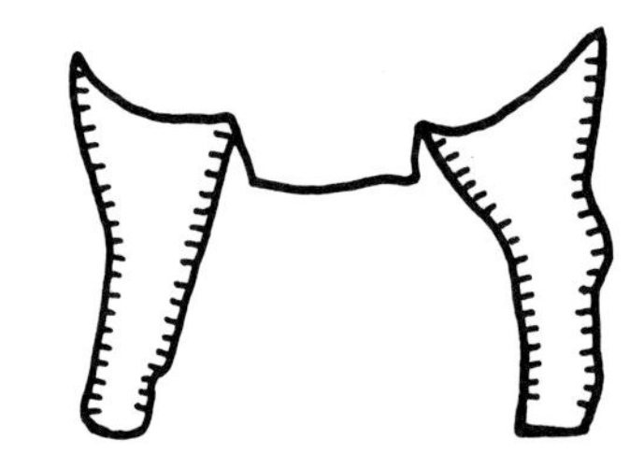

Fig. 1 *Stitching inner legs to body*

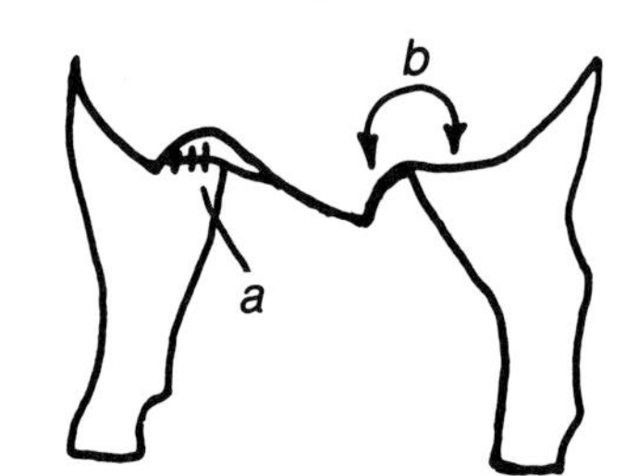

Fig. 2 *Stitching belly flap to inner legs*

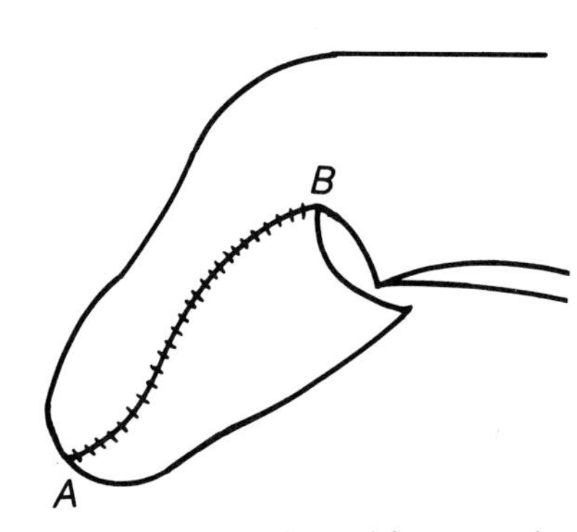

Fig. 3 *Stitching chin gusset to body*

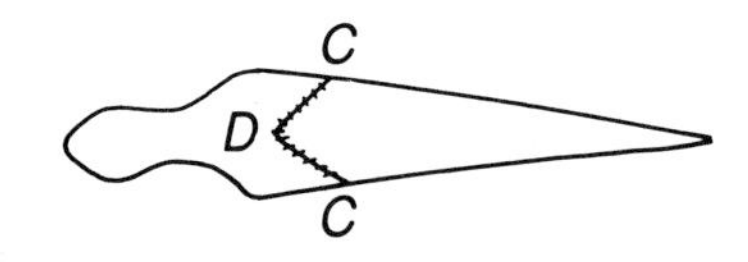

Fig.4 *Stitching face to mane*

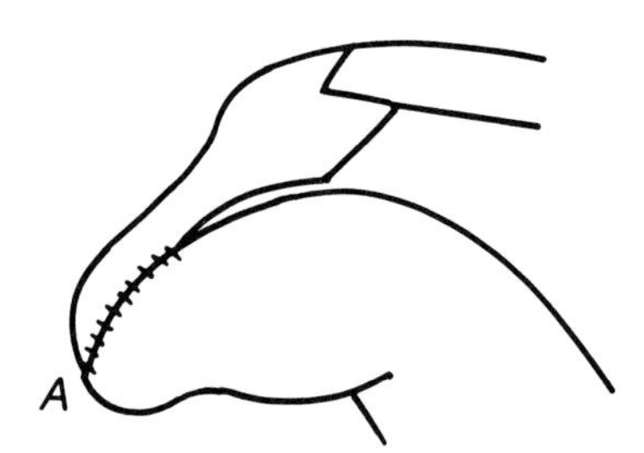

Fig. 5 *Stitching face/mane unit to body*

Note: Opening along chin gusset is not stitched. This will be closed later.

Stuff and finish

1. Stuff head and neck area firmly. Stuff balls of fiberfill into each foot for about 1½".

2. *If inner support* is to be used, prepare and add it now.

Refer to page 4. Cut a 12" length of wire for body and two 24" lengths for legs. Make a small loop in each wire end. Tape wires to hold in place, wrap with nylons or knit fabric, then wrap with fiberfill.

Position support in animal, adding fiberfill on all sides to keep support centered.

3. *With or without support,* finish stuffing animal firmly, and close opening with invisible stitches.

4. Adjust angle of head and close opening along chin gusset with invisible stitches.

5. To make tail, sew pieces right sides together, leaving 2" opening for turning. Turn to right side. Close opening with invisible stitches, and attach tail to body above hind legs.

6. To make each ear, pin matching pieces right sides together. Stitch, leaving straight edge open. Turn to right side.

Fold each ear down center, bringing curved edges forward, and stitch to animal.

7. Make and attach eyes; see *To make a felt eye,* page 5. Cut the large eye shape from the plastic lid and cover it with brown felt. Glue on a black felt circle, then add a white felt highlight.

BURRO

(color photo, page 68)

To make the basic pattern into a Burro, use long ears and a narrow tail, and cut the body from gray short-pile fabric. Add an inner support of wire if you want the Burro to stand up on all four legs.

MATERIALS
Follow list of materials for the Pony, page 109, using gray short-pile fur fabric (instead of brown). Use black long-pile fur fabric, 7½x12", for mane and tail trim (pile should run along the 12" length).

Add a 7x8½" piece of black felt for inner ears. Use gray, black and white felt scraps for eyes.

DIRECTIONS
Follow directions for the Pony, page 109, *with the following exceptions:*

Make pattern pieces
Use long Burro ears and omit Pony tail (Step 3).

Cut fabric
For Burro tail, mark and cut out a 4½x9" piece from the gray short-pile fabric (have pile running down the 9" length).

For tail tip, mark and cut out a 3½x4½" piece from the black long-pile fabric (have fur running down the 3½" length).

For ears, mark and cut out 2 ear pieces from the gray fur fabric. Then mark and cut out 2 ear pieces from the black felt (for inner ears).

Stuff and finish
To make tail (Step 5), fold gray piece in half lengthwise, with fur inside. Stitch a lengthwise seam, and turn to right side.

Fold black tail piece in half, with fur inside, so that the 3½" edges are together. Stitch along the 3½" edges and across one end. Turn to right side.

Join black tip to gray tail with invisible stitches, then stitch tail to body.

To make ears (Step 6), pin each gray piece to a black felt piece, right sides together. Stitch, leaving straight edge open. Finish ears and attach as for Pony (black felt will be folded to inside of ear).

To make eyes (Step 7), cover plastic shape with gray felt. Glue on a black felt circle, then add a white felt highlight.

To form hoofs, clip pile at end of each leg for about 1¼".

UNICORN

(color photo, page 67)

With some minor changes, our storybook farm can have its very own Unicorn. Because this is a mythical character, I thought the materials could be less realistic than those used for most of our other critters. I chose white crepe for the body, then added bulky yarn and gold braid for the trim.

I see this creation as a decoration for a girl's room. You may wish to use an inner support of wire, but this fanciful creature probably looks best without it, especially when stretched out among colorful pillows.

MATERIALS
¾ yd. white polyester crepe, 60" wide
18 yd. white bulky yarn or cord (sold on a spool for macramé), for mane and tail
21" narrow gold braid, for trimming horn
blue and black felt scraps, for eyes
transparent or matching thread, for machine stitching
button-and-carpet thread, for handwork
polyester fiberfill, for stuffing (about 1¼ lb.)
plastic lid, for eyes
glue

DIRECTIONS
Follow directions for the Pony, page 109, *with the following exceptions:*

Make pattern pieces
Trace pattern for Unicorn, following small broken lines as indicated. (Most of these outside pattern lines are ¼" wider than those for the Pony.)

Omit pattern for Pony tail and ear. Add patterns for Unicorn ear and horn, page 115.

Cut fabric
On wrong side of fabric, trace and cut out 2 body pieces (1 reversed), 2 inner front legs (1 reversed), 2 inner hind legs (1 reversed), 1 under gusset, 1 face, 1 chin gusset, 1 mane, 2 horns and 4 ears.

Assemble
Use ¼" seams and a straight machine stitch. You may want to baste some seams before stitching.

Before joining face to mane (Step 4), stitch along seam line C-D-C on face piece (single layer). Then clip seam allowance almost to stitching at D. This allows fabric to spread and fit against mane at pivot point.

Stuff and finish
To finish ears (Step 6), turn raw edges to inside before stitching to head.

To make eyes (Step 7), cover plastic shape with blue felt. Glue on a black felt circle.

To make horn, pin fabric pieces, right sides together. Stitch around curve, leaving the straight edge open for turning. Turn to right side, stuff and wrap with gold braid in spiral fashion. Turn raw edge under and center horn over the face/mane seam (at point D). Attach with a circular seam.

To make tail, cut 7 lengths of white yarn, each 24" long. Tie together in middle with thread. Sew middle of tail to body above hind legs. Unwind yarn and fluff it out.

To make mane, cut about 45 lengths of yarn, each 12" long. Pin center of each length to center of mane, starting behind horn and working down length of mane. Sew yarn to mane by hand, then unwind yarn and fluff it out.

STICK PONY

(color photo, page 68)

Most children would like to be carried away on a real horse that can walk, run and jump. With imagination, this action toy can do just that.

My Stick Pony has a white face, but you could cut both body and face from the same fabric. Use long-pile fabric for the mane and fabric-backed vinyl for the bridle.

MATERIALS

brown plush fabric, 9x27", for head and ears (pile should run along the 9" length)
white (or matching brown) plush fabric, 4½x7", for face (pile should run along the 7" length)
white long-pile fur fabric, 3½x12", for mane (pile should run along the 12" length)
brown, black and white felt scraps, for eyes
transparent thread, for machine stitching
button-and-carpet thread, for handwork
plastic lid, for eyes
glue
1¼"-wide strips of tan vinyl:
10½" for noseband
12½" for head strap
19" for reins
36" wooden dowel or P.V.C. (plastic) pipe with end caps, about ¾" outside diameter, for stick
strips of knit or cotton fabric, for anchoring head

DIRECTIONS
For tips on tracing patterns and working with fur fabric, see *Helpful Guides,* page 1.

Make pattern pieces
1. Trace sections 1 and 2 of body, page 116, joining sections on broken lines. On section 2, follow line at neck for Stick Pony. Also trace patterns for face, chin gusset and mane, page 114, and for Pony ear, page 113.
2. Cut out full pattern pieces. On body piece, slash along line at chin as indicated on pattern.

Cut fabric
1. Lay pattern pieces on back of fur fabric, making sure fur is running in correct direction. On brown plush, trace 2 body pieces (1 reversed), 1 chin gusset and 4 ears. On white (or matching brown) plush, trace 1 face.
2. On long-pile fabric, trace 1 mane.
3. Cut out fabric on traced lines; ¼" seam allowances are included. Slash body pieces at chin.

Assemble
Use ¼" seams and a zigzag machine stitch.
1. Refer to directions for Pony under *Assemble,* page 110. Follow Steps 3-5 for stitching chin gusset, face and mane.
2. Next, pin and stitch front neck seam.
3. By hand or machine, close seam along chin gusset.
4. Stitch bottom edges together, leaving an opening at center for turning Pony and for inserting stick. Turn to right side.

Stuff and finish

1. Stuff head firmly, leaving room to insert stick about 4".

2. Glue a wrapping of knit or cotton fabric strips around end of stick for about 4". When dry, spread glue on outside and bury stick in head stuffing.

3. Close bottom seam, sewing fabric tightly around stick. You might add a little more glue between stick and fabric to secure.

4. Make and attach ears (see Pony, *Stuff and finish,* Step 6, page 110).

5. Make and attach eyes (see Pony, Step 7, page 110).

6. To make bridle, fold each vinyl strip in half lengthwise, right side out, and straight-stitch along both lengthwise edges.

Take the 10½" noseband, overlap ends ½" and stitch a square to hold (Fig. 6).

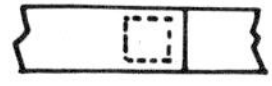

Fig. 6 *Stitching a square to join vinyl strip*

With seam in back, fold noseband to divide in half. At each fold, position one end of head strap at right angle to noseband, and stitch (Fig. 7).

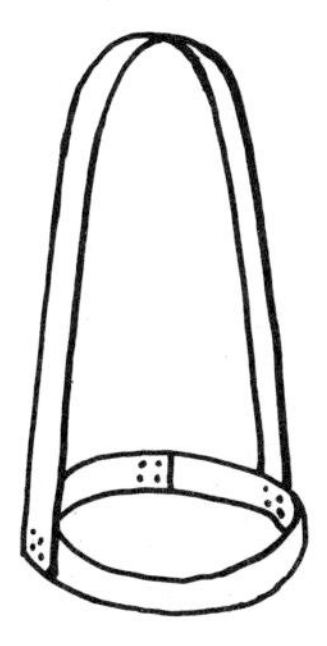

Fig. 7 *Stitching head strap to noseband*

Slip bridle on head. Position reins at correct angle. Remove bridle and machine-stitch reins in place.

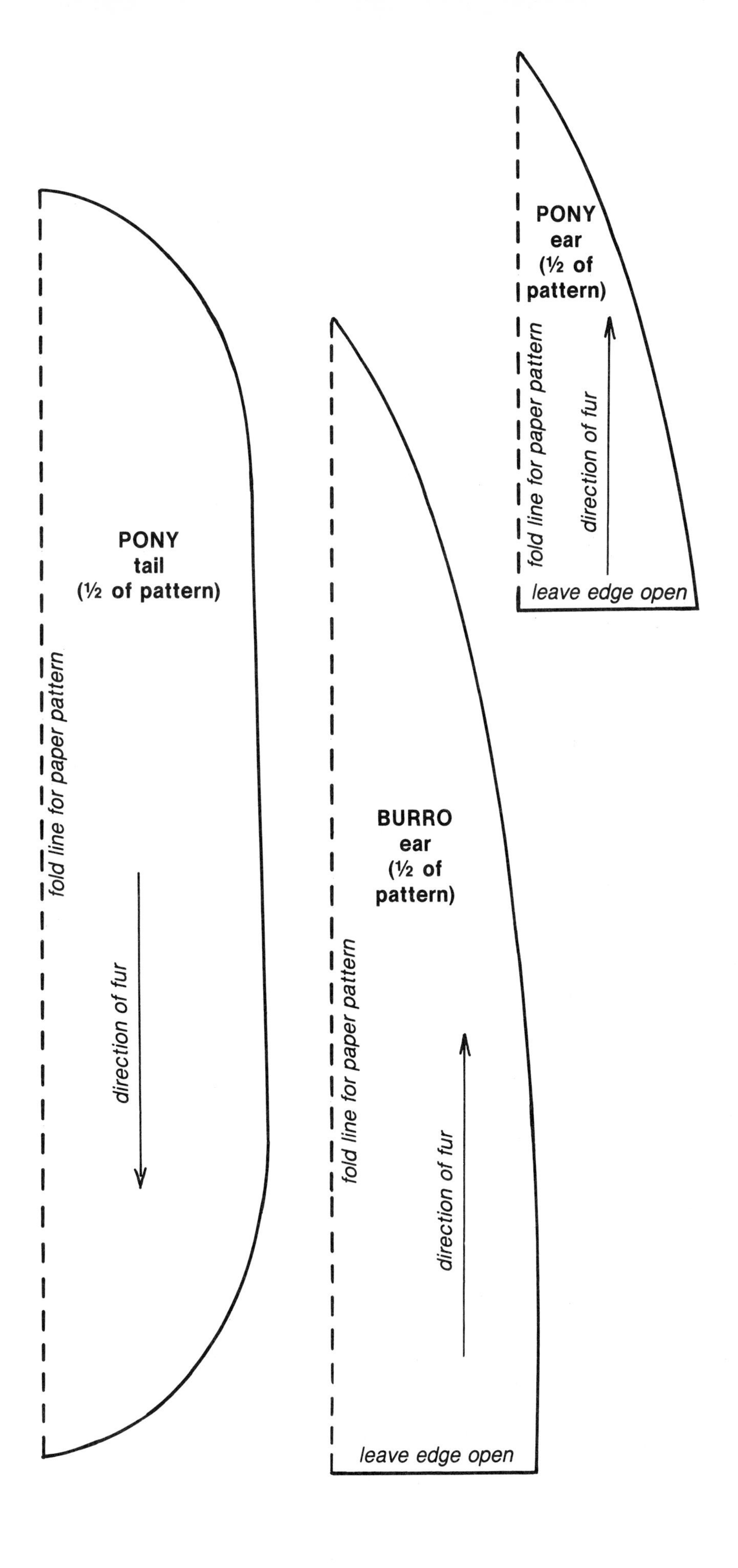

ACTUAL SIZE

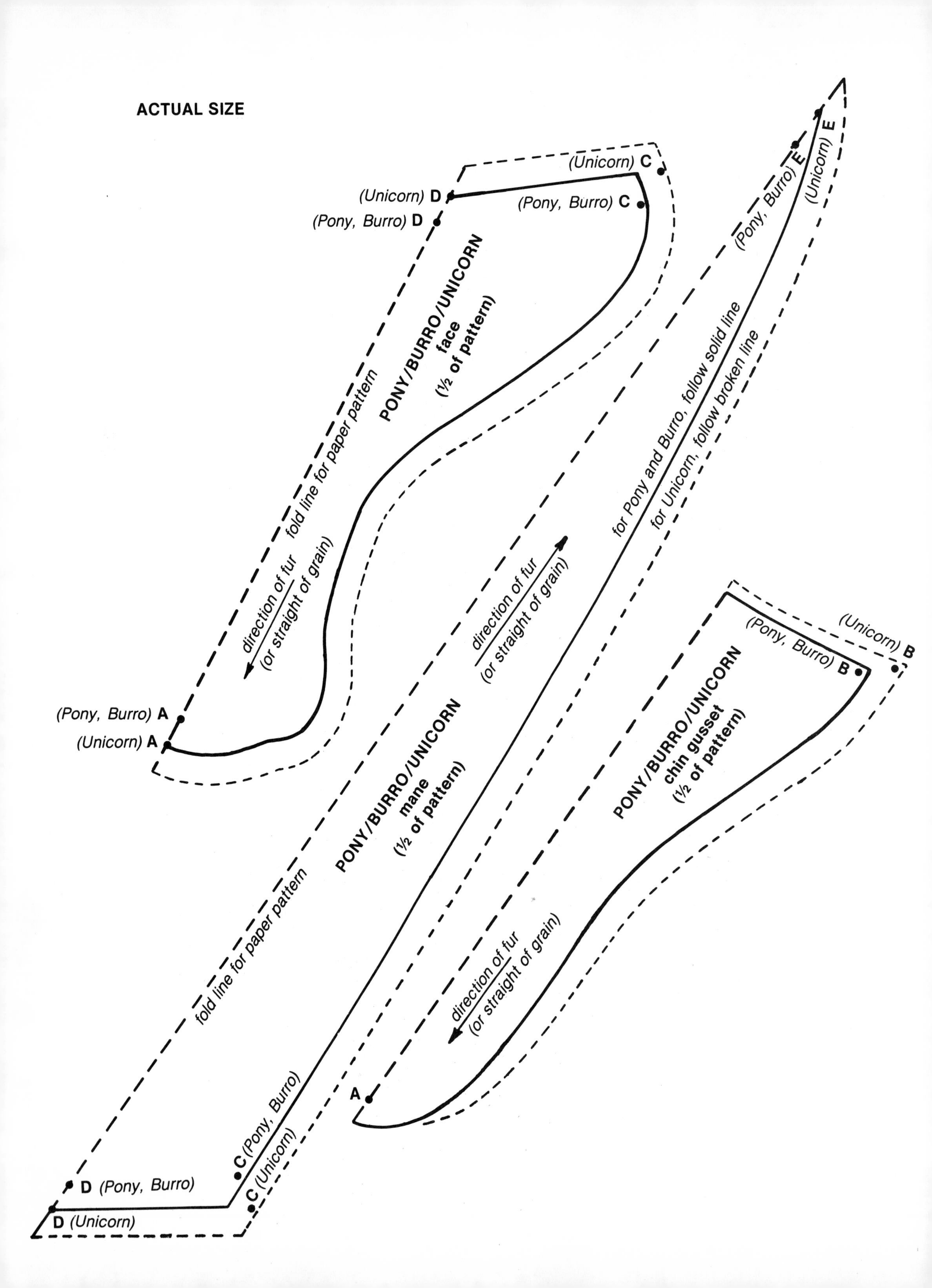

(Unicorn) C
(Unicorn) D
(Pony, Burro) C
(Pony, Burro) D
PONY/BURRO/UNICORN
face
(½ of pattern)
fold line for paper pattern
direction of fur
(or straight of grain)
(Pony, Burro) A
(Unicorn) A
(Pony, Burro) E
(Unicorn) E
for Pony and Burro, follow solid line
for Unicorn, follow broken line
direction of fur
(or straight of grain)
PONY/BURRO/UNICORN
mane
(½ of pattern)
fold line for paper pattern
(Unicorn) B
(Pony, Burro) B
PONY/BURRO/UNICORN
chin gusset
(½ of pattern)
direction of fur
(or straight of grain)
A
C (Pony, Burro)
C (Unicorn)
D (Pony, Burro)
D (Unicorn)

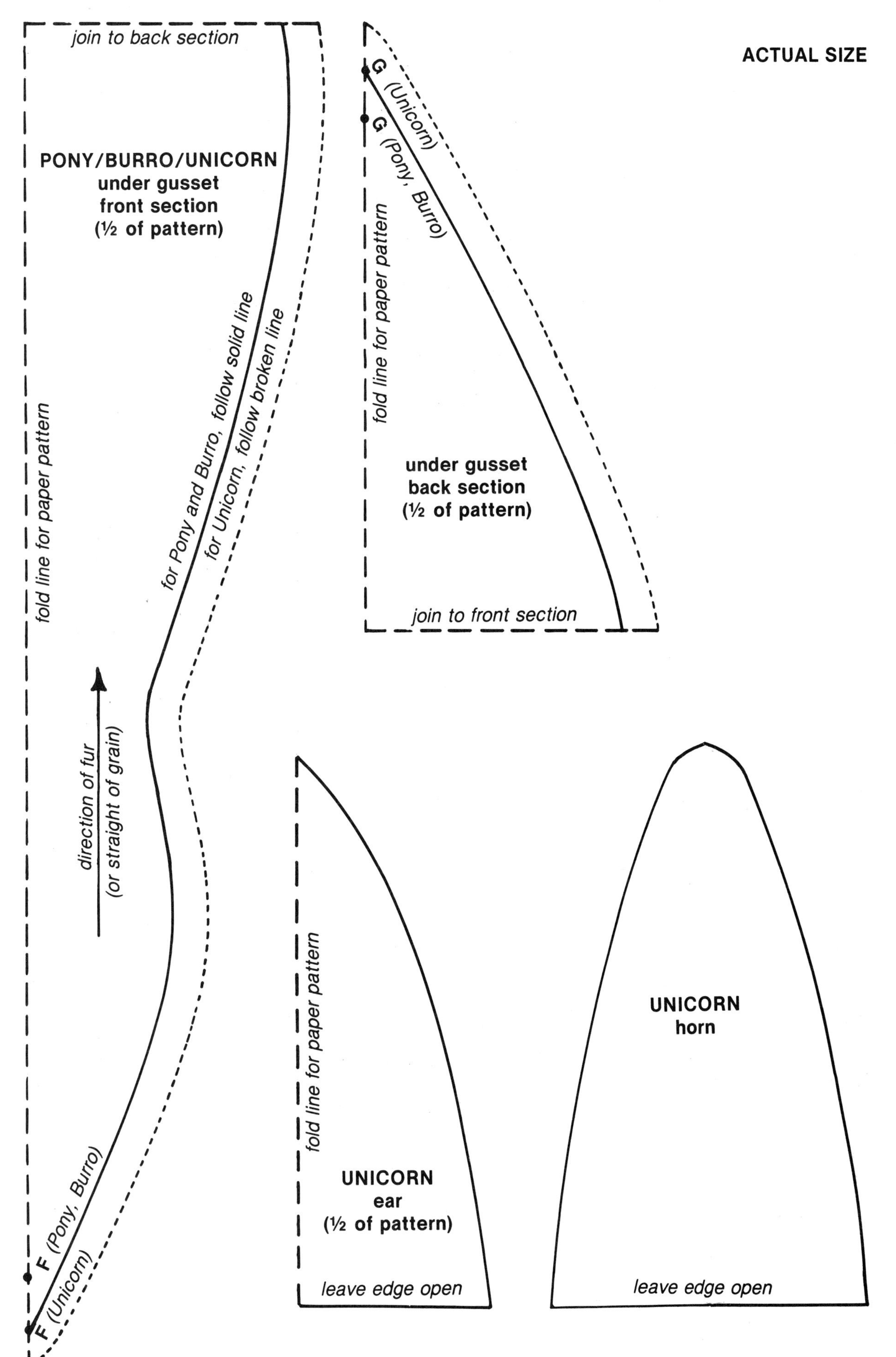
ACTUAL SIZE
join to back section
PONY/BURRO/UNICORN
under gusset
front section
(½ of pattern)
fold line for paper pattern
for Pony and Burro, follow solid line
for Unicorn, follow broken line
direction of fur
(or straight of grain)
F (Pony, Burro)
F (Unicorn)
G (Unicorn)
G (Pony, Burro)
fold line for paper pattern
under gusset
back section
(½ of pattern)
join to front section
fold line for paper pattern
UNICORN
ear
(½ of pattern)
leave edge open
UNICORN
horn
leave edge open

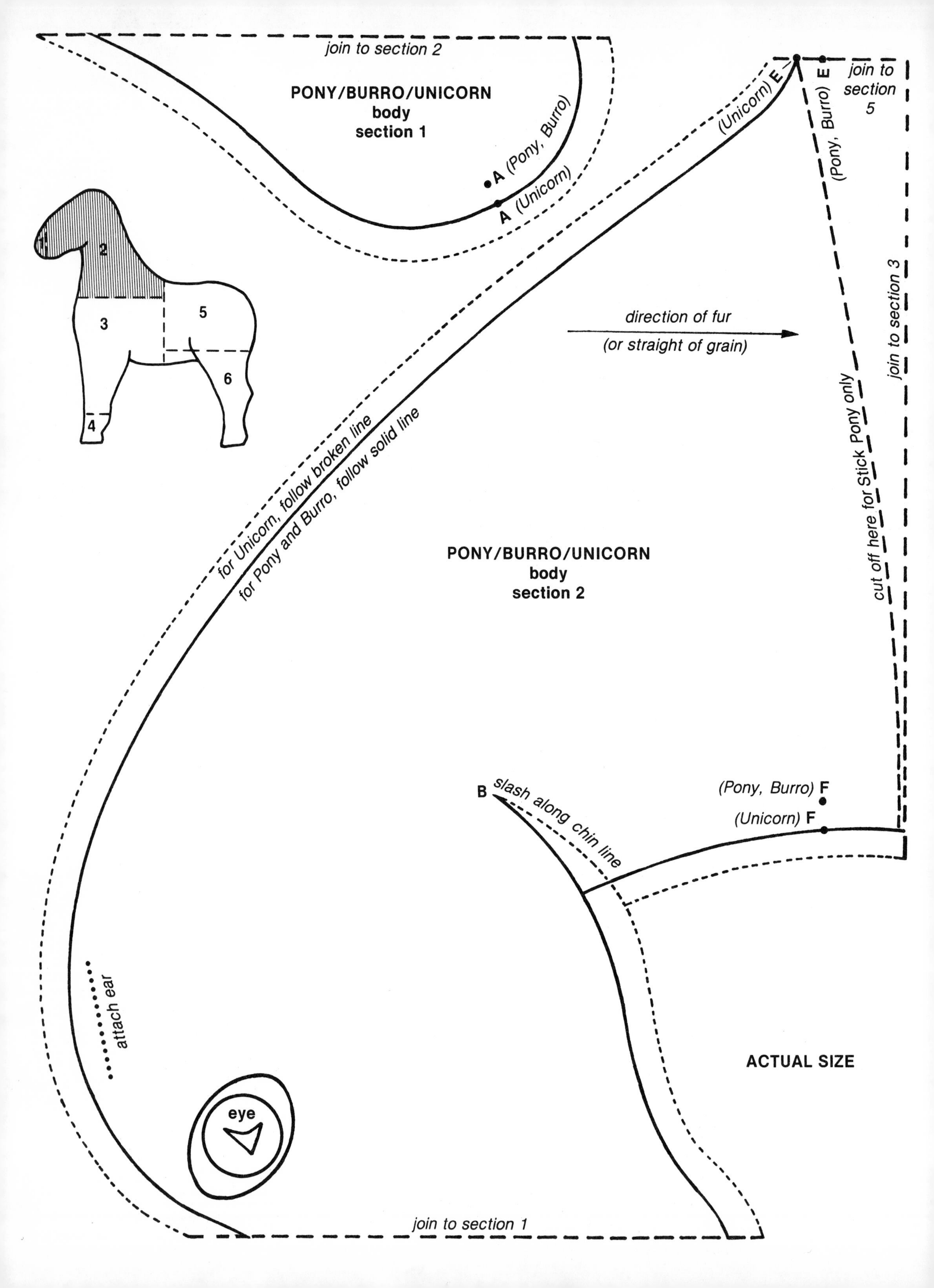
join to section 2
PONY/BURRO/UNICORN
body
section 1
A (Pony, Burro)
A (Unicorn)
1
2
3
4
5
6
(Unicorn) E
E
(Pony, Burro)
join to section 5
direction of fur
(or straight of grain)
join to section 3
cut off here for Stick Pony only
for Unicorn, follow broken line
for Pony and Burro, follow solid line
PONY/BURRO/UNICORN
body
section 2
B
slash along chin line
(Pony, Burro) F
(Unicorn) F
attach ear
eye
ACTUAL SIZE
join to section 1

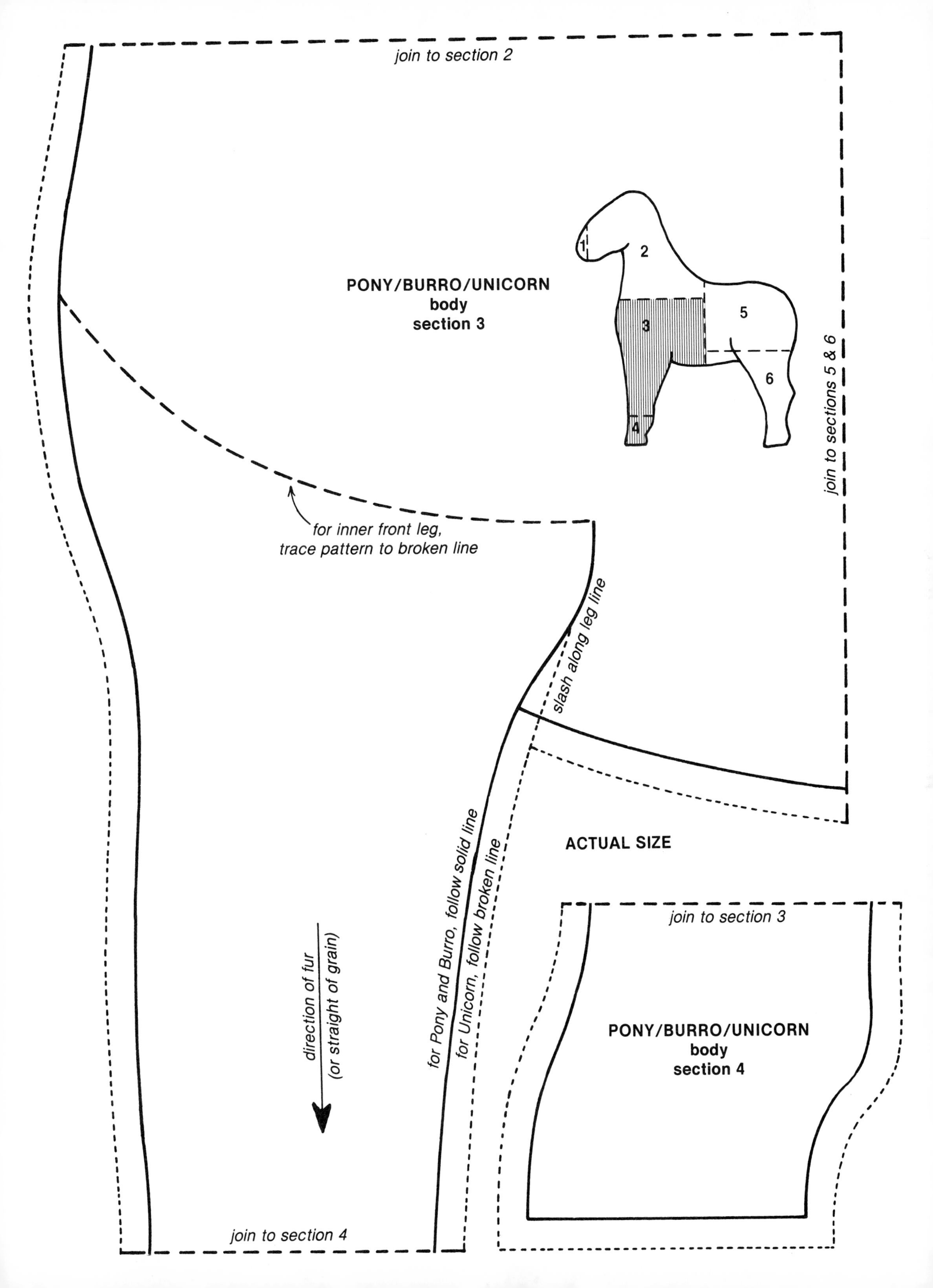
join to section 2
PONY/BURRO/UNICORN
body
section 3
1
2
3
4
5
6
join to sections 5 & 6
for inner front leg,
trace pattern to broken line
slash along leg line
for Pony and Burro, follow solid line
for Unicorn, follow broken line
direction of fur
(or straight of grain)
join to section 4
ACTUAL SIZE
join to section 3
PONY/BURRO/UNICORN
body
section 4

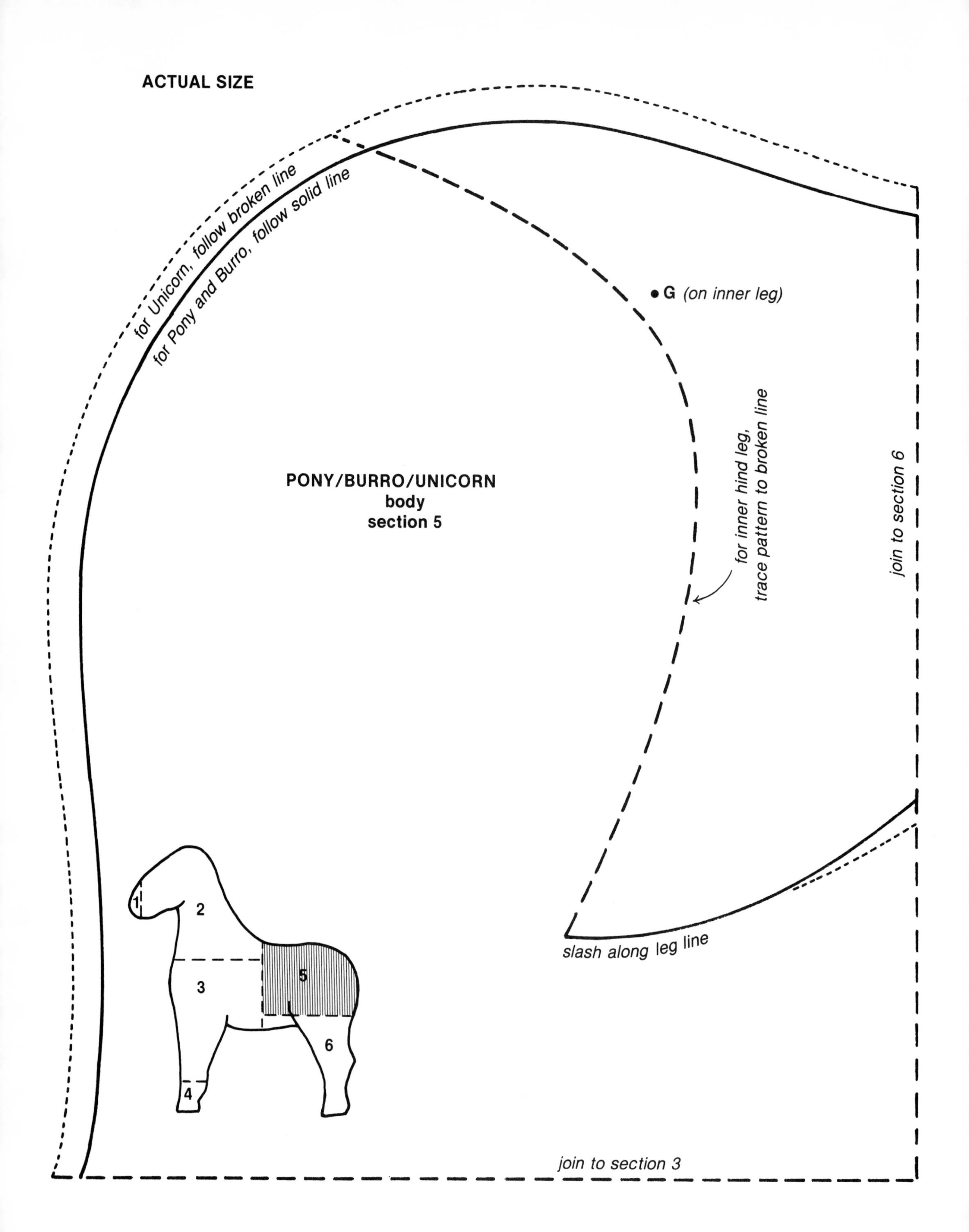
ACTUAL SIZE
for Unicorn, follow broken line
for Pony and Burro, follow solid line
• G (on inner leg)
for inner hind leg, trace pattern to broken line
join to section 6
PONY/BURRO/UNICORN
body
section 5
slash along leg line
1
2
3
4
5
6
join to section 3

ACTUAL SIZE

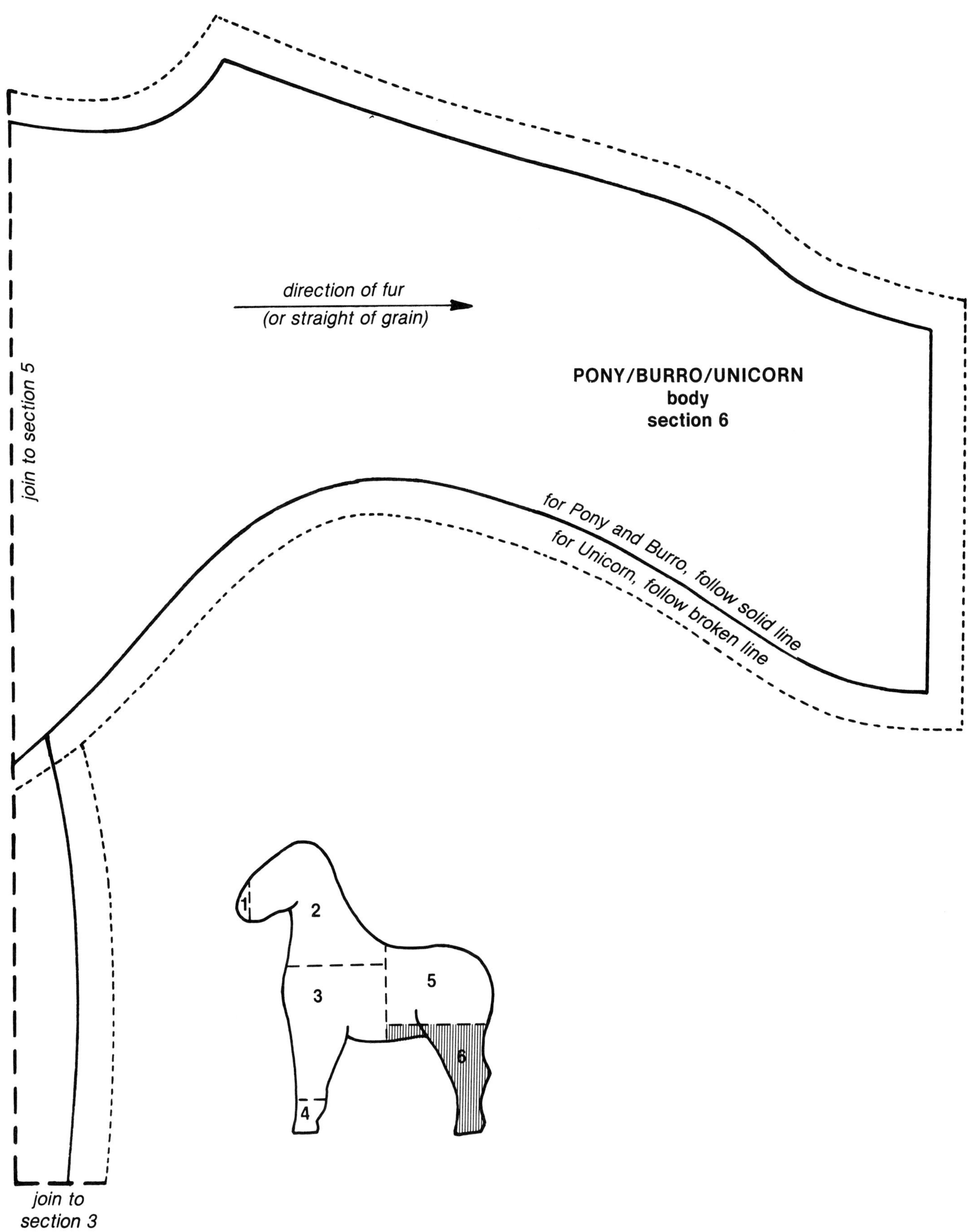
direction of fur
(or straight of grain)
PONY/BURRO/UNICORN
body
section 6
join to section 5
for Pony and Burro, follow solid line
for Unicorn, follow broken line
join to
section 3
1
2
3
4
5
6

Large animals

TV HORSE

(color photo, pages 104, 105)

This seated Horse has a saddle and bridle, and he's made for riding and "rassling." He doubles as a stool and is just the right size (30" long and 20" high) for watching television. If he ever begins to droop, fluff him back into shape like a pillow.

Two TV Horses are shown in color on pages 104 and 105. One is white with black spots (a lucky fabric find made this look like a Leopard Appaloosa). He has a white tail and mane, and blue and black eyes. The other Horse is black, with a hand-stitched white spot on its forehead and brown and black eyes.

The saddle and bridle are cut from vinyl, and directions for making them follow directions for the Horse.

MATERIALS
(for Horse)

1⅜ yd. short-pile fur fabric, 60" wide
long-pile fur fabric, 12x18", for mane and tail (pile should run along the 18" length)
felt scraps for eyes: brown, black and white for black Horse; blue, black and white for spotted Horse
transparent thread, for machine stitching
button-and-carpet thread, for handwork
polyester fiberfill, for stuffing (about 7 lb.)
plastic lid, for eyes
glue

DIRECTIONS

For tips on tracing and enlarging patterns, working with fur fabric, and making a fur "spot," see *Helpful Guides*, page 1.

Make pattern pieces

1. Use a 26x36" sheet of paper (marked in 2" squares) to enlarge pattern for body, pages 126-127; join front and back sections on broken lines.

2. From the enlargement, trace separate patterns for the inner front leg and inner hind leg.

3. Use a 12x34" sheet of paper (marked in 2" squares) to enlarge the half pattern for under gusset, pages 126-127; join front and back sections on broken lines. (You can enlarge the half pattern, then fold paper to cut out a full pattern piece.)

4. Trace patterns for tail, face, and mane, page 125; join sections for mane on broken lines. Also trace patterns for ear and chin gusset, page 128, and for inner mouth, page 129.

5. Cut out full pattern pieces. On body piece, slash along lines at mouth, neck and legs as indicated on pattern.

Cut fabric

1. Lay pattern pieces on back of fur fabric, making sure fur is running in correct direction. On short-pile fabric, trace 2 complete body pieces (1 reversed), 2 inner front legs (1 reversed), 2 inner hind legs (1 reversed), 1 under gusset, 1 face, 1 chin gusset, 1 inner mouth and 4 ears (see Fig. 1).

2. On long-pile fabric, trace 1 mane and 2 tails.

3. Cut out fabric on traced lines; ¼" seam allowances are included. Slash body pieces at mouth, chin and legs.

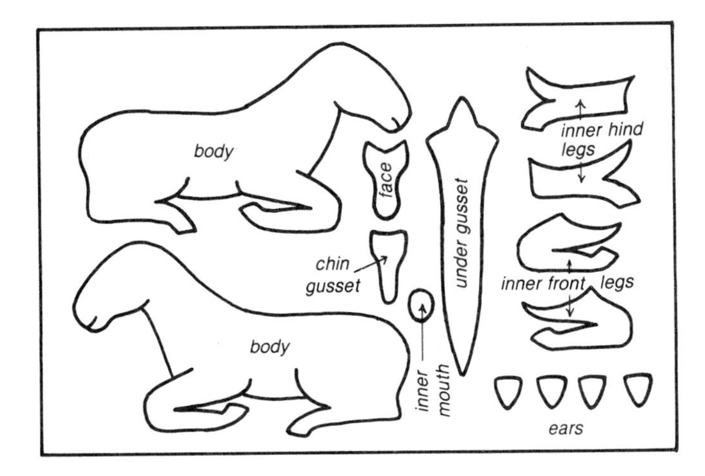

Fig. 1 *Layout for TV Horse, using 60"-wide fur fabric*

Fig. 2 *Stitching inner legs to body*

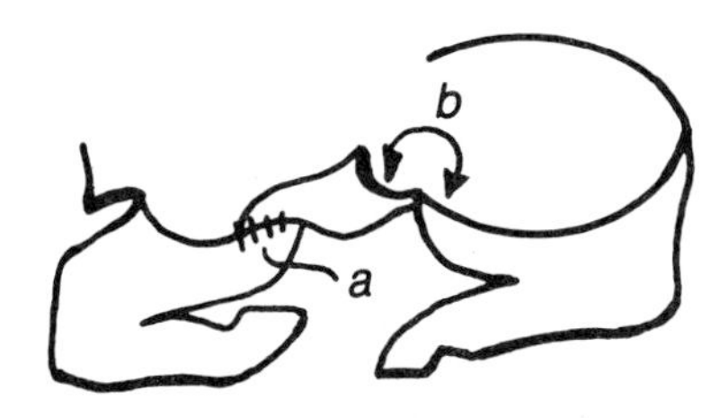

Fig. 3 *Stitching belly flap to inner legs*

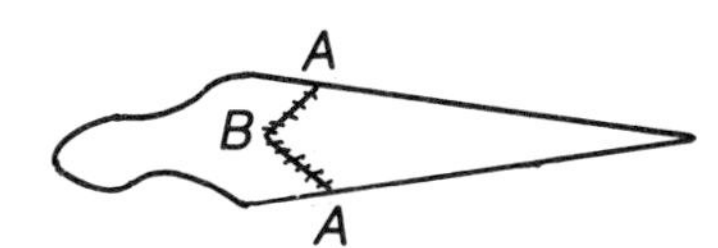

Fig. 4 *Stitching face to mane*

Fig. 5 *Stitching face to body*

Assemble

Use ¼" seams and a zigzag machine stitch.

1. Pin each inner leg to the matching body piece, right sides together (Fig. 2). Machine-stitch around leg, tapering seam to make it narrower at each end; leave top curve of inner leg open.

2. Lift belly flap between legs. Pin front cut edge to top curve of inner front leg, right sides together (Fig. 3, a). Stitch, tapering seam at each end.

Pin back cut edge of belly flap to top curve of back hind leg, right sides together (Fig. 3, b). Stitch in same manner.

3. To begin head assembly, join face to mane (Fig. 4), right sides together. Stitch seam in two steps, pivoting at center point B.

4. Stitch face/mane unit to each body piece, beginning at mouth C (Fig. 5) and ending at D on back.

5. Pin chin gusset to each body piece, matching points E and F (Fig. 6). Stitch, tapering seam at slash end (F).

6. Add under gusset. Begin pinning gusset to one body piece, right sides together, matching the H points (Fig. 7). Pin up about 4½" to tip of gusset at G. Pin along leg slash to I, then along leg curve and belly flap, and up hind quarters to J. Stitch the seam.

Note: Seam allowances should be tapered on one piece at points H and I to keep inside corners smooth. At H, make seam allowance narrower on gusset only. At I, make seam allowance narrower on body piece only (this is the end of a slash).

Pin under gusset to other body piece in same manner. Stitch seam, leaving 8" open for turning.

7. Pin and stitch front neck seam, joining body pieces above G (Fig. 8).

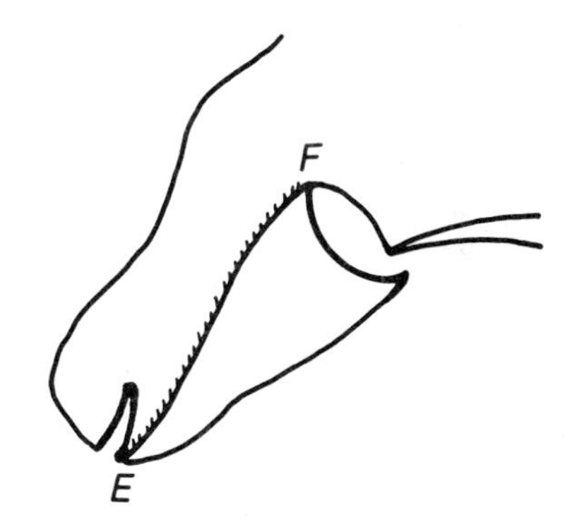

Fig. 6 *Adding chin gusset*

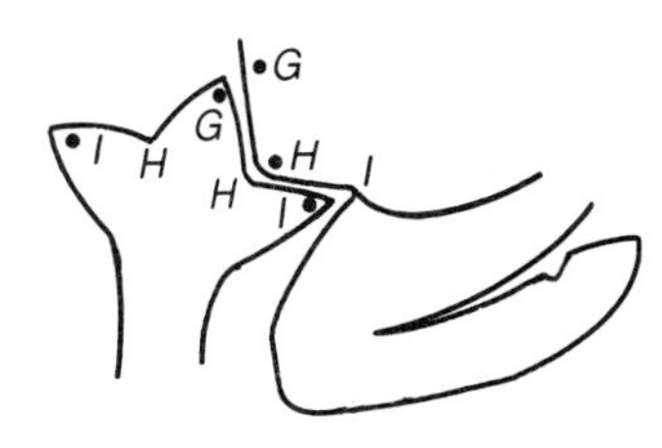

Fig. 7 *Adding under gusset*

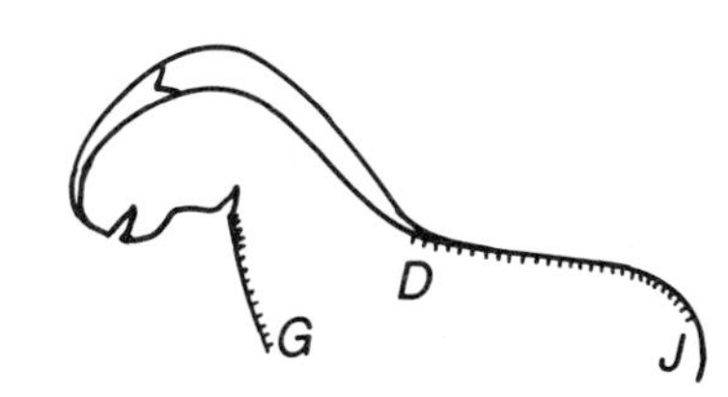

Fig. 8 *Closing neck and back seams*

8. Pin body pieces together along top of back between points D and J, and stitch.

9. Pin inner mouth to mouth slash, matching points C and E. Sew by hand with an over-cast stitch. Turn Horse to right side.

Note: Opening along chin gusset is not stitched. This will be closed later.

Stuff and finish

1. Begin stuffing nose, head and neck. (This is probably the most critical part of your work.) Work with small wads of fiberfill and pack it in firmly with a wooden spoon handle. Pack and shape so there are no holes or weak spots.

2. Stuff legs, making them tight and even. Then work into the body and make it firm. Close opening with invisible stitches.

3. Adjust angle of head and close opening along chin gusset with invisible stitches.

4. To make tail, pin pieces right sides together. Stitch, leaving 4" open for turning. Turn to right side, and close opening by hand. Stitch to body above J.

5. To make each ear, pin pieces right sides together. Stitch along curved edges, leaving straight side open. Turn to right side.

Fold ear in half along straight edge and stitch to head.

6. Trim fur pile at hoofs for about 2", and also trim around mouth.

7. Make and attach eyes; see *To make a felt eye*, page 5. Cut the large eye shape from the plastic lid and cover it with brown or blue felt. Glue on a black felt circle, then add a white felt highlight.

Bridle & Saddle

Choose all hardware in the same color—silver or gold.

MATERIALS

½ yd. brown fabric-backed vinyl, 54" wide
2 D rings, ¾" inside, for bridle
2 round, flat metal buttons, ¾" diameter, for bridle (optional)
1 buckle with prong and 2" center post, for saddle
transparent thread, for machine stitching
button-and-carpet thread, for attaching buttons
polyester fiberfill, for stuffing parts of saddle

DIRECTIONS

For tips on tracing patterns, and marking and cutting fabric, refer to *Helpful Guides*, page 1. Use a straight stitch for all machine stitching.

Make pattern pieces

1. Trace patterns for saddle seat and seat back, page 124; for horn, page 128; and for skirt, page 129.

2. Cut out full pattern pieces.

Cut vinyl

1. On back (wrong side) of vinyl, draw two straight strips, each 1½" wide, across the width. Along one strip, measure a section 36" long (for reins) and a section 10¾" long (for forehead strap).

Along the second strip, measure a section 21½" (for head strap) and a section 15½" (for noseband).

2. Draw a third strip 4" wide and 36½" long (for saddle cinch).

3. Lay pattern pieces for saddle on remaining vinyl, and trace 1 skirt, 1 seat, 2 back seat pieces and 2 horn pieces (1 reversed).

4. Cut out all pieces on traced lines; ¼" seam allowances are included where needed.

Assemble bridle

In place of pins, you can use paper clips to hold edges together for machine stitching.

1. Take the four 1½"-wide strips and fold each in half lengthwise, right side out. Straight-stitch cut edges together, about ⅛" from edge. Then stitch along folded edge in same manner.

2. Take the 15½" noseband and overlap ends ¾" to form a circle. Stitch a square to secure (Fig. 9).

3. Position the 21½" head strap so each end overlaps the noseband circle (Fig. 10). Have ends about 6" apart, with seam on noseband in center. Stitch a square at each end to secure.

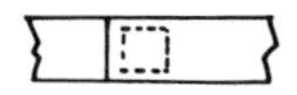

Fig. 9 *Stitching a square to join vinyl strip*

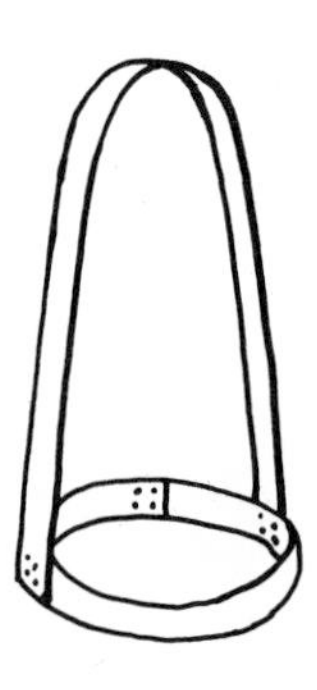

Fig. 10 *Stitching head strap to noseband*

4. Add the 10¾" forehead strap. Position bottom edge of each end 4½" from bottom of noseband, and stitch a square (Fig. 11). By hand, attach metal buttons (optional) to cover stitching.

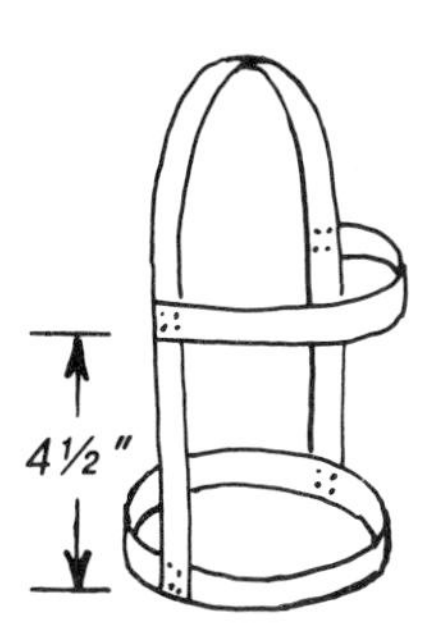

Fig. 11 *Adding forehead strap*

5. To make reins, fold each end of the 36" length over a D ring and stitch a square to secure (Fig. 12).

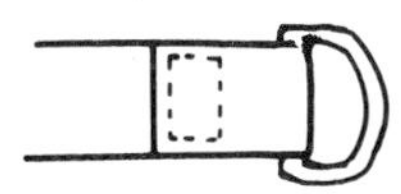

Fig. 12 *Stitching reins to D ring*

6. Turn rings to expose openings. Carefully open each ring with pliars (try not to mar the metal). Slip each ring over the noseband in front of the head strap, then pinch the ring closed. Turn rings again so that reins hide openings (Fig. 13).

7. Slip bridle on Horse.

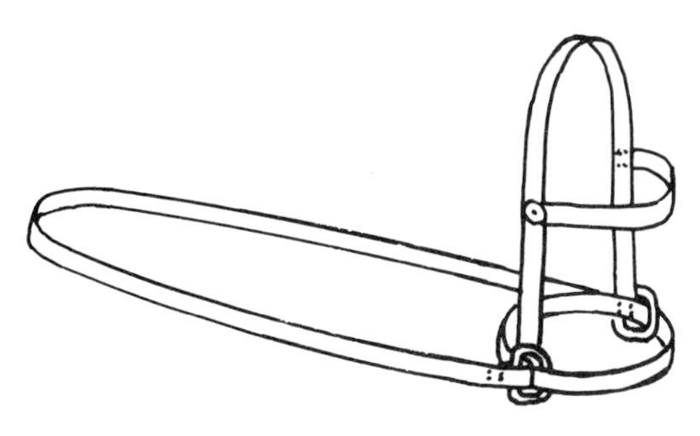

Fig. 13 *Attaching reins to noseband*

Assemble saddle

In place of pins, you can use paper clips to hold cut edges together, and masking tape to position sections for stitching.

1. Place horn pieces right sides together. Stitch a ¼" seam from A, over end curve, tapering off to edge at B (Fig. 14).

2. Turn right side out. Stuff curved end to form horn. Use fingers to press rest of seam flat on right side.

3. Position skirt over horn piece; match the C points and center the V point over the horn seam. Topstitch on each side of horn; leave ¼" at outside edge free so seam allowance on horn can roll under (Fig. 15).

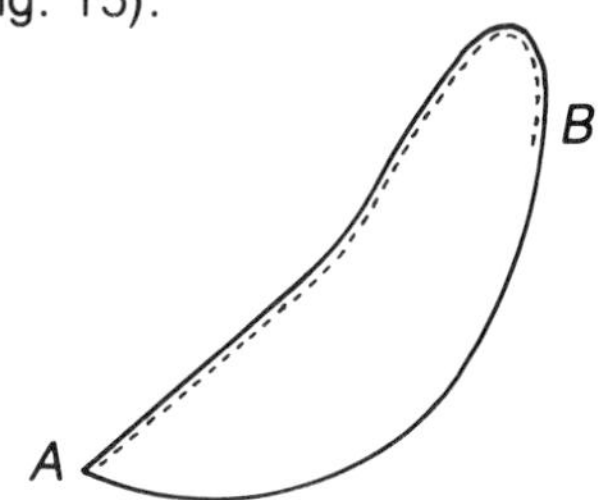

Fig. 14 *Stitching horn pieces together*

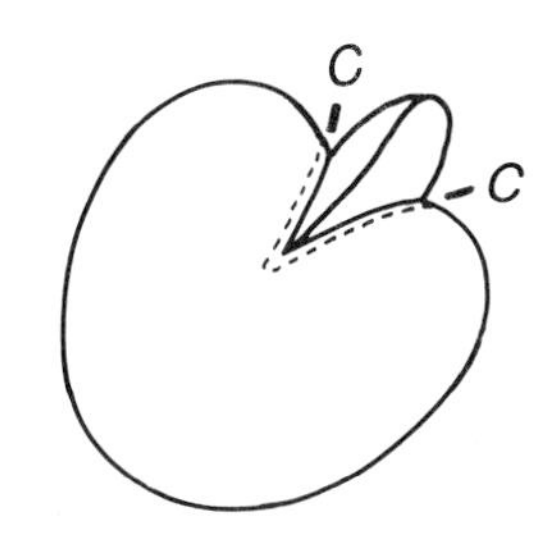

Fig. 15 *Adding skirt to horn*

4. To make cinch, fold the 4x36½" strip in half lengthwise, right side out. Stitch lengthwise, about ⅛" from cut edges, then stitch along folded edge in same manner.

5. Find center of cinch length. Position this over center of skirt, letting front edge of cinch meet the V point on skirt (Fig. 16). Topstitch

Fig. 16 *Adding cinch*

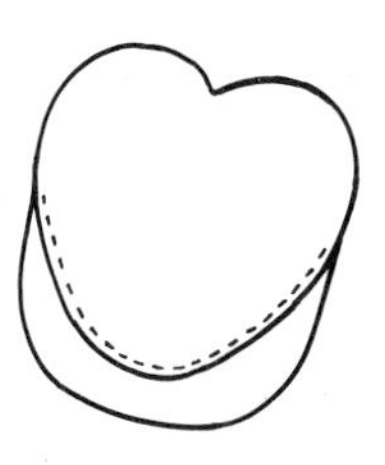

Fig. 17 *Stitching seat to seat back*

along front edge of cinch a short way to secure.

6. Place seat back pieces right sides together, and stitch around outside curve. Turn to right side and stuff lightly. Then hold inside edges together (paper clips help), and stitch.

7. Position seat so it overlaps back seat section about ¼". (Masking tape helps to hold this in place.) Topstitch along edge of seat (Fig. 17). If vinyl does not move easily, slip a sheet of typing-weight paper under it. Tear paper away after stitching.

8. Place seat unit over skirt/horn unit so back edges are even. Form a small tuck in the horn on each side of the seam to take care of extra fullness. Topstitch around edge of seat (Fig. 18).

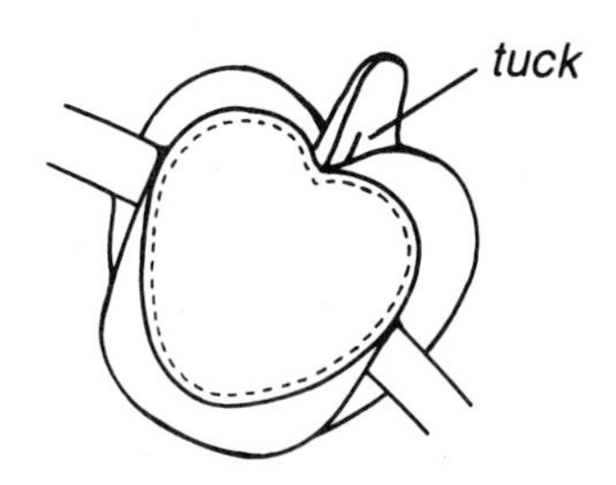

Fig. 18 *Adding seat unit to horn/skirt unit*

9. Cut slit for buckle prong about 1¾" from end of cinch (Fig. 19). Then stitch buckle to cinch (Fig. 20).

10. Try saddle on Horse to determine where holes for buckle prong are needed. Punch holes. Trim end of cinch to form point and stitch around point (Fig. 21).

11. Buckle saddle on Horse.

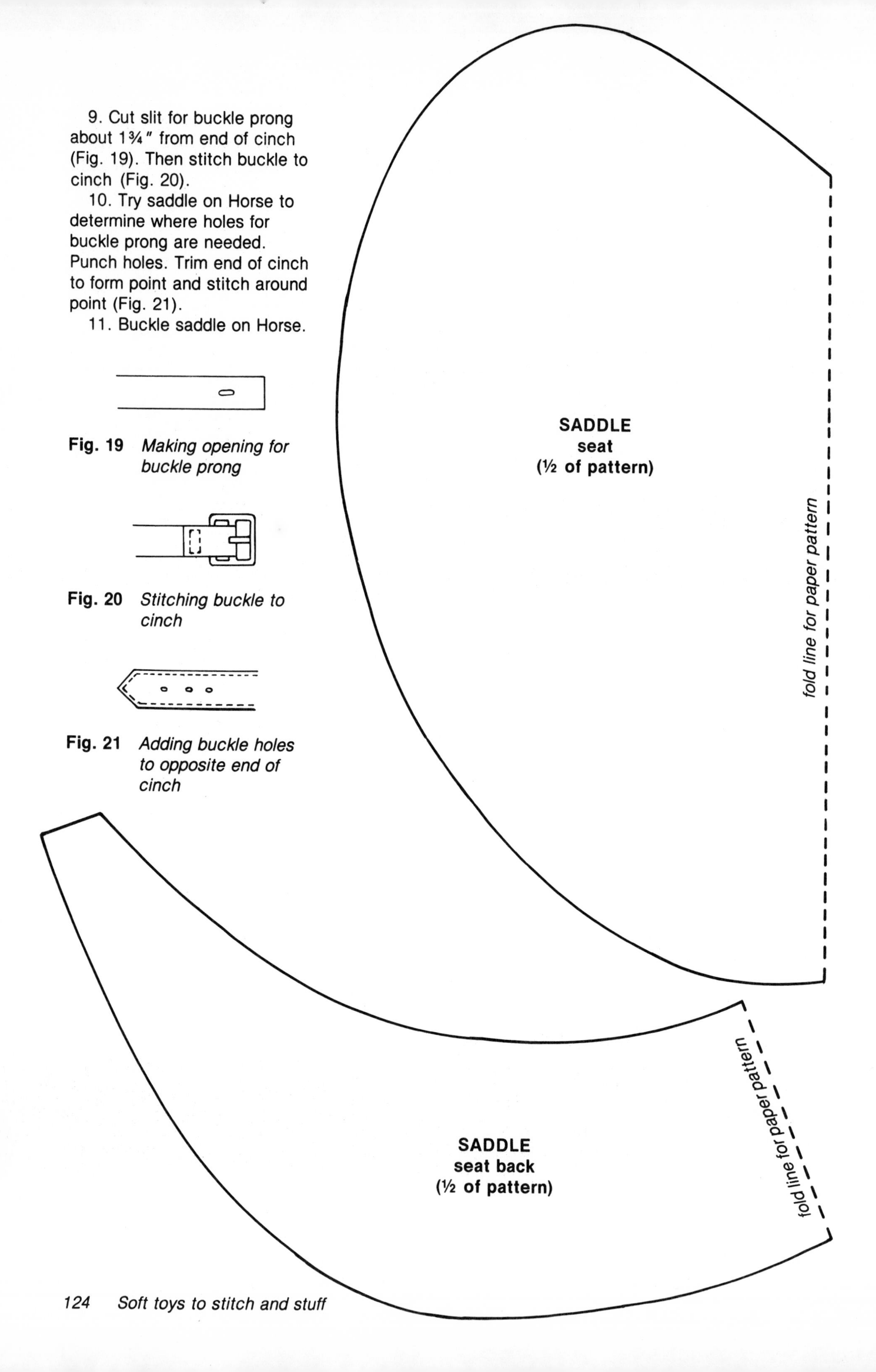

Fig. 19 *Making opening for buckle prong*

Fig. 20 *Stitching buckle to cinch*

Fig. 21 *Adding buckle holes to opposite end of cinch*

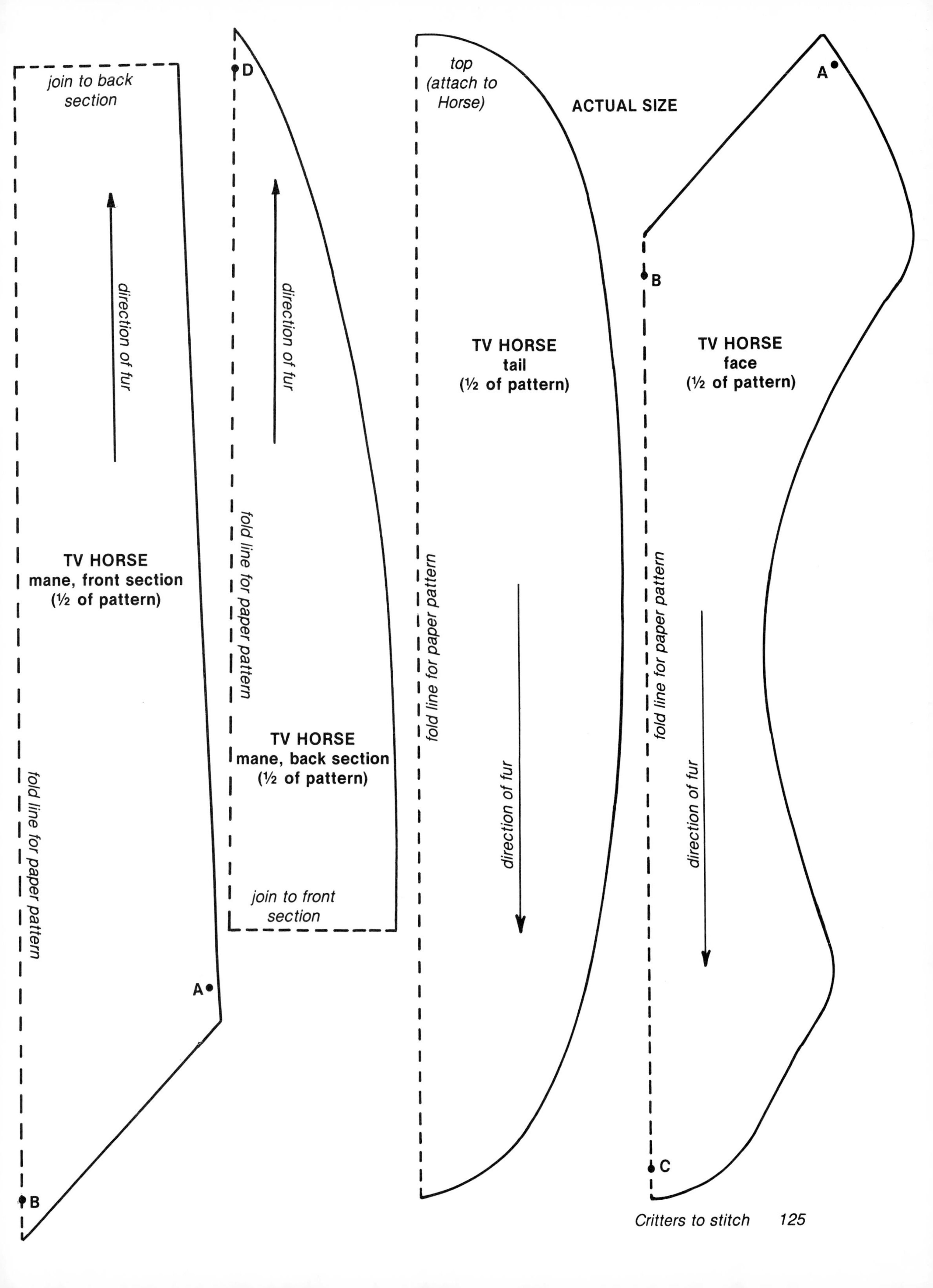
join to back
section
direction of fur
TV HORSE
mane, front section
(½ of pattern)
fold line for paper pattern
A
B
D
direction of fur
fold line for paper pattern
TV HORSE
mane, back section
(½ of pattern)
join to front
section
top
(attach to
Horse)
ACTUAL SIZE
TV HORSE
tail
(½ of pattern)
fold line for paper pattern
direction of fur
A
B
TV HORSE
face
(½ of pattern)
fold line for paper pattern
direction of fur
C

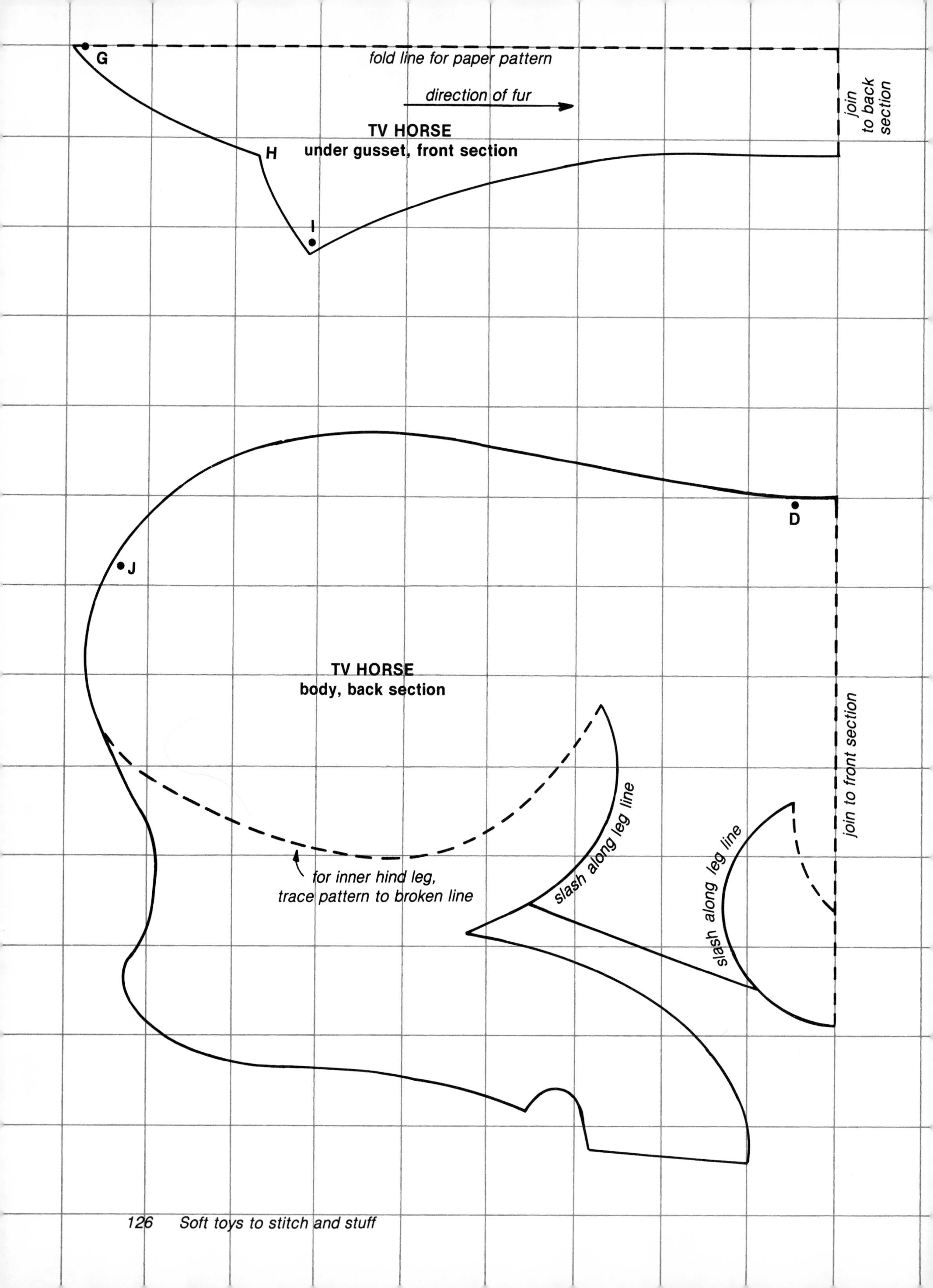
G
fold line for paper pattern
direction of fur
join to back section
TV HORSE
under gusset, front section
H
I
D
J
TV HORSE
body, back section
join to front section
slash along leg line
slash along leg line
for inner hind leg,
trace pattern to broken line

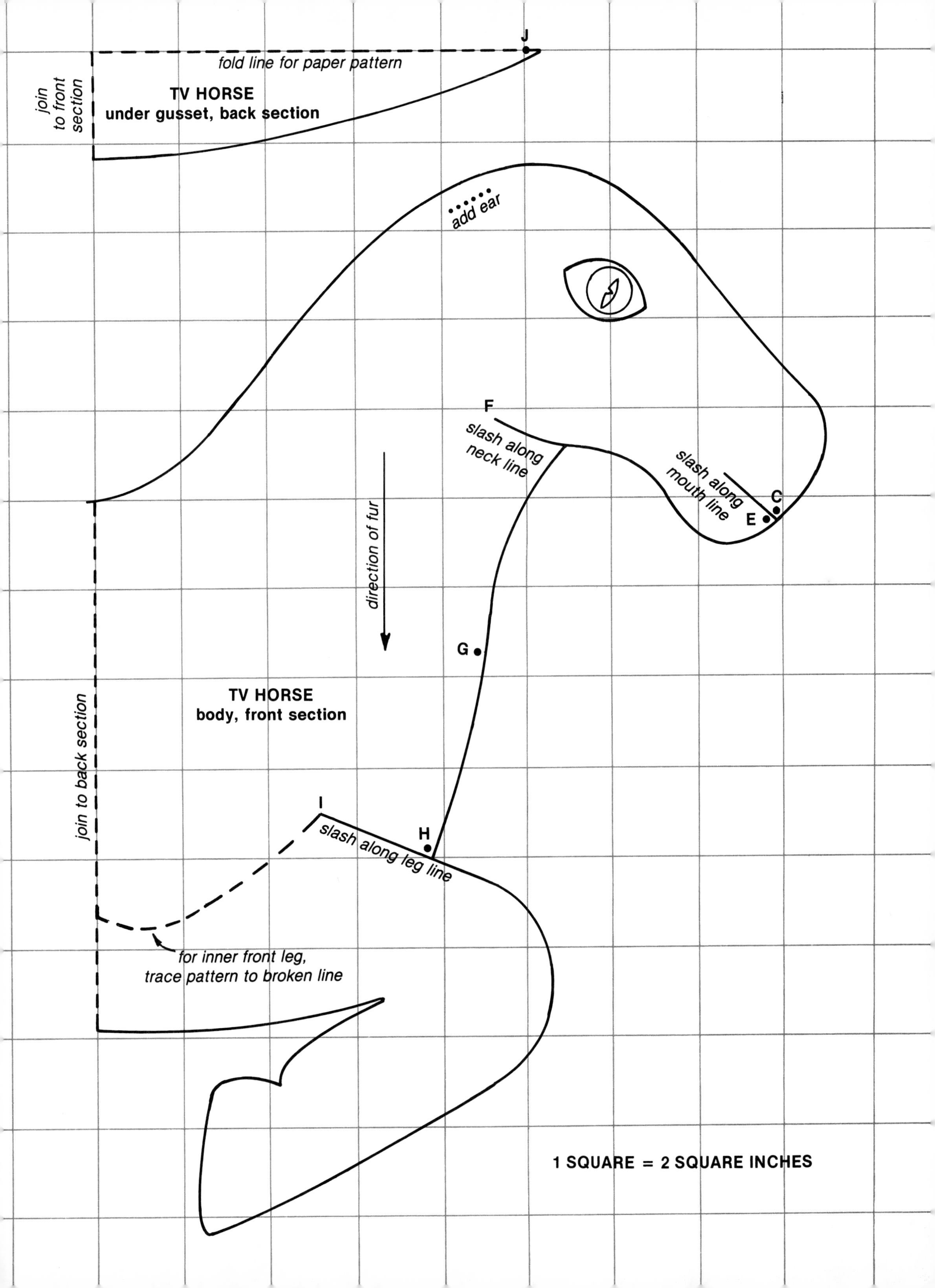
J
fold line for paper pattern
join to front section
TV HORSE
under gusset, back section
add ear
F
slash along neck line
slash along mouth line
C
E
direction of fur
G
TV HORSE
body, front section
join to back section
I
H
slash along leg line
for inner front leg, trace pattern to broken line
1 SQUARE = 2 SQUARE INCHES

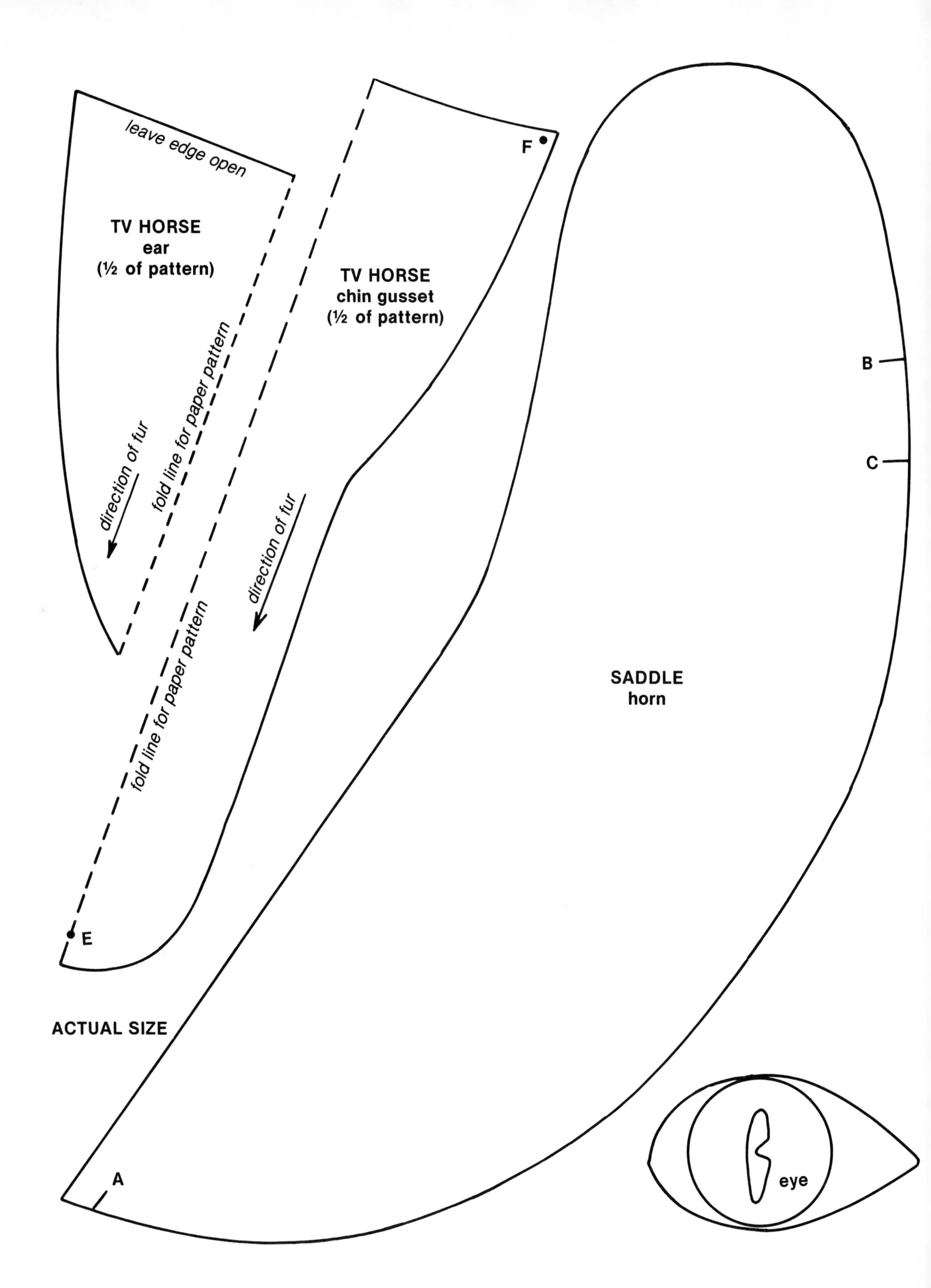
leave edge open
TV HORSE
ear
(½ of pattern)
direction of fur
fold line for paper pattern
TV HORSE
chin gusset
(½ of pattern)
F
direction of fur
fold line for paper pattern
E
B
C
SADDLE
horn
ACTUAL SIZE
A
eye

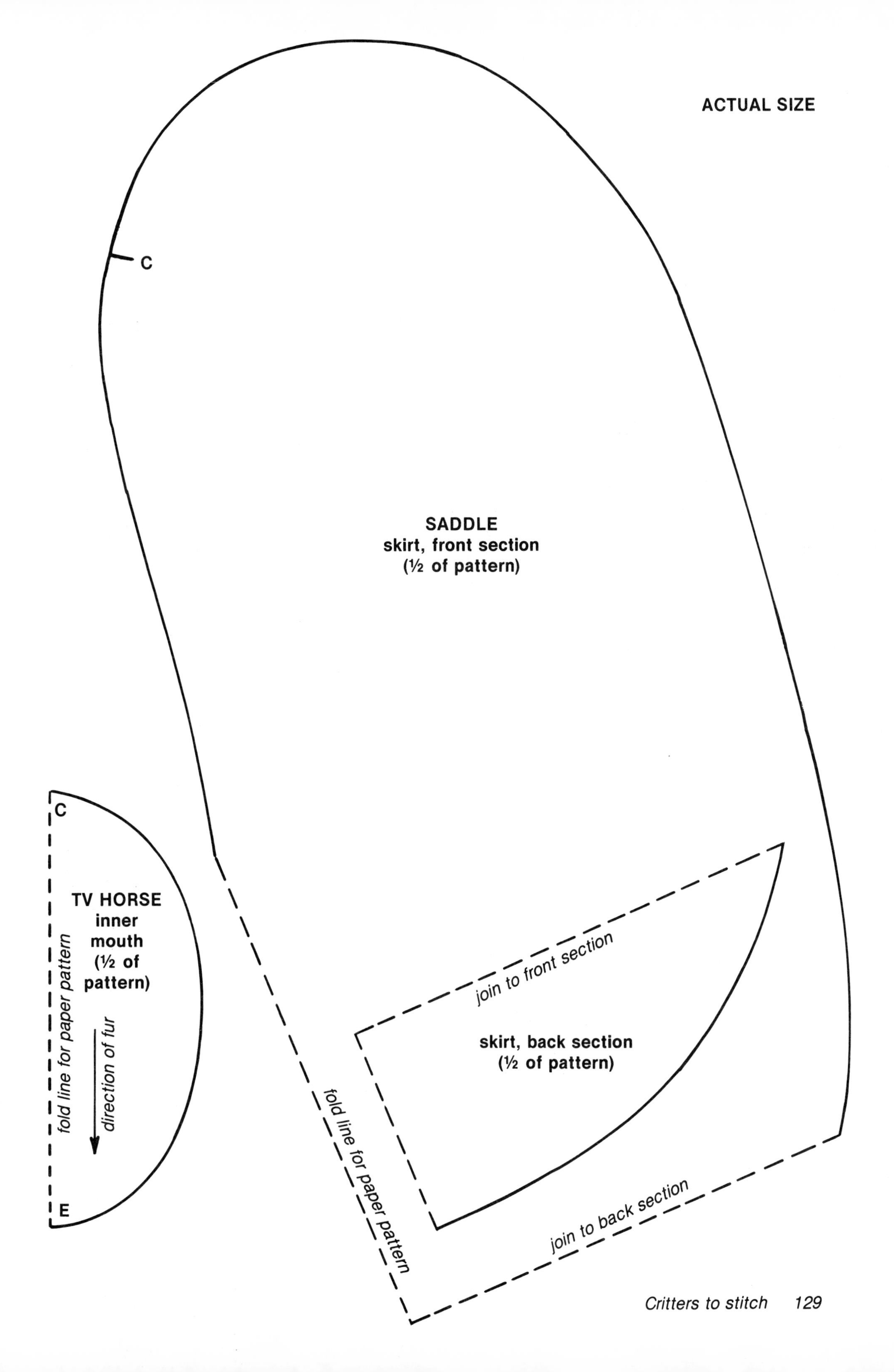
ACTUAL SIZE
C
SADDLE
skirt, front section
(½ of pattern)
C
TV HORSE
inner
mouth
(½ of
pattern)
fold line for paper pattern
direction of fur
E
join to front section
skirt, back section
(½ of pattern)
fold line for paper pattern
join to back section

APE

(color photo, page 106)

In some parts of the world—perhaps on a banana farm— an ape might be part of a farm family. (Think of the mischief an animal with such large hands could get into.)

I designed this Ape on request for a teenage girl. Everyone liked it so well, I decided to include the pattern here.

MATERIALS

1 yd. brown long-pile fur fabric, 60" wide
½ yd. brown velour knit, 44" wide (or ¼ yd. felt, 72" wide), for face, mouth, ears, hands and feet
white, blue and black felt scraps, for eyes
red felt scrap, for tongue
transparent thread, for machine stitching
button-and-carpet thread, for handwork
polyester fiberfill, for stuffing (about 2 lb.)
plastic lid, for eyes
glue

DIRECTIONS

For tips on tracing and enlarging patterns, and working with fur fabric, see *Helpful Guides,* page 1.

Make pattern pieces

1. Use a 26x28" sheet of paper (marked in 2" squares) to enlarge pattern pieces for body, front gusset, arm and leg, page 133. Use an 8x34" sheet of paper (marked in 2" squares) to enlarge the pattern for back gusset, page 132; join gusset sections on broken lines.
2. Trace patterns for ear, mouth and tongue, page 132. Trace separate patterns for hand, foot, face and eye, page 134.
3. Cut out full pattern pieces.

Cut fabric

1. Lay pattern pieces on back of fur fabric, making sure fur is running in correct direction. Trace 2 body pieces (1 reversed), 1 front gusset, 1 back gusset, 4 arms (2 reversed) and 4 legs (2 reversed).
2. On wrong side of velour or felt, trace 1 face and 2 mouth pieces.
3. Cut out fabric on traced lines; ¼" seam allowances are included.

Assemble

Use ¼" seams, with a zigzag machine stitch on fur fabric and a straight stitch on velour or felt.

1. Pin back gusset to one body piece, right sides together, matching points A and B. Stitch between points.

Pin back gusset to other body piece and stitch.

2. Pin front gusset to one body piece, matching points C and B. Stitch between points.

Pin front gusset to other body piece and stitch. Turn body to right side through face opening.

3. To make each arm and leg, pin matching pieces right sides together. Stitch the long seams, leaving both ends open. Turn to right side.

Stuff and finish

1. Stuff body firmly, and let stuffing curve out at the face opening.
2. Stuff arms and legs to make them medium-firm, leaving flared ends flat so they will blend into body.
3. To attach arms, keep flared edges together. Pin in position on body (long, heavy pins help here). Sew in place with invisible stitches, catching both layers of arm in one stitch, then catching body fabric in next stitch (Fig. 1). Raw edges of arm will turn under (against body) as you work.
4. Attach legs in same manner. Add a second row of stitching to catch inside of leg to body. To hold leg against body, add a few stitches closer to knee (see Fig. 1, point x).
5. To add face, place face piece over opening, right side up. Tuck edges under fur fabric

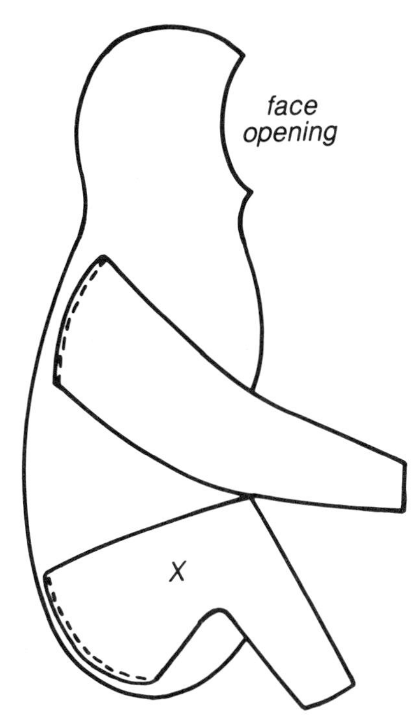

Fig. 1 *Attaching arms and legs*

and pin in a few places. Stitch face to body, using button-and-carpet thread and invisible stitches. Work on top half of face first and try to keep edge of face smooth; ease in any fullness at chin area.

6. To make mouth, place the two oval pieces right sides together. Pin upper half of mouth from E to F, then sew edges together by hand with small gathering stitches (Fig. 2). Gather slightly so that edge measures about 4″ across. (This will form indented center of mouth.)

Next, run a single gathering line around remaining edges, keeping them separate. (This will form outside of mouth.) Pull thread to gather; do not secure.

Stuff the two sections of mouth, keeping middle seam indented.

7. Pin mouth to face (Fig. 3), with raw edge of mouth turned under. Sew outside edge of mouth to face with invisible stitches. Then take a few stitches at center of mouth to hold indented seam in place.

8. To make each ear, pin or trace pattern on double thickness of velour or felt. (With *velour*, have right side of fabric inside.)

Straight-stitch around curve, leaving short edge open. Cut fabric along short edge and 1/8″ from stitching.

With *velour*, turn fabric to right side; then turn raw edges at opening 1/8″ to inside and pin to hold. With *felt*, do not turn; leave all edges flat.

Stitch inside lines on each ear. Stuff, using small wads of fiberfill; pack firmly with knitting needle or other slim tool.

9. Pin ears along edge of face and stitch (Fig. 3).

10. To add tongue, trace pattern on red felt and cut out. Stitch to center of mouth.

11. Make and attach eyes; see *To make a felt eye*, page 5. Cut large oval from the plastic lid and cover it with white felt. Glue on a blue felt oval, then a smaller black oval.

12. To make each hand and foot, pin or trace pattern on double thickness of velour or felt. (With *velour*, have right side of fabric inside.)

Straight-stitch around pattern, leaving straight edge open. Cut fabric along straight edge and 1/8″ from stitching. Slash to stitching in V areas between fingers and toes.

With *velour*, turn to right side. With *felt*, do not turn; leave stitching exposed.

Stuff, working small wads of fiberfill firmly and evenly into fingers and toes. Continue stuffing hands and feet tightly, then bend in a relaxed position.

13. Attach a hand to each arm and a foot to each leg, using invisible stitches.

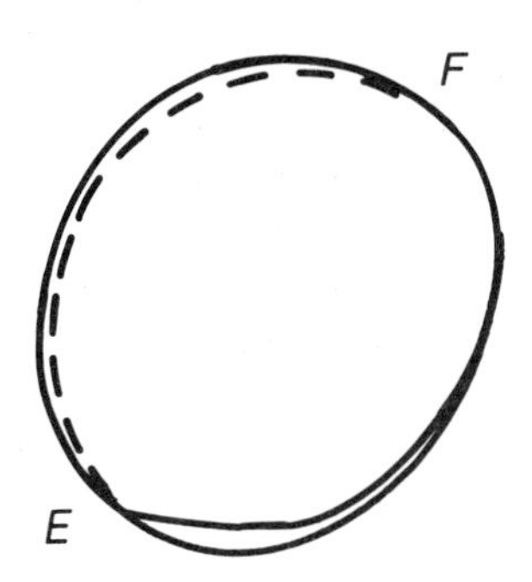

Fig. 2 *Joining mouth pieces with gathering stitch*

Fig. 3 *Adding features*

ACTUAL SIZE

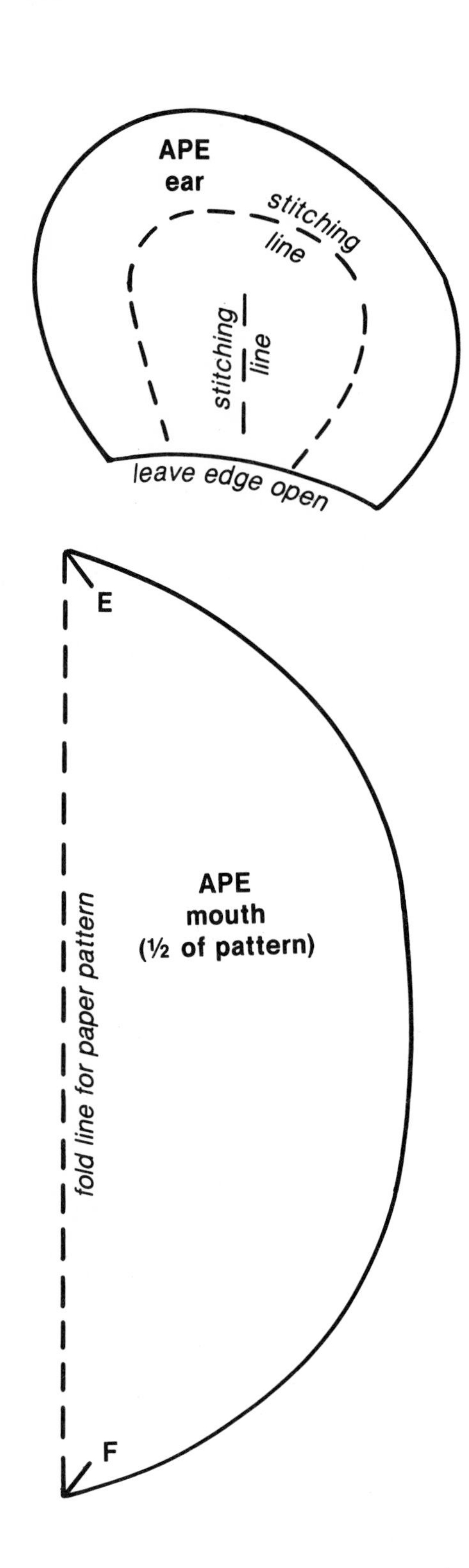
APE
ear
stitching
line
stitching
line
leave edge open
E
F
fold line for paper pattern
APE
mouth
(½ of pattern)

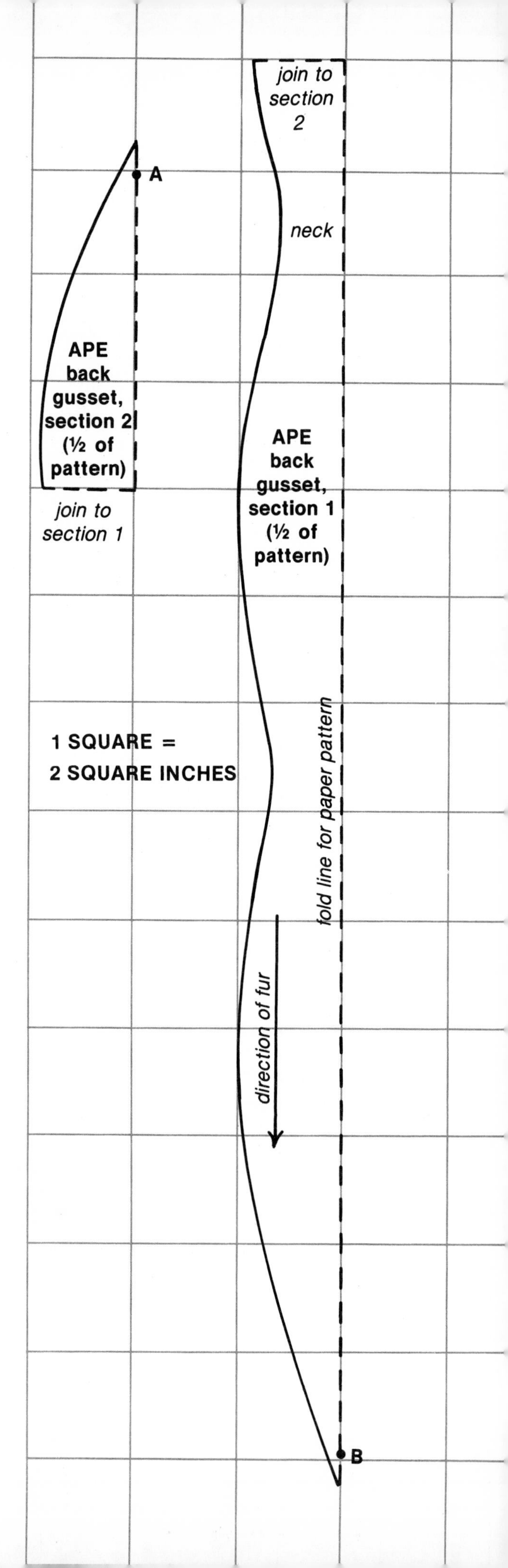
join to
section
2
A
neck
APE
back
gusset,
section 2
(½ of
pattern)
join to
section 1
APE
back
gusset,
section 1
(½ of
pattern)
1 SQUARE =
2 SQUARE INCHES
fold line for paper pattern
direction of fur
B

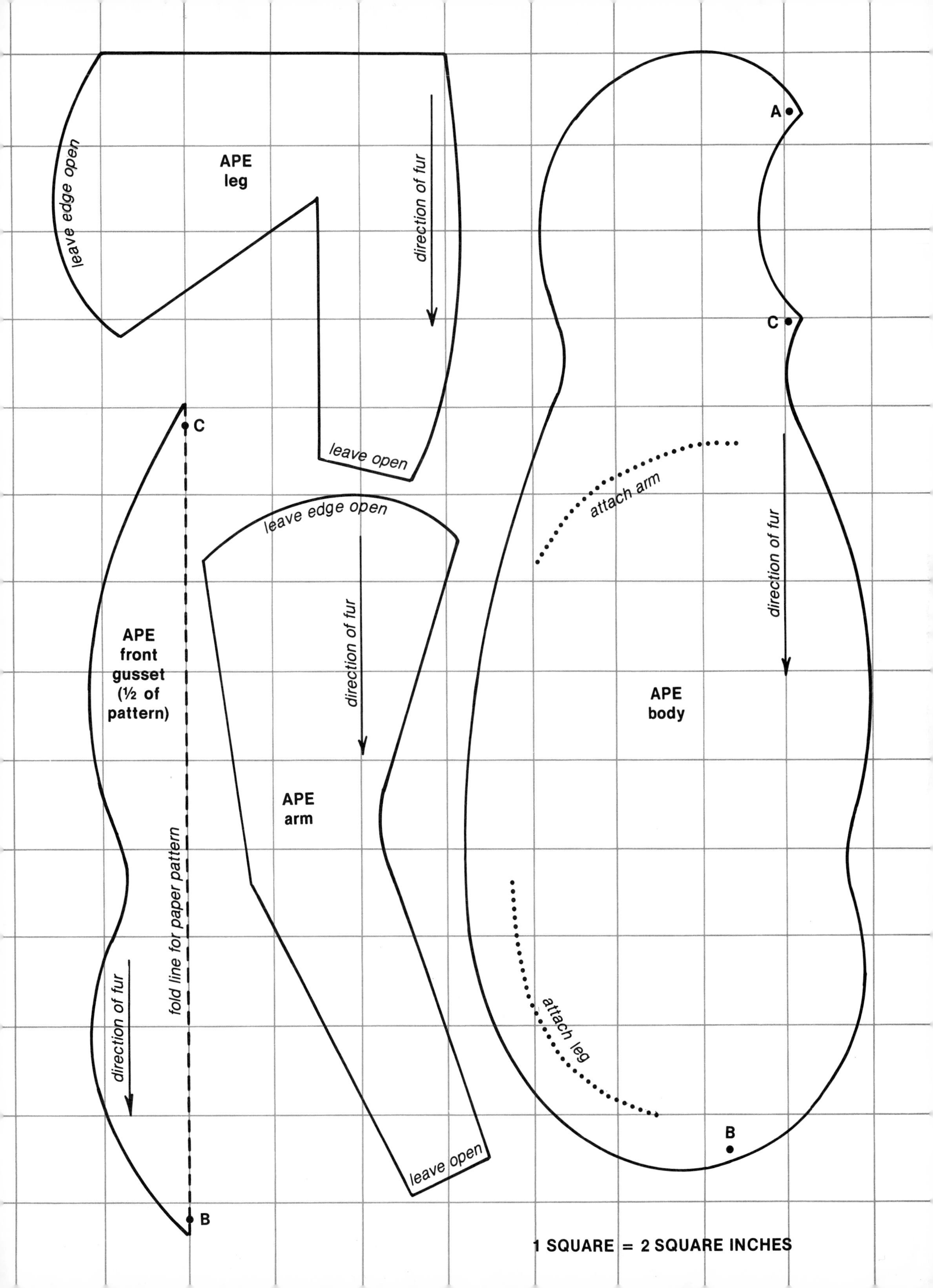

APE
leg
leave edge open
direction of fur
leave open
C
APE
front
gusset
(½ of
pattern)
fold line for paper pattern
direction of fur
B
leave edge open
direction of fur
APE
arm
leave open
A
C
attach arm
direction of fur
APE
body
attach leg
B
1 SQUARE = 2 SQUARE INCHES

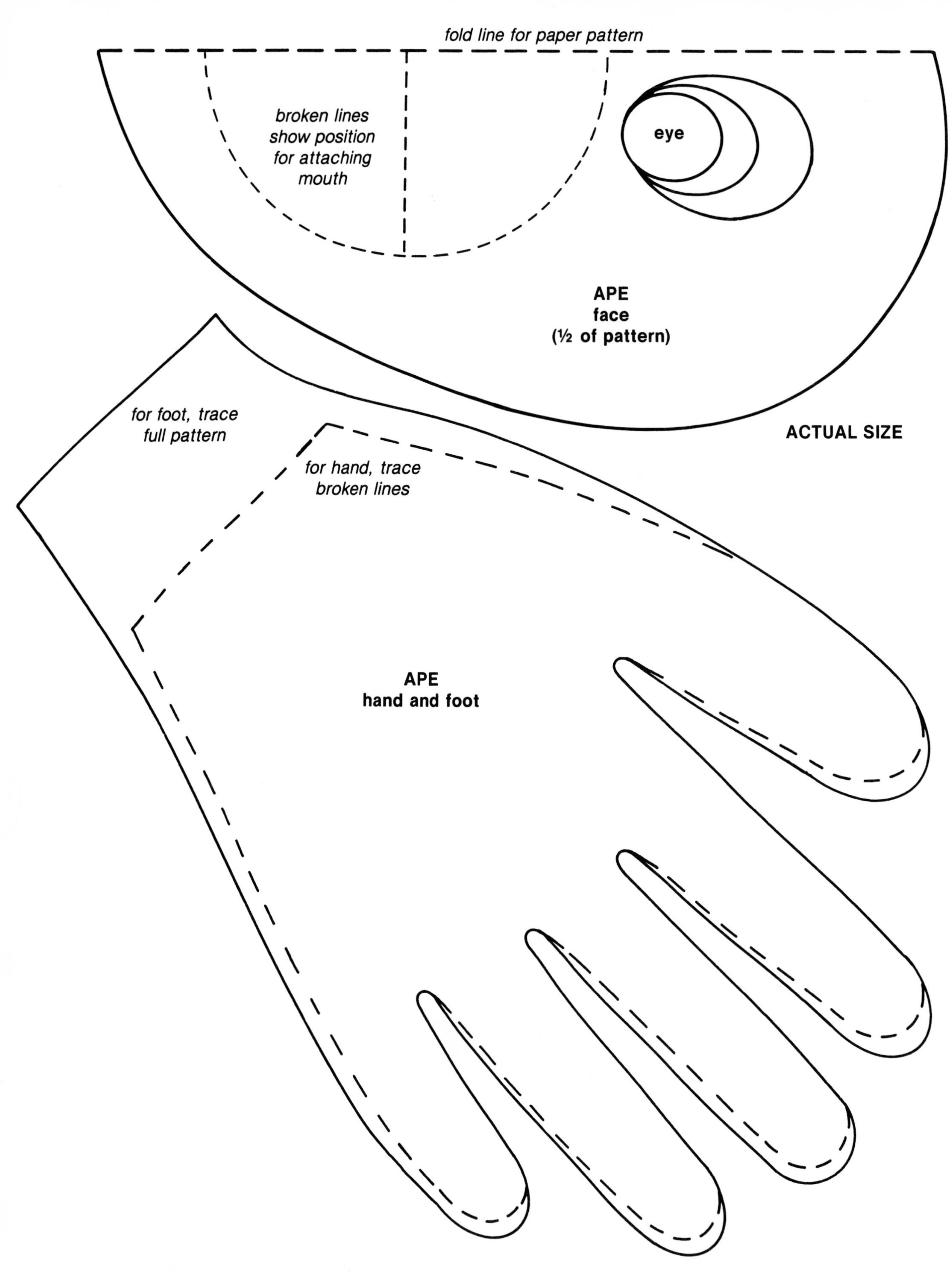
fold line for paper pattern
broken lines
show position
for attaching
mouth
eye
APE
face
(½ of pattern)
ACTUAL SIZE
for foot, trace
full pattern
for hand, trace
broken lines
APE
hand and foot

Barn & fence

A big red Barn with a white Fence can be the gathering place for many toy critters.

BARN

(color photo, pages 104-105)

The end door pulls down on this 23″-high, 26″-long Barn made of plywood. Children can march their critters in and out during playtime, then store the toys inside for the night.

MATERIALS

48x55″ piece of plywood, ½″ thick (interior grade)
13″ strip of 1x2″ lumber, for doorstop
12½′ flat trim, ¼x¾″ (add 6′ more if you want windows on both sides of Barn)
27″ of ½″ quarter-round molding, for roof top
3 doz. 3d finishing nails
1 pair 1″ rivited-pin hinges
2 round-head wood screws, ⅜″, for attaching door pull
lightweight magnetic catch (with magnet section about ⅝x1⅞″), for door
wood glue
wood putty, to seal cut edges of plywood
strip of leather or fabric-backed vinyl, 1x4″, for door pull
red and white nontoxic paint, ½ pt. each
1 pt. undercoat (or white paint), for first coat

DIRECTIONS

1. Trace actual-size pattern for top section of end wall,

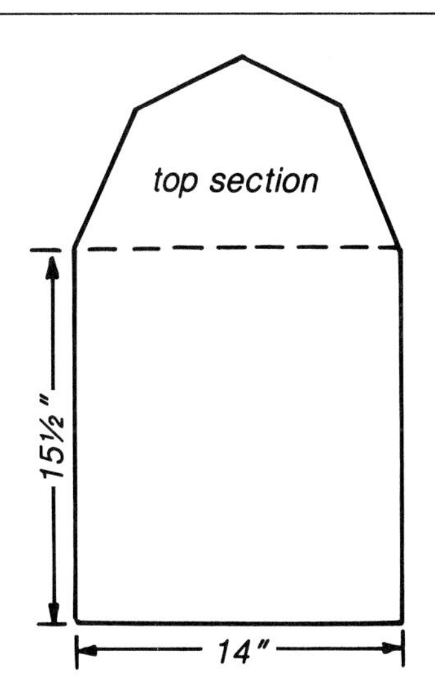

Fig. 1 *Adding top section to complete end wall pattern*

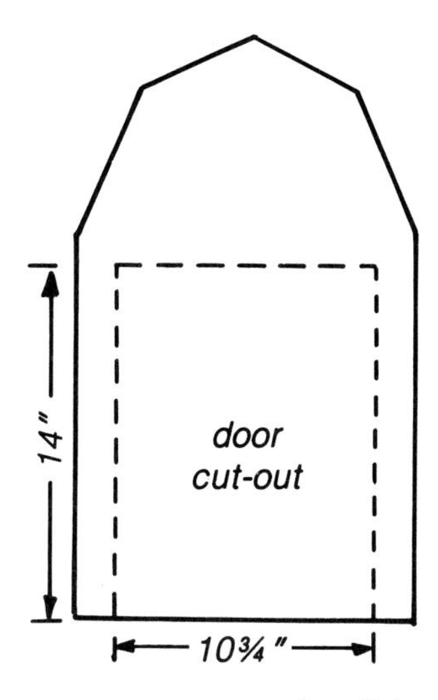

Fig. 2 *Marking end wall for door cut-out*

page 137, and cut out a full pattern piece. When marking plywood, add this pattern shape to a 14x15½" rectangle (see Fig. 1 and layout, page 137) to form the end wall. (End wall will be cut in one piece.)

2. To cut plywood, refer to layout, page 137. Mark 2 side walls; 1 floor; 2 top roof pieces, each 7x27"; 2 lower roof pieces, each 6X27"; and 2 end walls. Cut pieces and sand edges. Fill in any voids on cut edges with wood putty.

3. On one end wall, mark lines for door, 10¾" wide and 14" high (Fig. 2). Cut out and save piece to use as door.

4. Before assembling, paint all pieces with undercoat or white paint and let dry.

5. Center the 1x2" wood strip at top of door opening. Place narrow side of strip against inside of wall, with about half of strip width extending into opening. (This will act as a doorstop to hold door in place when closed.) Glue and nail in place.

6. To assemble Barn, glue floor to side walls (floor will be on the bottom when finished). Nail in place.

7. Add each end wall, overlapping both floor and side walls. Glue and nail in place.

8. Position both top roof pieces on end walls so they meet at the peak; overhangs should be the same at both ends. Glue and nail in place.

9. Place each lower roof piece against next slant of end wall, sliding it up and under top roof piece as far as it will go. Glue and nail in place. (There will be a small area on the end wall that does not touch the roof.)

10. To finish roof, place the quarter-round strip between the two top roof pieces to fill in the gap. Glue in place.

11. Fit cut-out door piece to opening. (You will have to cut off about 1" along the bottom to accommodate hinges which will be attached to floor and inside of door.)

12. Paint outside walls and both sides of door red. Paint roof and inside of Barn white. Paint trim strips white. Let paint dry. (It's easier to paint trims before cutting; you can touch up ends before gluing pieces in place.)

13. Add door hinges, fastening one side of each hinge to floor, and other edge to inside of door.

14. Cut flat trim in strips to outline windows and door. For each window, cut two 7" strips, three 5½" strips and two 2³/₈" strips. For each door, cut two 11¾" strips, two 10⁷/₈" strips, one 15" strip (for diagonal) and two 7" strips (for diagonal).

15. Glue trim strips along outside edges of door, referring to photo as a guide. Use a 10³/₈" strip across top and bottom, and a 11³/₈" strip along each side. For diagonal strips, miter ends to fit into corners. Glue the long strip in place first, then add the two shorter strips.

16. To make door pull, form a loop from the leather or plastic strip and screw to door.

17. For each window, glue a 7" horizontal strip 5" from bottom of Barn, and 3½" from end wall. Place a 5½" vertical strip at each end (on top of first strip) and another up the center. Add a 7" horizontal strip at top, and two 2³/₈" horizontal strips across the center.

18. Add magnetic catch. Center magnet section on bottom of the 1x2" wood strip (at top of door opening), and screw in place. Screw strike plate to inside of door.

FENCE

(color photo, page 69)

Make four or or more of these units to fence in a few critters. The two-foot long units hook together at the ends, and they'll stand alone if you set them at angles.

MATERIALS
(for four units)

4 (1x2") wood strips, each 8' long
3 doz. 3d finishing nails
wood glue
1 pt. white (or any color) nontoxic paint
1 pt. undercoat (or use paint for first coat)
4 screw eyes and 4 screw hooks, size 110

DIRECTIONS

1. Cut wood to make 12 strips, each 2' long, and 8 strips, each 1' long.

2. Paint all pieces with undercoat or paint. Let dry.

3. To assemble each unit, refer to the photo. Glue and nail a 2' piece (top) to two 1' pieces (ends), keeping all edges even.

Glue and nail a second 2' strip in place, 2" below first strip.

Add a third 2' strip, 2" below middle strip.

4. Paint finished units and let paint dry.

5. Add fasteners to each unit. Install a hook at left end and an eye at right end. Hook units together.

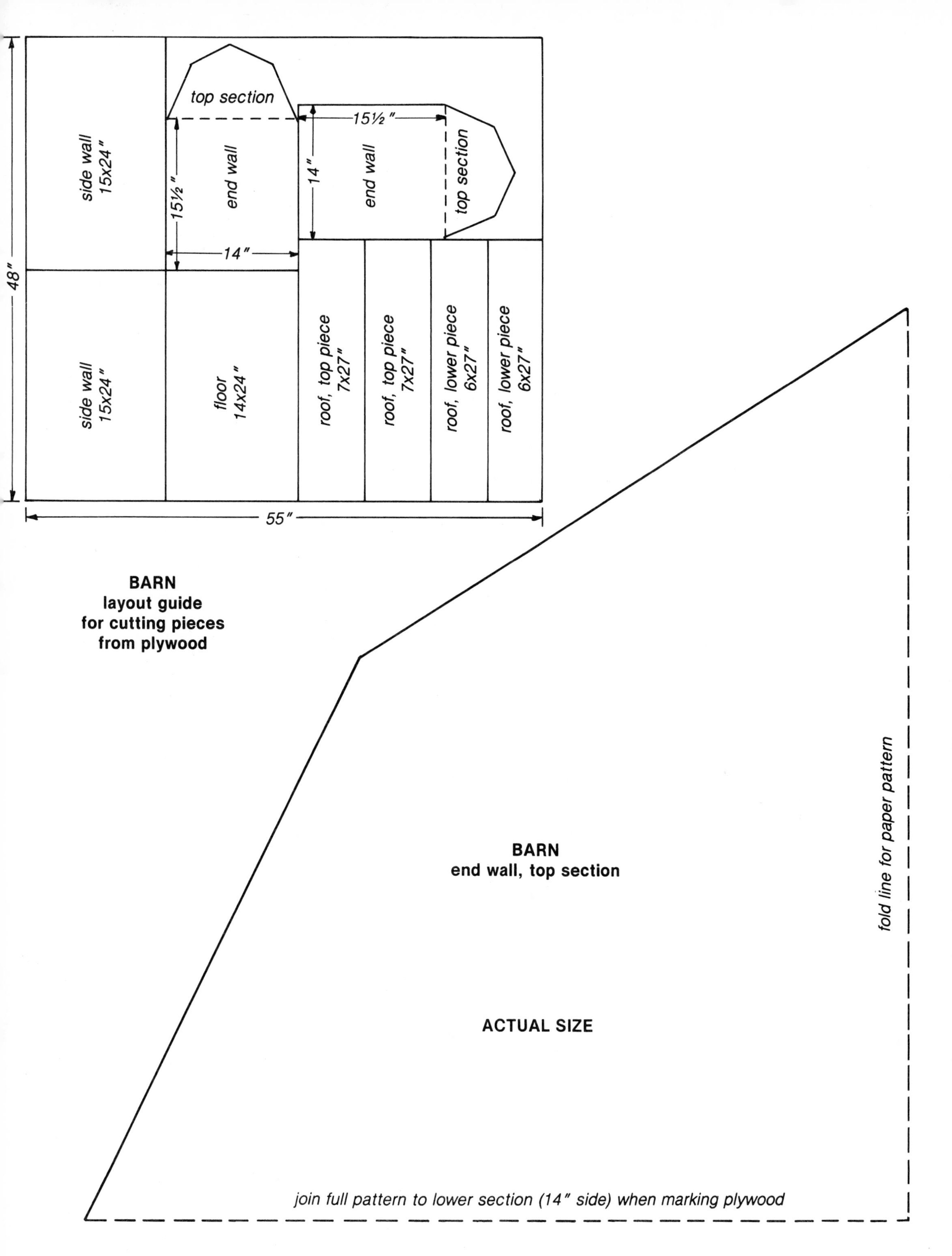
top section
15½″
14″
end wall
top section
side wall
15x24″
15½″
end wall
14″
48″
side wall
15x24″
floor
14x24″
roof, top piece
7x27″
roof, top piece
7x27″
roof, lower piece
6x27″
roof, lower piece
6x27″
55″
BARN
layout guide
for cutting pieces
from plywood
BARN
end wall, top section
fold line for paper pattern
ACTUAL SIZE
join full pattern to lower section (14″ side) when marking plywood

Index

Page numbers for color photos are in boldface type

Ape, **106,** 130-31
Apple Pillow, 29, **31**

Barn toy box, **104-105,**135-36
Basic supplies, 6
Bear, Lovey, 100-101, **103**
Black Sheep, **11,** 21-22
Bluebird Circle Critter, 37, **104, 105**
Bunny Slippers, **69,** 86-87
Burro, **68,** 111

Cat, Siamese, **31,** 91-92
Circle Critters, Simple
 Bluebird, 37, **104, 105**
 Chick, 37-38, **68**
 Duck, 38, **68**
 Kitten, **34,** 36
 Leopard, **34,** 35-36
 Puppy, **34,** 37
 Rabbit, **34,** 35
 Robin, 37, **68**
Circular seam, 5
Chain stitch, 6
Chick
 Circle Critter, 37-38, **68**
 Slippers, **69,** 86-87

Dog, Shag, **34,** 88
Dolls
 Baby, **32,** 52-53
 Boy, **33,** 55
 Dad, **32,** 57-58
 Girl, **33,** 53-54
 Grandma, **33,** 56
 Grandpa, **33,** 57-58
 Mom, **32,** 56
Dress or shirt with sleeves (for doll), 58
Duck(s)
 Circle Critter, 38, **68**
 Cotton Print, **13,** 45-46
 Wild, **13,** 44-45

Embroidery stitches, 6
Enlarging patterns, 2
Eyes
 felt, 5-6
 ready-made plastic, 5

Fabrics
 choosing, 1
 cutting, 2-3
 fur, 1
Felt eye, how to make, 5-6
Fence, **69,** 136
Fish, **12,** 42, 44
Fish Pole, **12-13,** 42, 44
Fox puppet, **70,** 75
Frog puppet, **70,** 71-73
Fur fabrics
 choosing, 1
 cutting, 2-3
Fur "spots," how to make, 3-4

Goose with Egg, **13,** 46

Hen Pajama Bag, **69,** 82-83
Horse, TV, **104, 105,** 120-24

Inner support of wire, 4-5
Invisible stitches, 5

Kitten Circle Critter, **34,** 36

Leopard Circle Critter, **34,** 35-36
Lovey Bear, 100-101, **103**

Monkey, 96-97, **106**
Mouse
 Gray Fur, 10, **14,** 15
 Peach Fur, **14,** 15
 Print Cotton, **14,** 15

Overcast stitch, 3

Pajama Bag, Hen, **69,** 82-83
Pants and Overalls (for doll), 58
Parrot puppet, **70,** 78-79
Patterns
 enlarging, 2
 tracing, 2
Pig, 15-16, **69**
Pillow
 Apple, 29, **31**
 Fish, **12,** 42, 44
Pony, **68,** 109-10
 Stick, **68,** 112-13

Puppet, hand
 Fox, **70,** 75
 Frog, **70,** 71-73
 Parrot, **70,** 78-79
Puppy
 Circle Critter, **34,** 37
 Slippers, **69,** 86-87

Rabbit Circle Critter, **34,** 35
Robin Circle Critter, 37, **68**
Rooster, 7-8, **105**

Satin stitch, 6
Seams
 circular, 5
 stitching, 3, 5
Shag Dog, **34,** 88
Sheep, Black, **11,** 21-22
Siamese Cat, **31,** 91-92
Simple Circle Critters. *See* Circle Critters
Slippers
 Bunny, **69,** 86-87
 Chick, **69,** 86-87
 Puppy, **69,** 86-87
Snake, 50, **69**
Squirrel, 26, **105**
Stem stitch, 6
Stick Pony, **68,** 112-13
Stitches
 Chain, 6
 Invisible, 5
 Overcast, 3
 Satin, 6
 Stem, 6
 Zigzag, 3
Stitching seams, 3, 5
Stuffing, 4

Toy box, Barn, **104-105,** 135-36
Tracing patterns, 2
TV Horse, **104, 105,** 120-24

Unicorn, **67,** 111-12

Wire supports, 4-5
Worm, 29-30, **31**

Zigzag stitch, 3